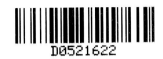

Taunton's COMPLETE ILLUSTRATED *Guide to*

Period Furniture Details

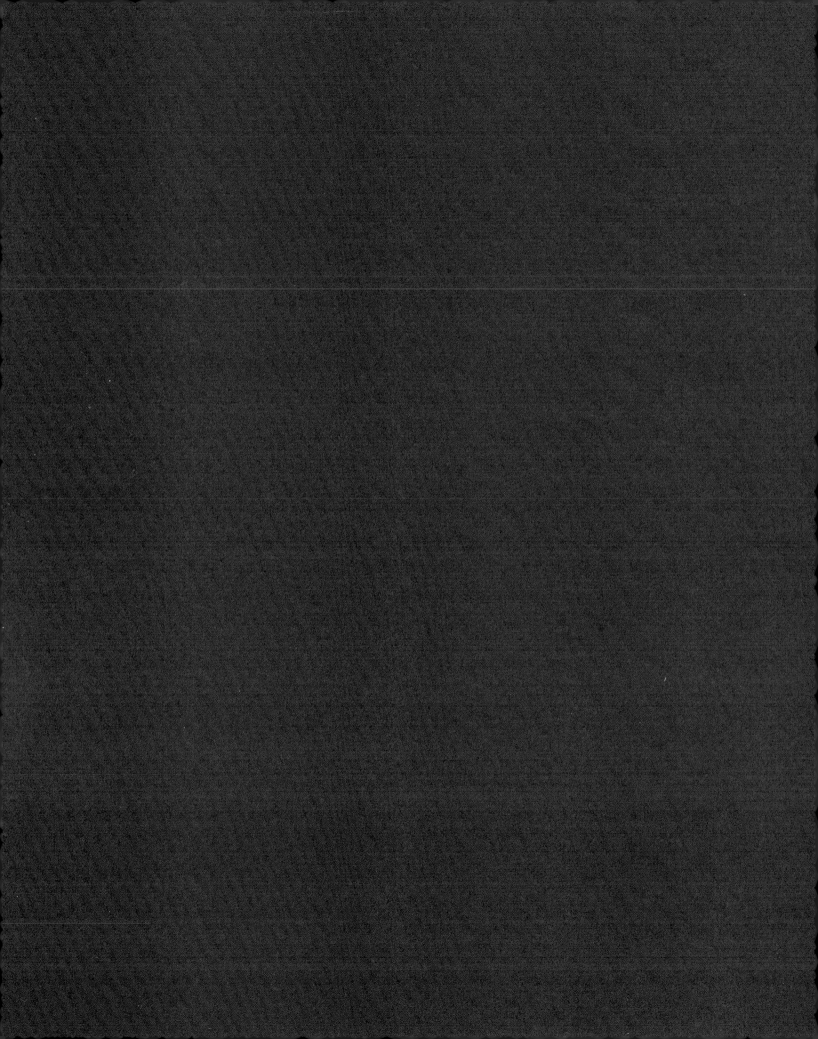

Taunton's COMPLETE ILLUSTRATED *Guide to*

Period Furniture Details

LONNIE BIRD

The Taunton Press

The Taunton Press
Inspiration for hands-on living®

The Taunton Press, Inc., 63 South Main Street, PO Box 5506, Newtown, CT 06470-5506
e-mail: tp@taunton.com

Distributed by Publishers Group West

DESIGN: Lori Wendin
LAYOUT: Susan Lampe-Wilson
ILLUSTRATOR: Mario Ferro
PHOTOGRAPHER: Lonnie Bird

LIBRARY OF CONGRESS CATALOGING-IN-PUBLICATION DATA:

Bird, Lonnie.
Taunton's complete illustrated guide to period furniture details / Author, Lonnie Bird.
p. cm.
Includes index.
ISBN 1-56158-590-4
1. Furniture making--Amateurs' manuals. 2. Furniture, Colonial--United States--Reproduction. 3. Furniture--United States--History--18th century. 4. Furniture--United States--Reproduction. I. Taunton Press. II. Title.
TT195 .B573 2003
684.1'04'097309033--dc21
2003005688

Printed in the United States of America
10 9 8 7 6 5 4 3 2 1

About Your Safety: Working with wood is inherently dangerous. Using hand or power tools improperly or ignoring safety practices can lead to permanent injury or even death. Don't try to perform operations you learn about here (or elsewhere) unless you're certain they are safe for you. If something about an operation doesn't feel right, don't do it. Look for another way. We want you to enjoy the craft, so please keep safety foremost in your mind whenever you're in the shop.

To my parents, Lee and Pat Bird.

Acknowledgments

Writing a book is a team effort that requires the ideas, support, and work of many people. Through this work, new friendships are often forged and old friendships are deepened. With this in mind, I want to say thanks to the many people who helped me with this project:

Helen Albert of The Taunton Press, for her patience and words of encouragement. Jason Bennett, woodworker, friend, and patient stand-in, for many of the photos in this book.

Most of all, I want to thank my wife and best friend, Linda. Without her love, patience, and hard work, this book would not have been possible.

Contents

SECTION 6 Chairs • 63

SECTION 7 Casework • 85

Introduction

Furniture from 18th-century America continues to be among the most popular styles of all time. While other forms of furniture come into style and soon appear dated, period furniture continues as a best-selling classic.

And for good reason—period furniture is rich with detail. It was produced during a time when there was a broad separation between classes of people. Those with means, just as with people today, sought ways to display their wealth and status in society. One of the primary ways to display opulence in the eighteenth century was through finely crafted furniture. In large, wealthy cities, such as Philadelphia, Boston, and Newport, Rhode Island, furnituremakers crafted highly developed furniture artforms. Embellishment became the norm as artisans pierced, carved, sculpted, inlaid, and gilded what is recognized today as some of the finest examples of furniture ever produced.

As a furnituremaker for over twenty years, I enjoy the challenge of reproducing American period furniture both for its level of technical difficulty as well as its timeless beauty. As you study, draw, and reproduce these classic examples of Americana, you can't help but to be immensely impressed with the period craftsman's sense of design and proportion, as well as his tremendous skill with a few relatively simple tools.

As a woodworker, if you're not accustomed to using hand tools, then I encourage you to begin by accumulating the essential edge tools such as planes, chisels, and a dovetail saw and enjoying learning to use them. Furniture produced entirely with machines is void of the fine details that define period furniture. Quite simply, machines for all their sophistication can't duplicate what's created by a trained eye and a skillful hand. In other words, while it is acceptable and desirable to use machines to saw curves, shape moldings, and even cut some types of joints, hand tools are still required for many of the details. In the process you'll experience the delight of cutting a dovetail by hand and hearing the unique sound of a sharp plane as it slices the surface of a board.

No book or even several volumes of books can contain the wealth of furniture details created by America's colonial craftsmen. But, it is my hope that this book will inspire you to deeper study and appreciation of period furniture, and, most importantly, to develop your skill in building it.

Moldings

Ogees

Coves

Beads

Crown Moldings

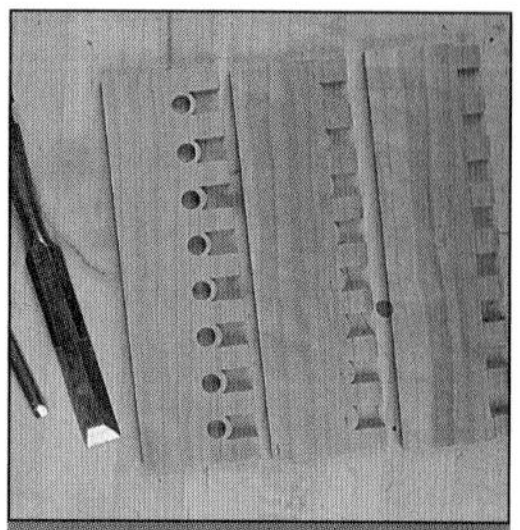

Dentil Moldings

All moldings, even seemingly complex ones, are comprised of shapes derived from about a half dozen basic profiles: The bead, thumbnail, ovolo, ogee, chamfer, and cove. Simple moldings typically use just one of these profiles while complex moldings use a number of them. By mixing sizes and variations of the basic profiles the options can become nearly endless.

Moldings are integrated into furniture in one of two ways: a strip of molding is mitered and attached to the work, or the edge of a surface is shaped. Strip moldings perform several functions: They unify separate cases, frame the work, establish visual parameters, and provide visual unity. Most of all, strip moldings add visual interest by reflecting light and creating interesting shadow lines.

Strip moldings are shaped on lengths of stock and then attached to the work with glue and/or fasteners. Strip moldings can consist of one or more profiles shaped onto a single wood strip or several strips joined together to make a wide and/or deep complex molding.

Stock selection for moldings

Select straight-grain stock when making strip moldings to prevent tearout when using handtools such as planes and scratch-stock; straight-grain stock will produce less tearout. When using machines it's safer to shape a wide board and rip the molding free afterwards. This method will position your hands a safe distance from the cutter or bit. If you select straight-grained stock the strips will be less likely to distort when you rip them free.

Attaching moldings

Parallel strips such as those that wrap around a table edge must be of the exact same length for the miter to fit. Use a stop on the miter saw for exact cuts.

When fitting molding to casework, miter the front strip first, and then the returns or side strips. If adjustments need to be made for a precise fit they can be made to the returns. Afterwards the ends of the returns are cut ninety degrees to be flush with the caseback.

When attaching strip molding, remember to allow for cross-grain, seasonal wood movement. Small moldings can be effectively fastened with brads, which are set below the wood surface. As the wood moves the soft brads will flex. For large moldings such as a crown molding on casework it works well to fasten the molding with screws from the inside of the case. Slot the holes in the case for the screws to slide as the case expands and contracts. Always use glue in the miter joints of moldings; it keeps the joint closed tight through the years.

MOLDINGS ON A CORNER CABINET

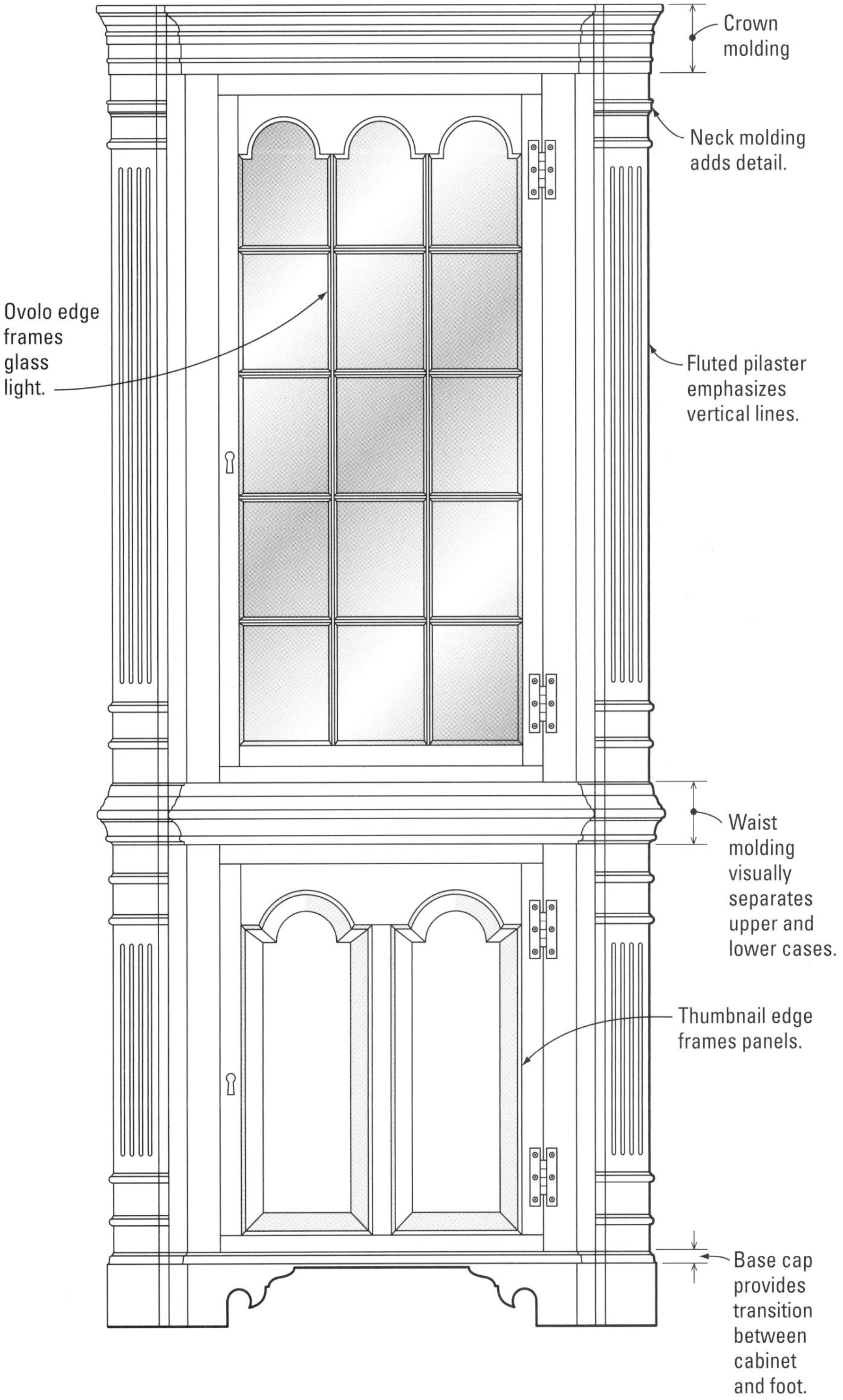
Crown molding
Neck molding adds detail.
Ovolo edge frames glass light.
Fluted pilaster emphasizes vertical lines.
Waist molding visually separates upper and lower cases.
Thumbnail edge frames panels.
Base cap provides transition between cabinet and foot.

MAKE A LITTLE EXTRA MOLDING

A little extra molding is always useful. If you run short, it will match the grain and profile exactly. If you do it later, you'll have to set up your machinery again and it has to be spot on to match. Always save a short section of molding when the job is complete as reference sample.

BASIC MOLDING PROFILES

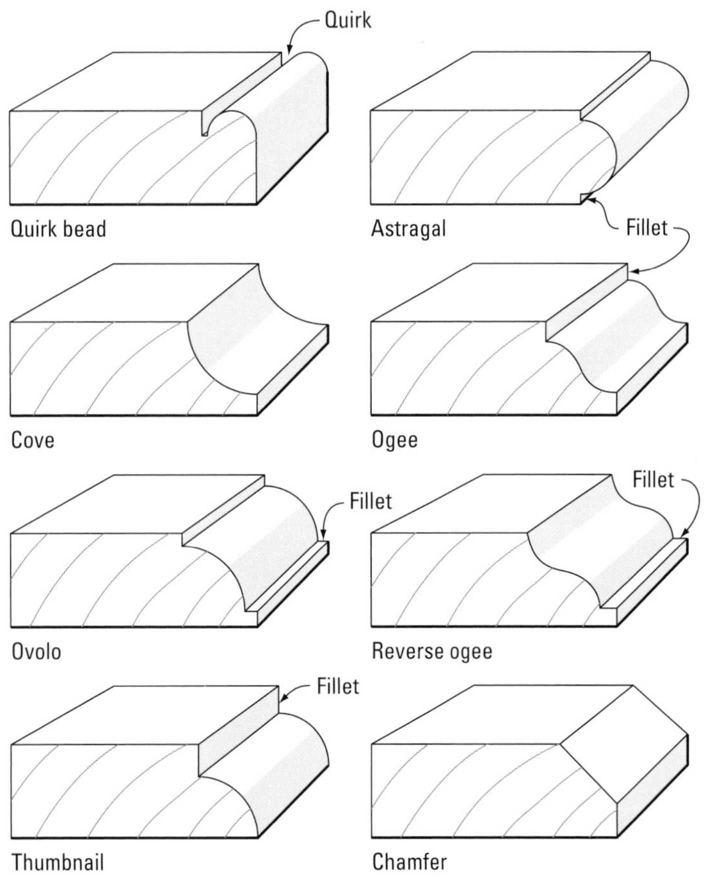

Using handtools to create moldings

Using handtools is quiet work and for period projects you get the tool marks and slight imperfections that lend an authentic look. Molding planes were once made in an amazing variety of profiles and can be found at flea markets or in antique shops.

The so-called universal plane, the Stanley #55, was developed about 100 years ago to replace a multitude of wooden planes.

For small moldings, a scratchstock can be used. A scratchstock is simply a scraper with a profile. By pushing the tool across the wood surface a molding profile is produced. Why use a scratchstock instead of a router? There are several reasons. A scratchstock can shape tiny profiles that a router can't. Also, a scratchstock can easily shape a profile along a freeform curve. And you can easily customize the shape to suite your design requirements.

Making a scratchstock

These days you can buy a scratchstock but it's just as easy to make your own. You can shape a scratchstock from a wood block or you can use an old wooden marking gauge. Pieces of an old handsaw work well for the blade. To shape the profile into the blade I use small files of various shapes.

The versatile bead

There's probably not a more versatile molding profile than the bead. A bead is a semicircular or semi-elliptical profile. It can be shaped flush along the edge of a table apron or proud around the perimeter of a drawer front. Used along the edge of backboards in casework the bead will embellish the back while hiding the expansion joint between the boards. Beads are easily shaped with a router, plane, hand beader, or a scratchstock. Undoubtedly it's this versatility and ease of use that has made the bead so popular for centuries. Next time you need to soften a hard edge or add a bit of decoration remember this simple, versatile profile.

When shaping beads, remember that you need to get to the full depth of the cutter's profile to achieve the right shape. Beads that aren't cut to full depth can appear flattened on one or more sides.

Complex moldings

Complex moldings are combinations of two or more simple profiles. They are used when a more dramatic or formal look is desired. A typical example of a complex molding is the

MAKING A SCRATCH STOCK

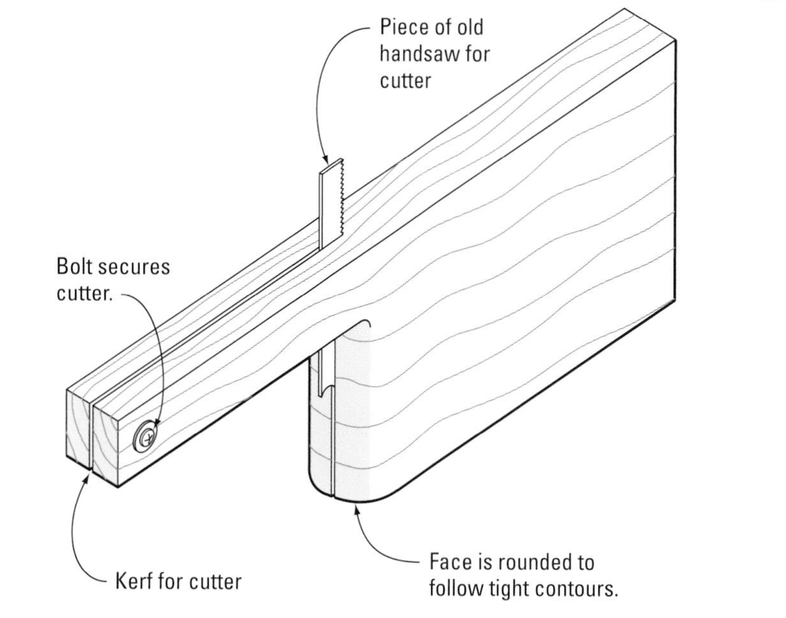
Piece of old handsaw for cutter
Bolt secures cutter.
Kerf for cutter
Face is rounded to follow tight contours.

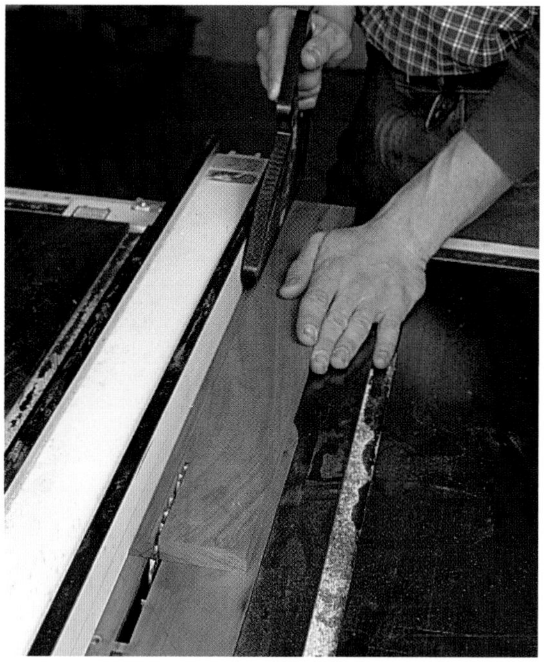

For an applied molding, rip the molded profile from the main board on the table saw. For safety, always use a push stick to feed the stock.

A simple scratch can be constructed by cutting a kerf in a block of wood. Shape the fence to a round to ensure good contact with the edge of the stock.

Old bandsaw blades make good stratch-stock blades. Small files are used to shape the profiles.

USES FOR THE VERSATILE BEAD

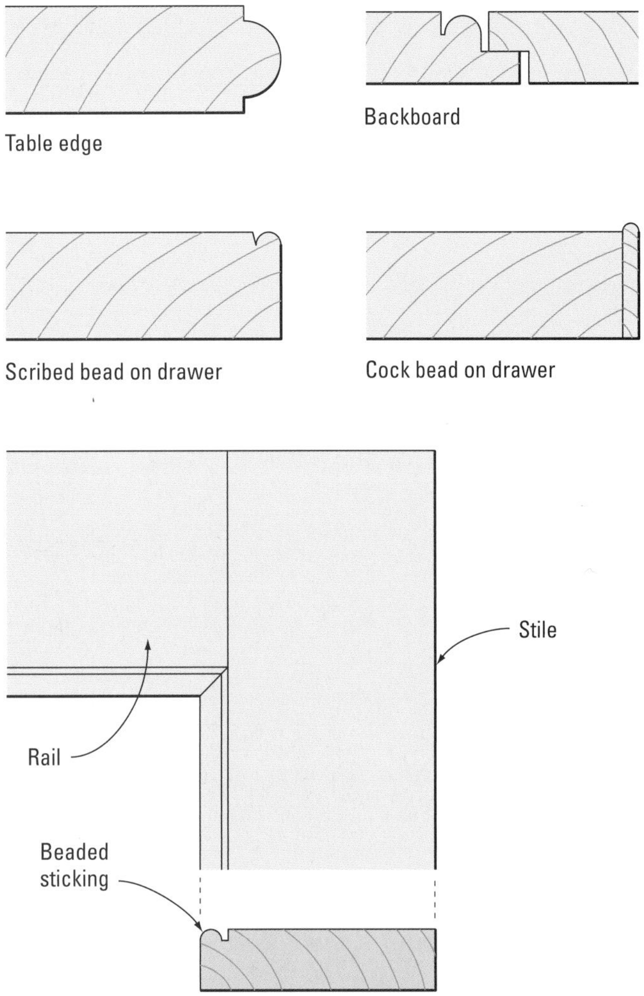

crown molding on most casework. A typical crown may consist of a large cove flanked by smaller profiles such as a thumbnail, bead, or ogee. As the molding steps upward it also steps outward to 'look' down toward the observer.

Waist moldings on casework are another example of complex moldings. Chests, clocks, desks and other tall examples of casework are usually constructed of several cases or 'boxes.' To unify the separate cases, a waist molding is used at the junction of the cases.

There are three options for making a complex molding: shaping thin, flat stock and attaching it to the case at an angle, shaping thick stock, and shaping and stacking strips of simple profiles. You can also use a combination of the methods to create a cornice. But first let's discuss each method individually.

A SAMPLE OF COMPLEX MOLDINGS

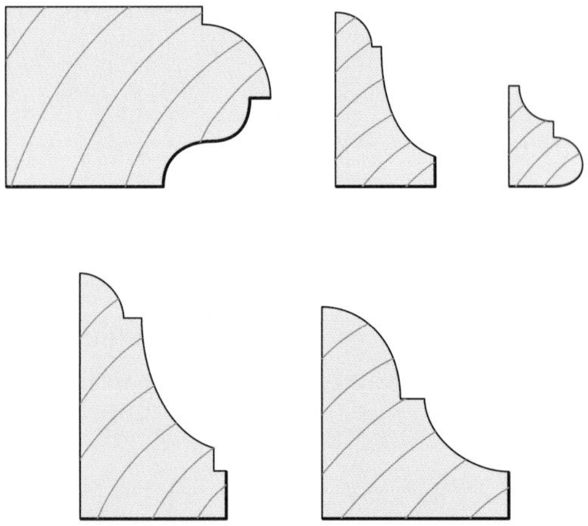

COMBINING A FLAT CROWN MOLDING WITH STACKED STRIPS

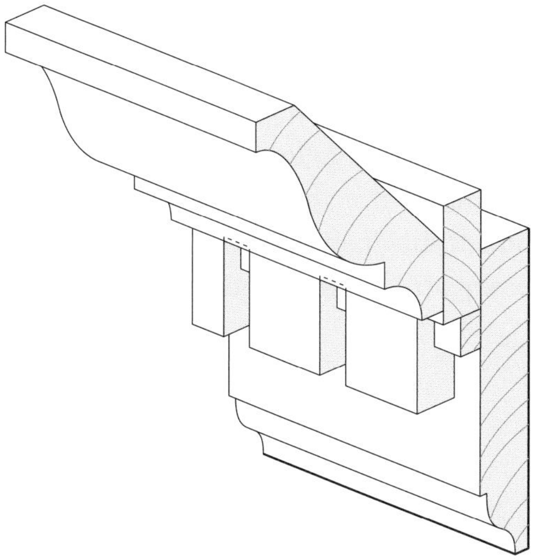

Flat stock moldings

Shaping flat stock and mounting at an angle is commonly used for architectural crown moldings. It also works well for furniture. A flat crown molding is beveled on bottom edges and applied at an angle. This method uses thinner stock, yet gives the appearance of depth. The downside is that flat moldings are difficult to apply; it's awkward to align the molding and attach it. Additionally, if the molding isn't capped off will need to be supported by triangular glue blocks.

The main advantage to this method is that it avoids using thick stock. To shape wide, flat stock you'll need a shaper with a long spindle, molding planes, or a table saw molding head. Unfortunately, a router can't reach to shape wide stock.

MOLDINGS ON A CHEST

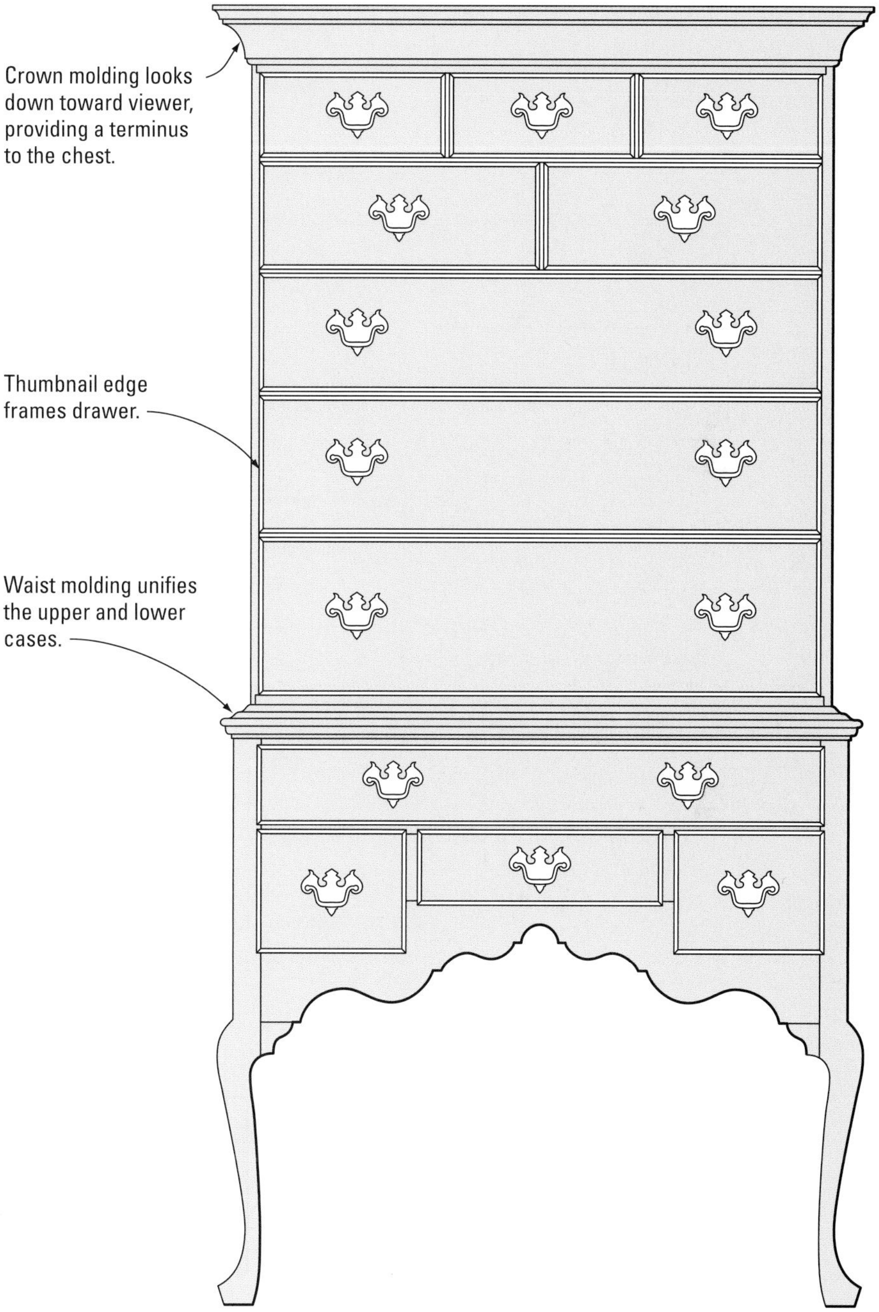

Crown molding looks down toward viewer, providing a terminus to the chest.
Thumbnail edge frames drawer.
Waist molding unifies the upper and lower cases.

THREE METHODS FOR SHAPING CROWN MOLDING

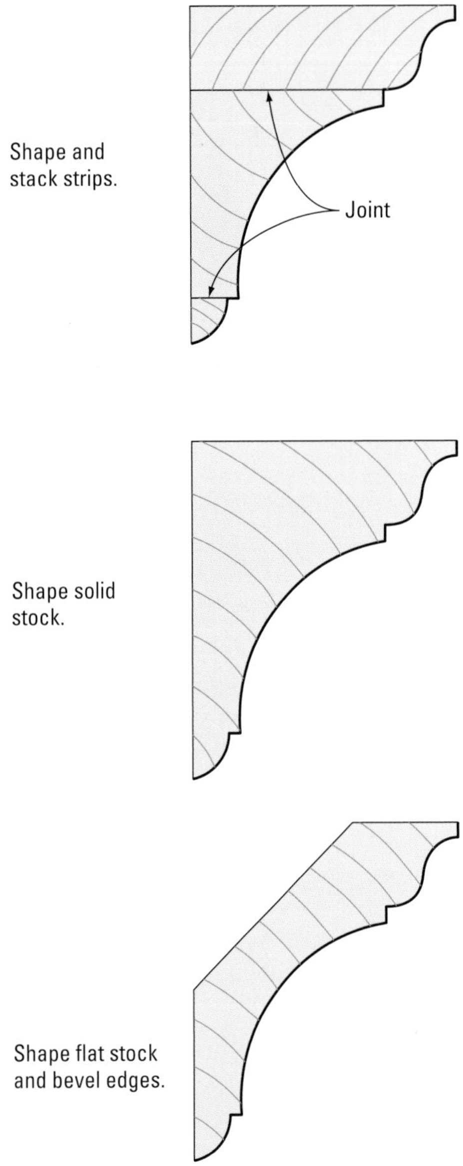

Shape and stack strips.
Joint
Shape solid stock.
Shape flat stock and bevel edges.

STRIP MOLDINGS

This corner cupboard cornice was shaped as two separate strips to avoid waste; then it was fastened to the case.

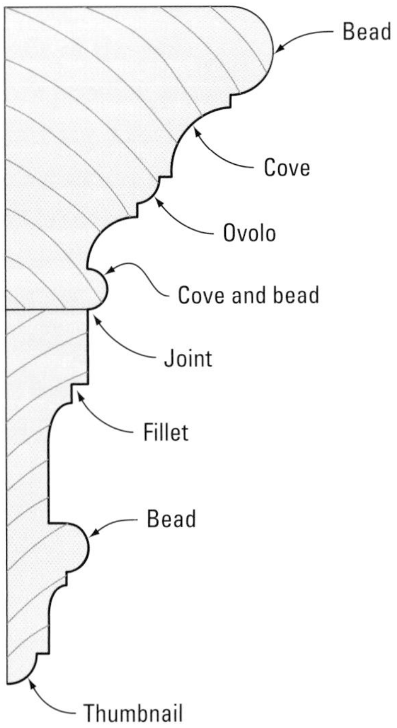

Thick stock moldings

The second method of shaping a complex molding uses thick stock. This method works well when a large, elliptical cove is the centerpiece of the molding. The cove is cut first on the table saw, then smaller profiles are shaped on each side of the cove. Because it's shaped from thick stock, the molding is self-supporting and easier to apply to a case than flat stock. It appears more finished, too. This can be especially important when the case is short enough to view from the top. Also, this method is a great choice when the molding curves, such as a semi-circular or gooseneck pediment molding.

Stacked moldings

The third method involves stacking strips of simple molding profiles to create a wide, dramatic effect. To avoid using a lot of valuable stock, the strips can be glued to a secondary wood such as poplar. Once the strips are stacked the secondary wood will be hidden.

Still another option is to combine the methods described above. The decision of which method to use is often based upon the tools and materials at hand.

SAFETY GUIDELINES FOR CUTTING COMPLEX MOLDINGS

- Make the largest cut first. While the stock has the greatest mass and resistance to chatter and kickback.
- Make certain that there is sufficient surface area in contact with the table and fence. Ensuring that there is adequate surface area in contact with the table and fence prevents the possibility of the stock tipping into the cutter and spoiling the work.
- Position the workpiece to expose the least amount of cutter. When possible position the cut underneath the stock so that the stock shields your hands.

SHAPING A COMPLEX MOLDING ON THICK STOCK

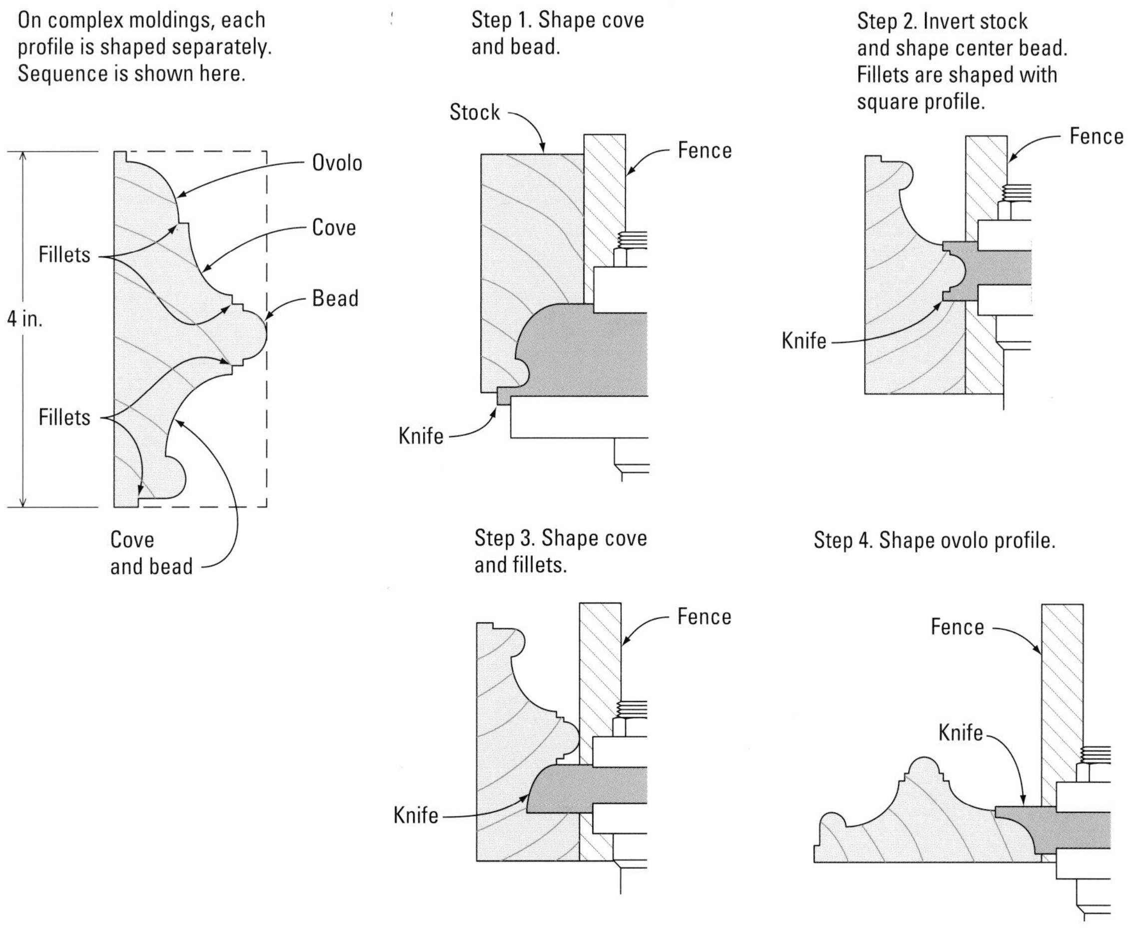
On complex moldings, each profile is shaped separately. Sequence is shown here.
Ovolo
Cove
Bead
Fillets
4 in.
Fillets
Cove and bead
Step 1. Shape cove and bead.
Stock
Fence
Knife
Step 2. Invert stock and shape center bead. Fillets are shaped with square profile.
Fence
Knife
Step 3. Shape cove and fillets.
Fence
Knife
Step 4. Shape ovolo profile.
Fence
Knife

A

B

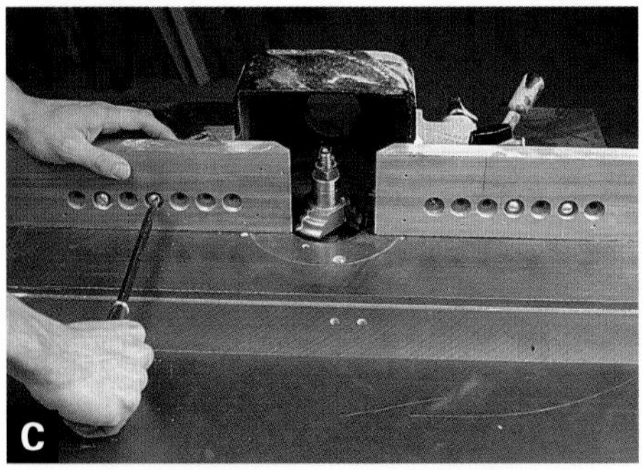
C

D

E

F

Ogee on the Shaper

When using the shaper, safety is always the most important issue, even when shaping a basic profile. Resist any temptation to shape narrow stock without a power feed or appropriate jig. Instead, select wide stock, which positions your hands a safe distance from the cutterhead.

After mounting the cutterhead, check the height with a combination square (**A**). Next, adjust the fence tangent to the smallest cutting circle (**B**); then adjust the fence for the smallest possible opening (**C**). Next, check the spindle rotation. To position the cutterhead underneath the stock for safety requires reversing the spindle to a clockwise rotation (**D**). Now add a featherboard for additional safety and make the cut (**E**). Afterward, rip the molding free on the table saw (**F**).

Ogee with a Molding Plane

Wooden molding planes have been around for centuries. Despite the array of power tools available, the wooden plane is still an effective and enjoyable tool for shaping moldings. Molding planes are readily available from tool dealers and flea markets; if you've never experienced the pleasure using them, I encourage you to find one and give it a try.

Stock selection is important; wooden molding planes are lightweight and work best on straight-grain stock.

Check the iron for sharpness and set it for a light cut (**A**). Most asymmetrical profiles (like the ogee in this example) require that you hold the plane at an angle in relationship to the work. As an aid in gauging and maintaining the correct angle, planes usually have spring lines scribed into the front end of the plane (**B**). As you begin each cut, keep the spring lines parallel to the stock and the fence in contact with the edge of the stock (**C**). When you reach the full depth of the profile, the stop will contact the surface of the work and prevent the plane from cutting farther (**D**).

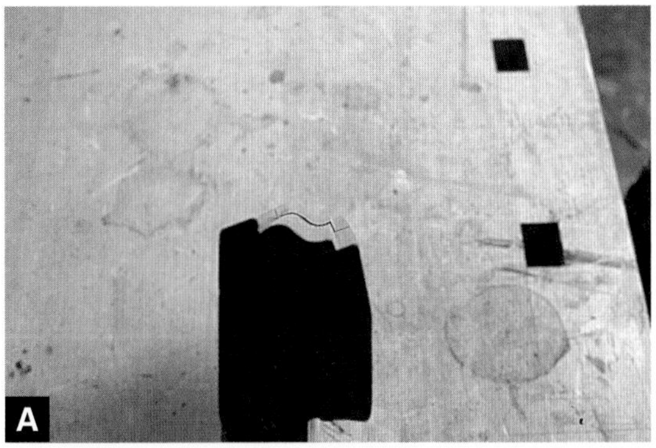
A

B

C

D

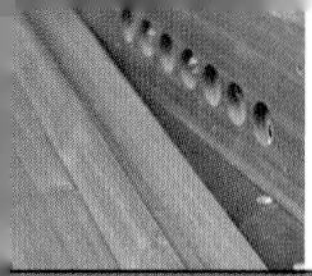

A

Ogee with a Universal Plane

Begin by selecting the stock. Anything but the straightest grain makes planing difficult. Although soft woods plane easily, you can also achieve good results with a moderately hard wood, such as walnut or cherry. The next step is to set the iron in place and adjust the cutting depth (**A**).

[TIP] Check the iron for sharpness first; like any chisel or place iron, the edge should be smooth and polished.

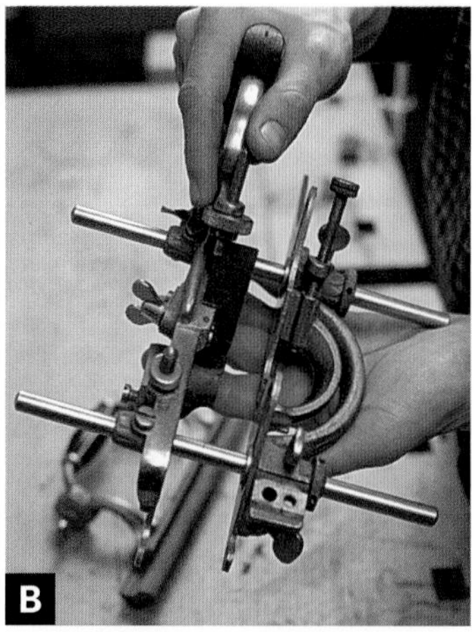
B

C

Adjust the iron with the thumbwheel for a light shaving. Next, set the second skate in position flush with the cutter or slightly inset (**B**). Then slide the fence onto the arms and lock it in place with the thumbscrews (**C**). When shaping asymmetrical profiles such as this ogee, it works best to position the cut inward slightly from the edge of the stock. This way, the cutter will be trapped by the stock as you plane, which prevents it from sliding off of the profile.

D

E

Now you're ready to make the cut. Keep the fence against the stock with one hand and push the plane firmly with the other (**D**). As the shavings peel away and the profile is revealed (**E**), set the plane's stop to bear against the stock (**F**). The stop will ensure that all subsequent moldings are identical in profile depth.

F

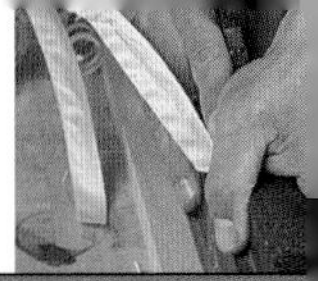

Cove Cut with a Molding Plane

One of the most common molding planes is called a round. It's aptly named because of the semicircular, convex shape of its sole. Hollows, as the name implies, have a concave sole. Hollows and rounds were once produced together in matching pairs for making moldings—and they're still useful today.

To make a cove with a wooden plane, begin by laying out the parameters of the cove on the stock (**A**). Next, cut a V groove down the length of the stock. This type of plane does not use a fence, so the V is required to keep it running in a straight path.

To cut the profile, make several passes down the V to establish a cove (**B**). Then widen and deepen the cove until the full profile is reached (**C**).

A

B

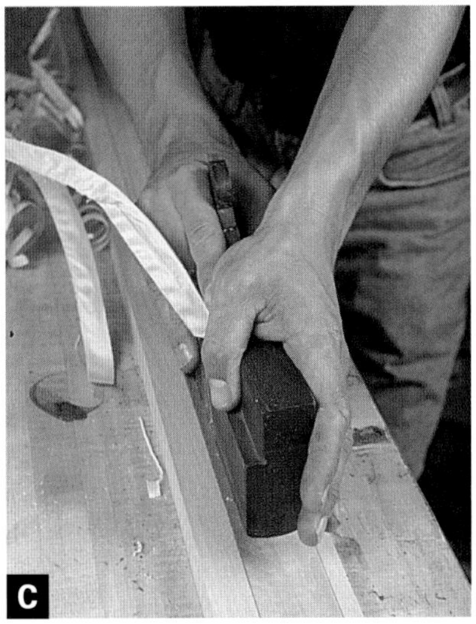

C

A

B

C

Quirk Bead on a Compound Curve

Remember that a compound curve is one that flows in two directions simultaneously. Some furniture components that have compound curves use simple profiles such as a quirk bead to provide additional detail and draw the eye to the flowing lines of the curve.

The easiest method for shaping a profile on a compound curve is to use a scratch stock (**A**).

➤ See *"Making a Scratch Stock"* on p. 7.

After bandsawing and smoothing the curves, secure the workpiece in a vise. Using the scratch stock, gently scrape the quirk-bead profile onto the surface (**B**). As you work, keep the body of the scratch stock against the work and tilt it slightly in the direction of the cut (**C**).

Quirk Bead with a Wooden Plane

Wooden quirk-bead planes are still widely available, and they're a pleasure to use. Best of all, the quirk bead has a wide variety of applications.

Begin by selecting clear, straight-grain stock for planing. Sight down the sole of the plane to set the plane iron for a light cut (**A**).

To make the cut, use one hand to keep the fence of the plane against the stock (notice I've added a strip a wood to my plane as a fence), while pushing the plane with the other hand (**B**). A quirk bead should have a full, round profile. If the plane comes away from the stock, the bead will be flat on the side. If you don't plane to the full depth, the bead will be flat on top. The plane's built-in stop will ride against the stock to prevent further cutting once the full profile is reached.

A

B

Beaded Backboard with a No. 45 Plane

You've probably seen no. 45 planes at your local flea market (**A**). Stanley Tools manufactured them for many years, and so they're quite common. They work well for shaping beaded backboards. The idea behind a beaded backboard is to hide the expansion joints in a solid-wood case back (**B**).

Begin by milling the stock for the backboards. I prefer to use random-width boards with minor defects. This allows me to use stock I have on hand that may not be suitable for more visible areas.

After milling the stock, cut a rabbet along both edges of each board. Keep in mind that the rabbets must be on opposite faces. First, mount a square cutter in the main body of the plane and position the second skate flush with the outside edge of the cutter. Lock the skate in position with the thumbscrews. Now adjust the cutter for a light cut and lock it in place. Finally, slide the fence in position on the arms and lock it in place next to the cutter (**C**). While cutting the rabbet, keep the fence firmly against the stock (**D**). As you reach the full depth of the rabbet on the first piece, adjust the depth stop to bear against the work.

After cutting the rabbets on all the stock, shape the bead (**E**). Follow the same set-up procedure as you did earlier: set the iron, then the second skate, and finally the fence. The no. 45 plane is equipped with a special fence for beading that rides the edge of the rabbet. To make use of it, you'll first need to remove the wood fence (**F**).

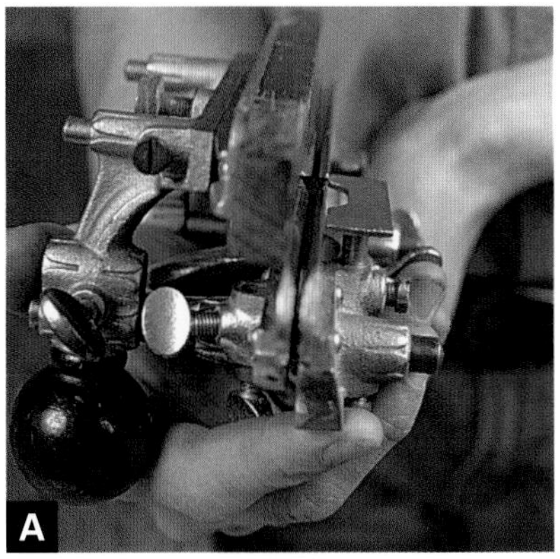

A

B

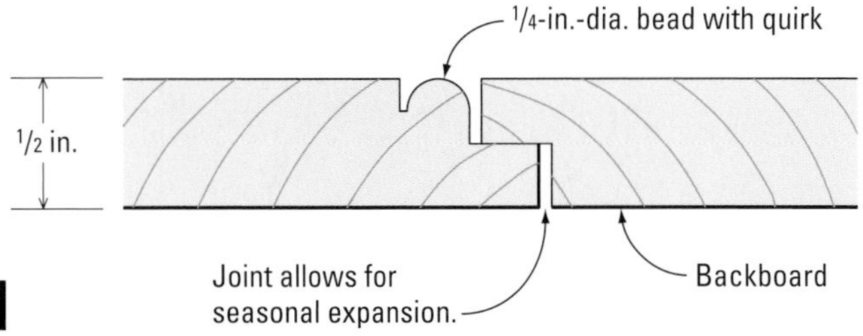

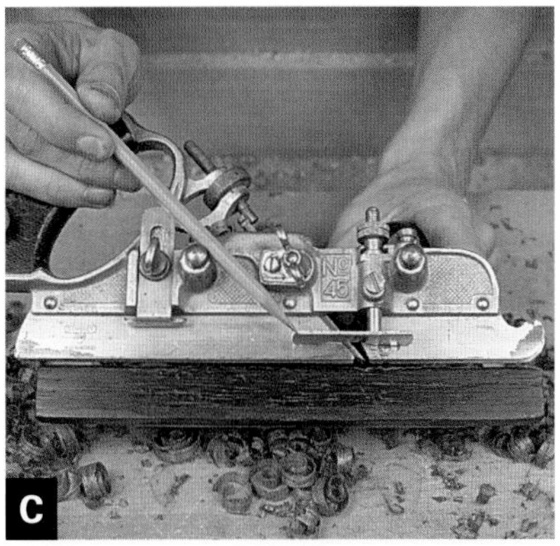

C

D

E

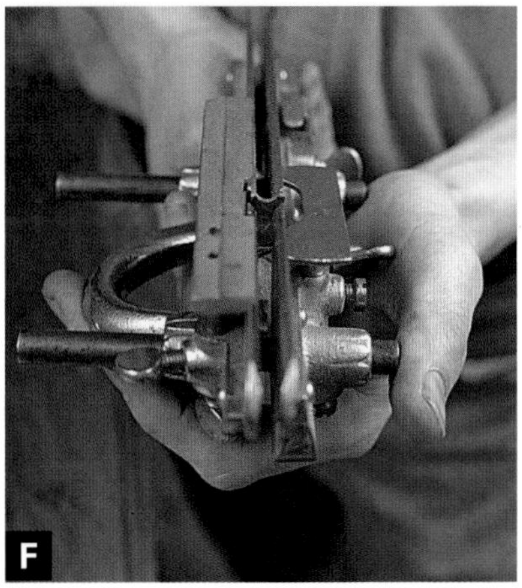

F

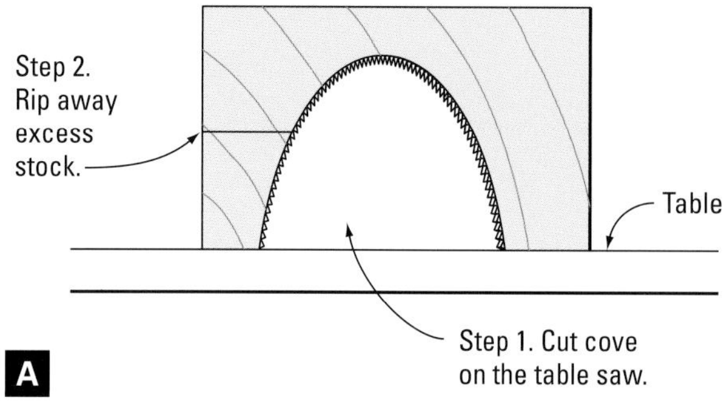
Step 2.
Rip away
excess
stock.
Table
Step 1. Cut cove
on the table saw.

A

B

C

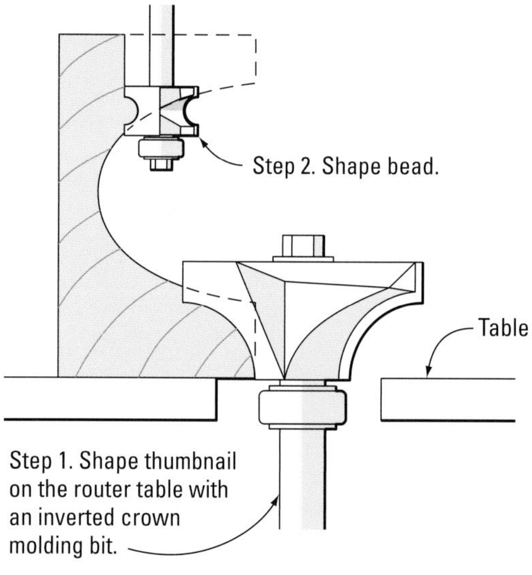
Step 2. Shape bead.
Table
Step 1. Shape thumbnail
on the router table with
an inverted crown
molding bit.

D

Large, Solid Crown Molding on the Table Saw and Router Table

The molding shown here is used as a crown for a large case, such as a Connecticut-style tall chest. But the technique, like most in this book, has broad applications.

Many furniture crown moldings use a deep, elliptical cove as the large focal point, with smaller, basic profiles flanking it. Making the molding from one piece of solid stock ensures continuity of grain and color and greatly simplifies application to the casework

Begin by drawing the profile full-scale. This ensures good proportions and allows you to plan each cut more easily. Next, shape the cove on the table saw while the stock is still square (**A, B**).

Before you begin shaping with the router, rip away the excess stock at the base of the molding. Now turn your attention to the thumbnail profile at the top of the molding. If you have a shaper, you can invert a roundover cutter (**C**); or you can use a special inverted router bit, available from CMT USA, Inc. (**D**).

Shape the bead next. The tall fence that came with your router table will obstruct the cut. Instead, use a flat, wide piece of stock. Cut it the same length as your router table and clamp it to the top after cutting a small opening for the bit. Now stand the molding on edge and shape the bead (**E**).

There is only one profile remaining: the small cove at the base. To cut the cove, you can use the shaper (**F, G**) or a corebox bit on the router table.

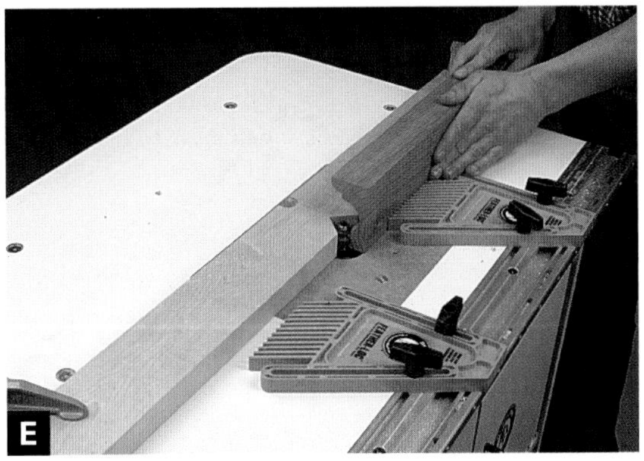

E

F

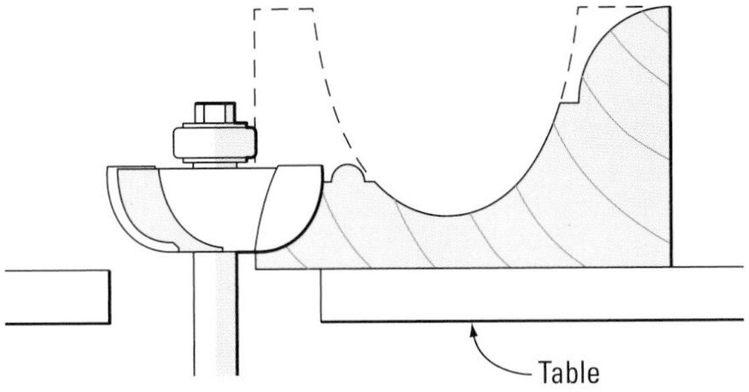

G Cut the cove on the shaper with an inverted cutterhead.

Another Large, Solid Crown Molding on the Table Saw and Router Table

Here's another example of a solid crown molding. Many design variations can be accomplished with the use of different profiles. This example uses a large cove flanked by an ogee at the top and a thumbnail profile at the base (**A**).

Begin by shaping the large cove on the table saw (**B**) and then rip off the excess stock (**C**).

Next, invert the molding to shape the ogee at the top (**D**). Finally, lay the molding on its back to shape the thumbnail (**E**).

(This cutter is from the CMT USA, Inc., crown-molding set.)

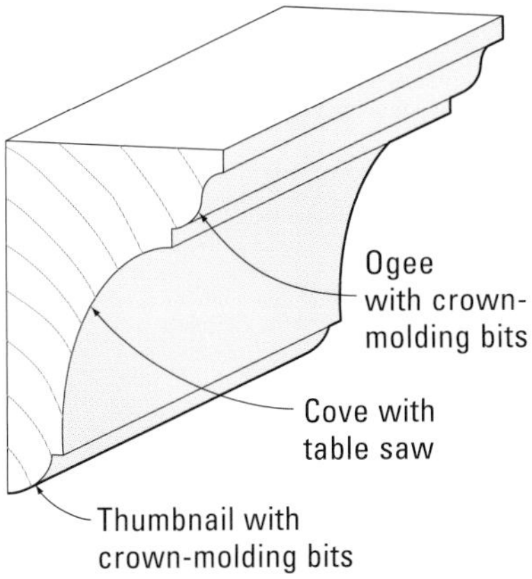

A

B

C

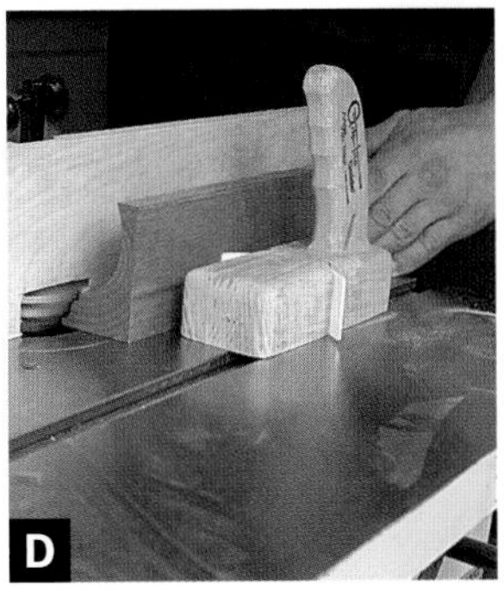

D

E

Flat Crown Molding on the Router Table

Like an architectural cornice, this molding is attached to a case at a 45-degree angle (**A**).

After milling wide stock for safety, start by shaping the cove. I've removed the bearing on the cove bit to allow it to cut deeper. Shape this profile with the stock face down (**B**). Next, shape the thumbnail profile at the base of the molding (**C**). Now turn the stock on edge and shape the second thumbnail (**D**).

Because the back of this molding can be seen inside the lid, it's necessary to bevel the back corner for refinement. Begin by tilting the table-saw blade to 45 degrees and lowering the blade so that it doesn't penetrate the stock thickness. Now rip a kerf along the back of the molding (**E**). Return the blade to 90 degrees and set the height just above the stock thickness. Position the fence for the width of the molding and rip it free (**F**).

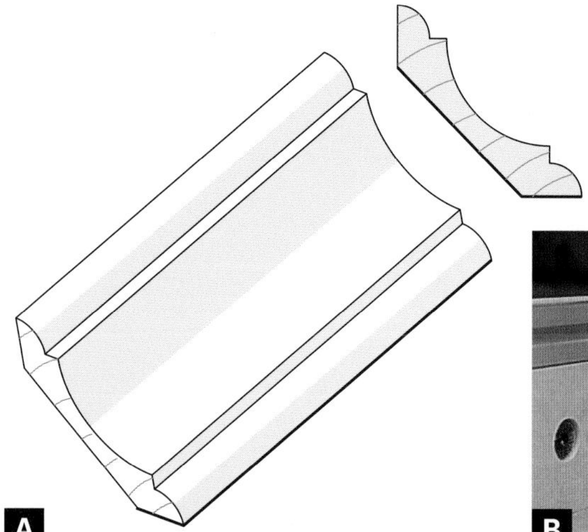
A

B

C

D

E

F

A SAMPLE OF FLAT CROWN MOLDINGS

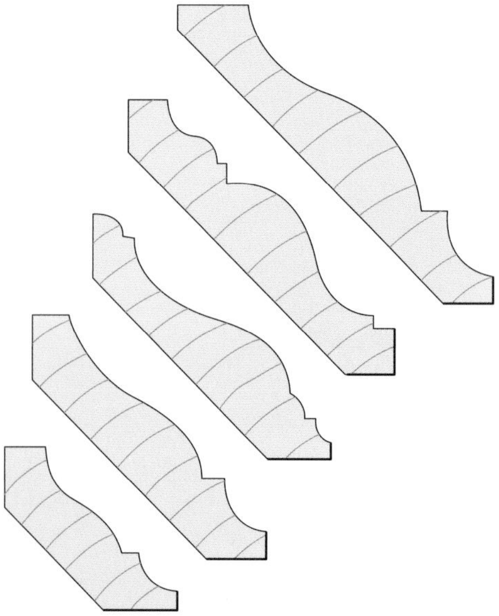

Flat Crown Molding with Wooden Handplanes

Wooden handplanes still have a place in the small shop. Here's a good example: To shape a wide, flat crown by a machine method, you would need a large shaper or a molder. Yet you can easily shape crown moldings with a few hollow and round planes.

Begin by drawing the crown molding full-size. Next select clear straight-grain stock for the molding (**A**).

The first step in shaping is to saw the fillet that separates the two profiles. Tilt the sawblade to 45 degrees and position the fence to align with the drawing you made earlier. Next, saw V-grooves to guide the planes (**B**). Now, shape the cove that is part of the ogee. Then shape the cove that is adjacent to the fillet (**C**).

The final step of the process is to bevel the edges of the molding to 45 degrees. Simply tilt the blade and position the fence for this ripping cut. This completes the crown molding (**D**).

A

B

C

D

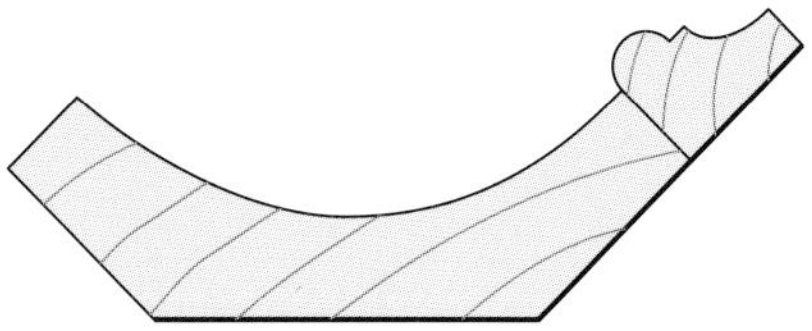

Shape cove separately; then glue on bead strip.

A

B

C

E

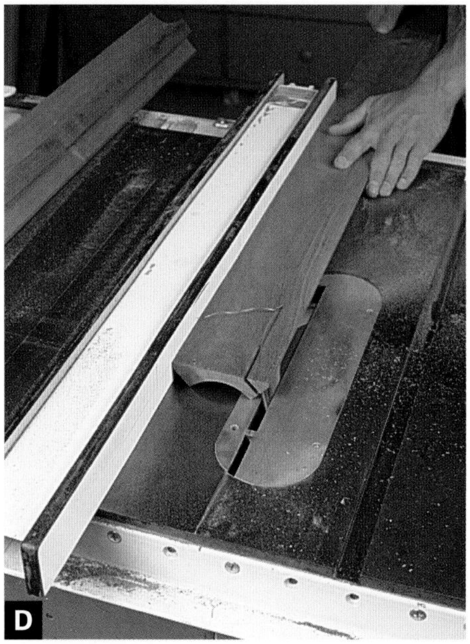

D

F

G

Complex Flat Crown Molding

Many crown moldings, including the one in this example, incorporate a large cove flanked by a small bead at the base (**A**). With this style of molding, it becomes necessary to shape the cove and bead separately and join them after shaping. Otherwise, the bead will be cut away during the cove-shaping process.

Begin by shaping the cove (**B**). Next, bevel the edges of the cove strip. First bevel the front edges (**C**); then the back edges (**D**).

Now shape the small secondary molding strip. Start by shaping the bead (**E**) and then complete the strip with the cove (**F**). Finally, glue the strip onto the base of the cove (**G**).

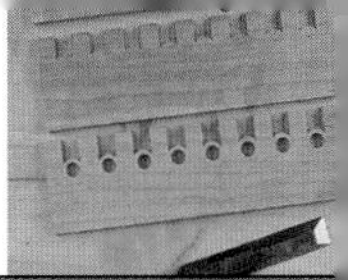

Dentil with a Carved Detail

Furniture dentil is often more elaborate than architectural dentil. The dentil shown here is a good example (**A**). The bottom of the space between each dentil block is carved with an arch. Above each arch is a small hole, which accentuates the arch, adding even greater detail. The time involved in producing many linear feet of this dentil for a room is more than most people are willing to spend. But 7 ft. or so for a chest isn't enormously time consuming.

Before beginning, it's essential to understand the importance of accurate spacing on furniture dentil molding. The miters at each end should fall precisely on the edge of a dentil block instead of at a space or in the middle of a block. Therefore, the brad-spacing technique used in the previous examples isn't effective here. Even the smallest spacing error is multiplied many times over, which may affect the location of the blocks at each end.

Thus it's best to lay out the entire length of dentil strip with dividers (**B**) and a square (**C**). After making the layout, saw each space to the line (**D**). It's not nearly as tedious as it sounds, because you need only a few feet of molding.

The next step is to carve the arch at the top of each kerf. Finally, drill a small hole above each kerf to complete the job (**E**).

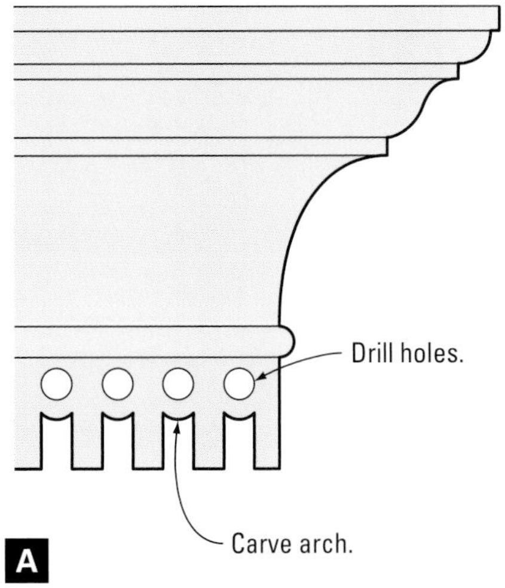

A

B

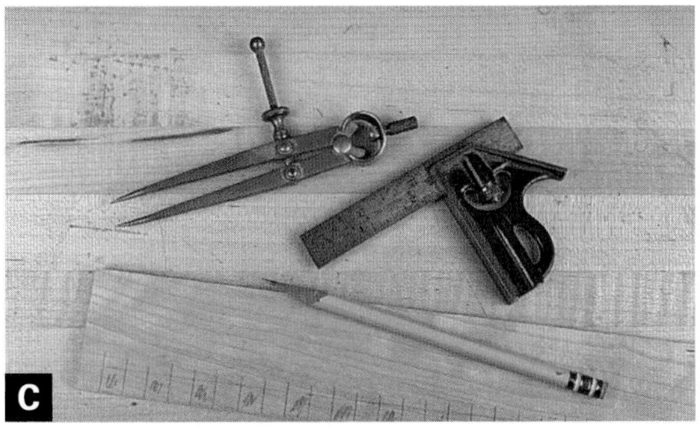
C

D

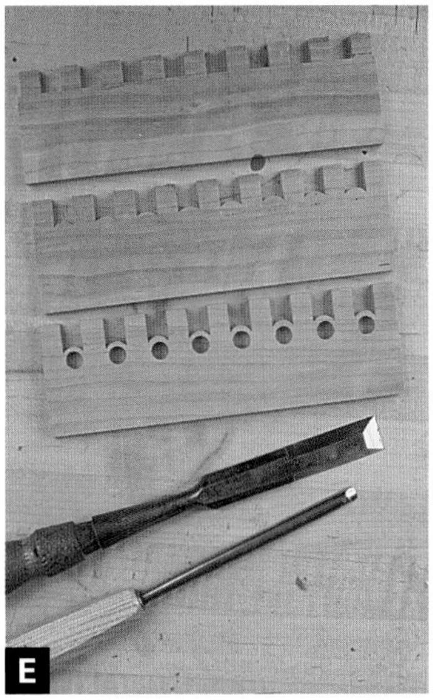
E

Legs

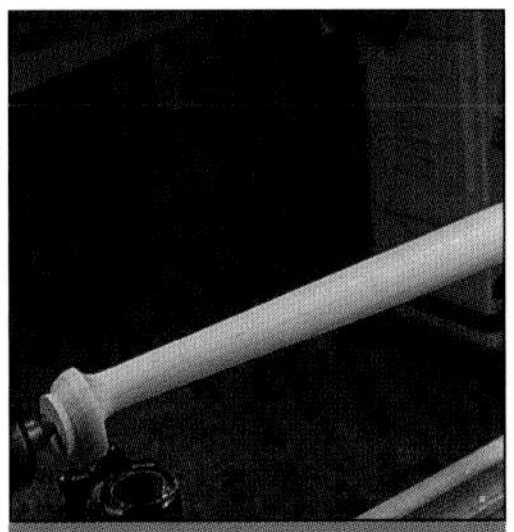

Tapers

Knee Blocks

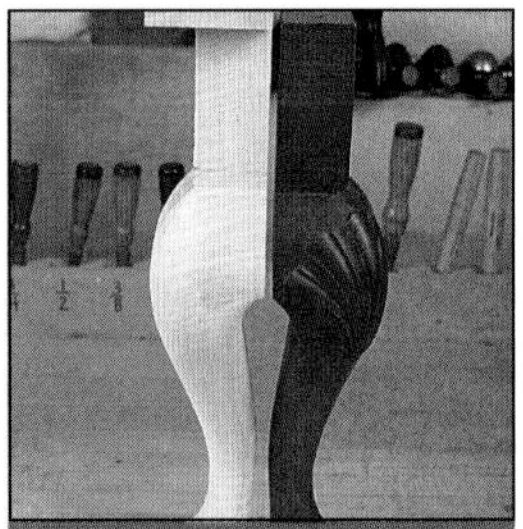

Cabriole Leg

NOTHING SYMBOLIZES 18TH-century furniture more than the cabriole leg. It was integrated into every form of furniture casework, tables, chairs—even beds.

Cabriole legs exhibit tremendous variation; in fact, furniture historians can often determine the origin of an antique based upon the legs and feet. Pad feet are the most common and easiest to reproduce; its circular form is easily turned on a lathe. Pennsylvania and Delaware Valley furniture often feature trifid, or three-toed, feet. Undoubtedly, the most familiar design is the claw-and-ball foot. Because it was so time-consuming to carve, it was a status symbol for the wealthy.

➤ **See *"Feet"* on p. 42 for information.**

Cabriole legs are not difficult to make; they are essentially a compound curve which requires bandsawing two adjacent faces. However, designing and drawing a leg with balance, proportion, and flowing curves can be quite a challenge. When designing a cabriole leg, it is always best to begin by looking at good examples for inspiration and direction.

Cabriole Proportions

Begin by establishing dimensions for the knee, post block, ankle, and foot. Knees usually fall within a range of 1/2 in. to 2 7/8 in. The foot is proportional to the knee or slightly smaller. Ankles can range in size from 13/16 in.on a slender leg of a diminutive tea table to 1/2 in. on a bed or large case piece. The post block is usually 3/4 in. to 1 in. smaller than the knee. A post block that is too small will not allow sufficient room for joinery; it can also make the knee appear swollen.

Undoubtedly, the most important part of a cabriole leg is the graceful "S" curve; the finest legs have smooth continuous curves that lead your eye from the post block to the foot. Stiff, straight legs lack appeal and should be avoided. When designing legs for a new piece of furniture I'm developing, I'll carve a prototype and study it from all angles. Only after I'm satisfied with the prototype do I begin construction of the piece.

Tapered legs

Not all period legs were curved; many pieces, from simple to refined, feature tapered legs. In fact, tapered legs were in vogue during the Federal Period (1780–1810) and featured contrasting stringing and delicate inlays.

Tapered legs can be tapered on two, three, or four sides with the two-sided taper probably most common. The taper usually begins immediately below the rail or apron and ends at the floor. Typically, the tapered end of the leg is half the width of the leg at the starting point. This creates a graceful slender leg with a small footprint without sacrificing strength in the post area where the joinery occurs.

Turned legs

During the early years of the 18th century before most the design details of William-and-Mary furniture dissipated, turned legs were quite common on tables, chairs, and even casework. Probably the most familiar form of turned leg from this period is the ring-and-vase. Widely used on table legs, it

LEG DIAGRAM HEAD

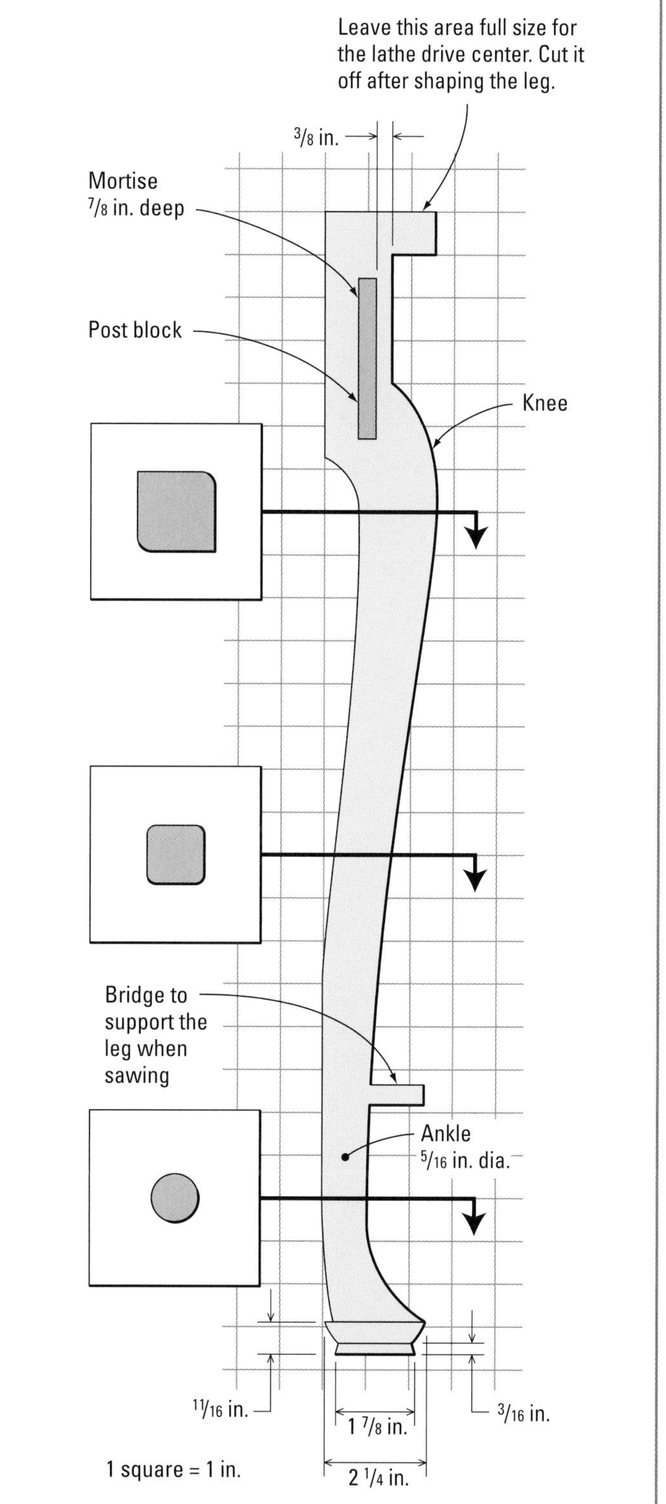

A well-designed cabriole leg has fluid lines, a graceful curve that draws your eye from the post block to the foot.

was also a popular architectural form and frequently used on balustrades.

Turned legs are usually reinforced with turned stretchers. To accommodate the joinery, a short portion of the leg is left square a few inches from the floor. Additionally, the top of the leg is also square to accept tenons on the ends of the rails.

Another popular turned leg of the period is the offset leg. Obviously designed to resemble a cabriole leg, the offset leg is much less labor intensive to craft. The pad foot is turned first; afterwards, the turning is positioned offset in the lathe to turn the ankle. Although the result isn't a true cabriole leg, it is still an attractive variation that was—and is—quite popular.

Two-Sided Tapered Leg Freehand on the Bandsaw

Begin by laying out the taper on the stock (**A**). To simplify construction, tapers usually don't extend into the area of joinery (**B**). It's best to lay out and cut the leg mortise while the stock is still square (**C**).

Next, mount a wide blade, such as ¾ in., on the bandsaw. Using a wide blade greatly reduces the tendency for the blade to wander in the cut (**D**). Start at the foot and closely follow the layout line (**E**). Turn the leg 90 degrees and make the second cut (**F**). After all the cuts are made, remove the saw marks with a sharp bench plane (**G**).

A

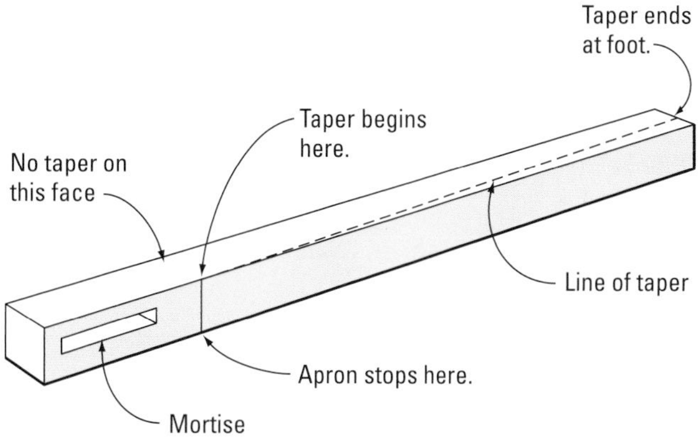

C

D

E

F

G

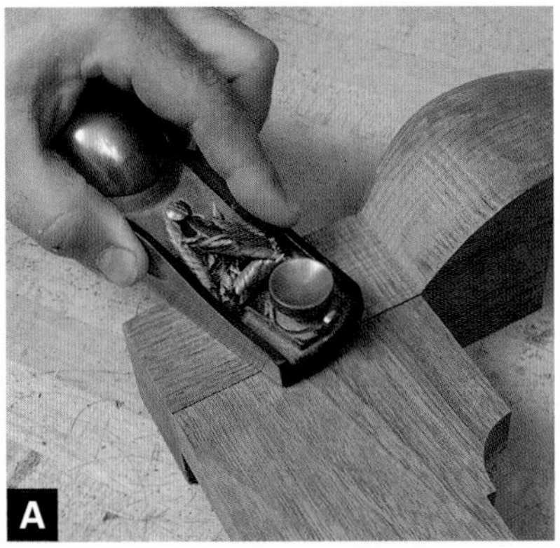
A

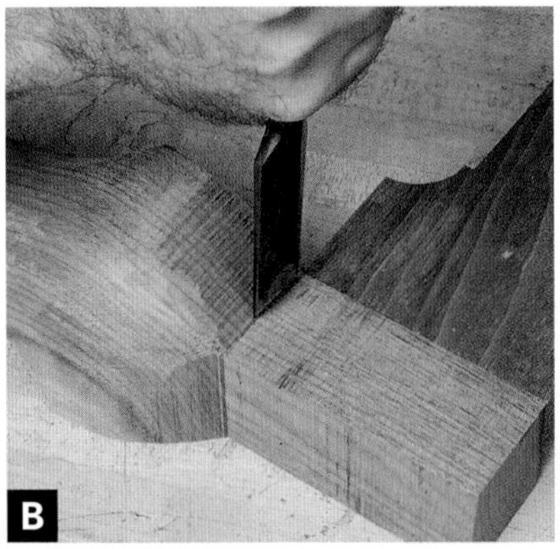
B

C

D

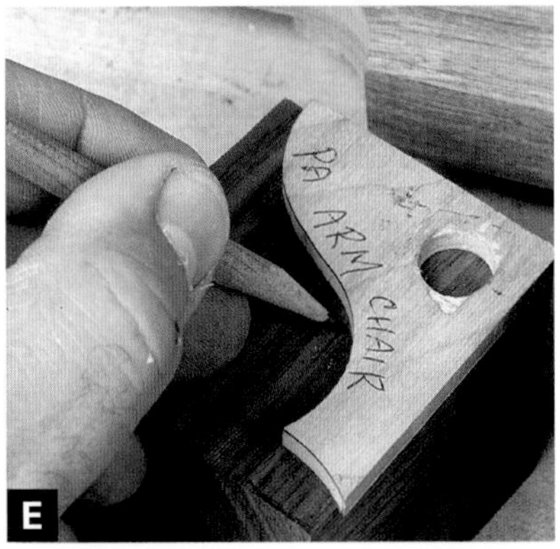

E

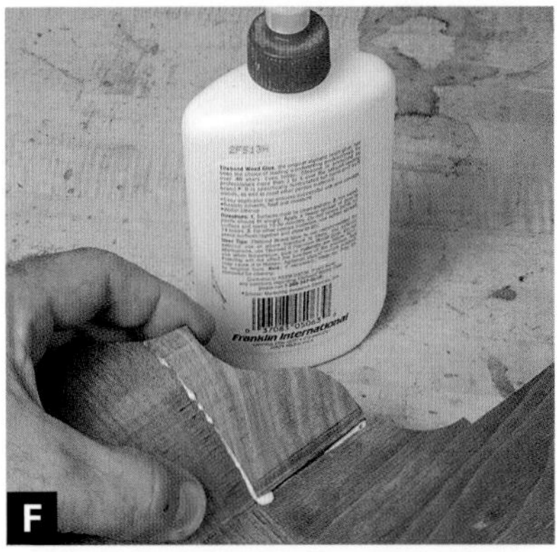
F

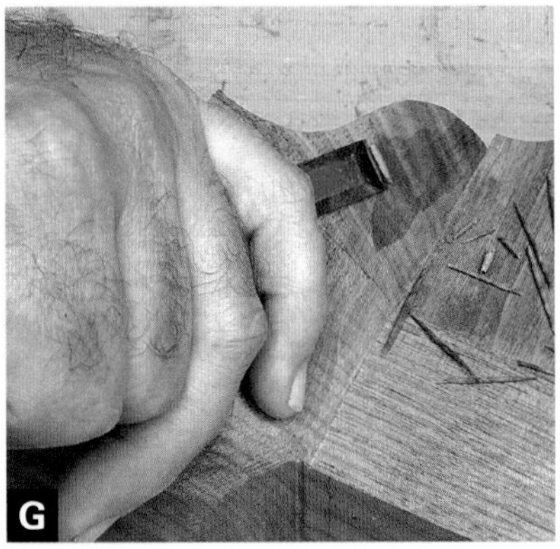
G

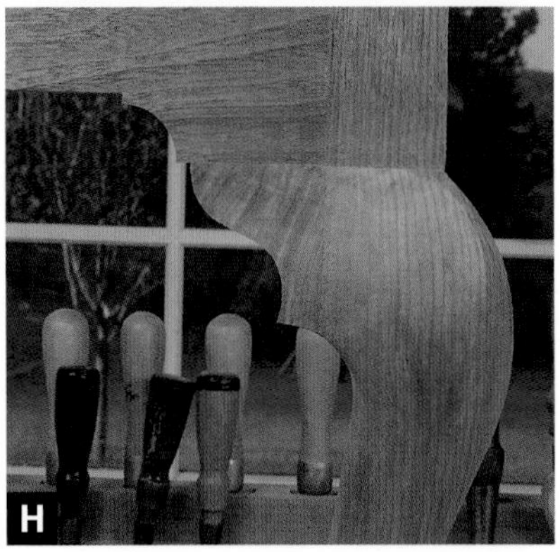
H

Under-the-Apron Knee Blocks

Knee blocks, sometimes referred to as transition blocks, visually unite the compound curves of a cabriole leg with the curves on a rail or apron. For the under-the-apron type, begin by gluing together the leg to the rail or apron. Then work the post block flush with a block plane (**A**). You can work the inside corner with a chisel (**B**) and a shoulder plane (**C**).

Next, trace the knee profile onto the knee block (**D**) and track the pattern contour on the block face (**E**). Bandsawing the knee block requires taping the offcut back in position after the first cut. After sawing the second cut, glue the knee block in position (**F**). Finally, pare the knee block flush with the surface of the knee (**G**). The finished knee block (**H**).

Over-the-Apron Knee Blocks

The process of shaping over-the-apron knee blocks is similar to the under-apron type. Glue the leg to the rail or apron. After working the post block flush, trace the knee profile (**A**) and the knee pattern onto the block (**B**). Next bandsaw the face contour and glue the knee block to the backing board for carving (**C**). Heavy paper in the glue joint will allow you to pry the block up later. Carefully carve the face of the block with a 1 in. #2 gouge. As you carve, follow the layout line that you traced from the knee. After gluing the knee block to the apron, blend the surfaces with the knee (**D**). The finished knee block (**E**).

A

B

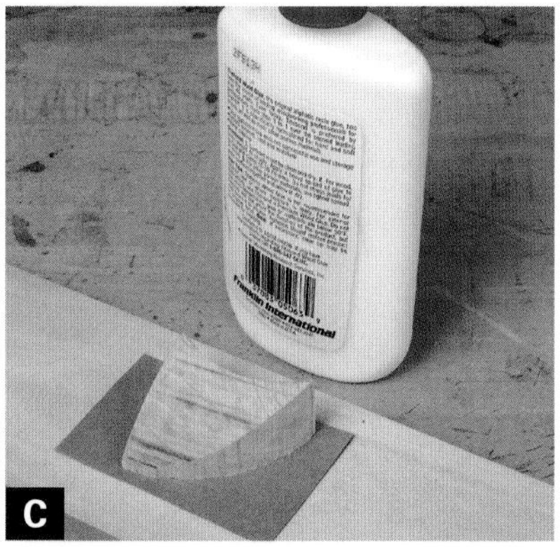
C

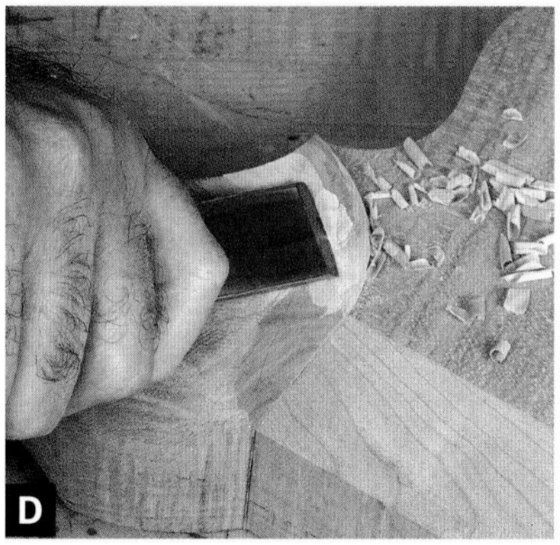
D

E

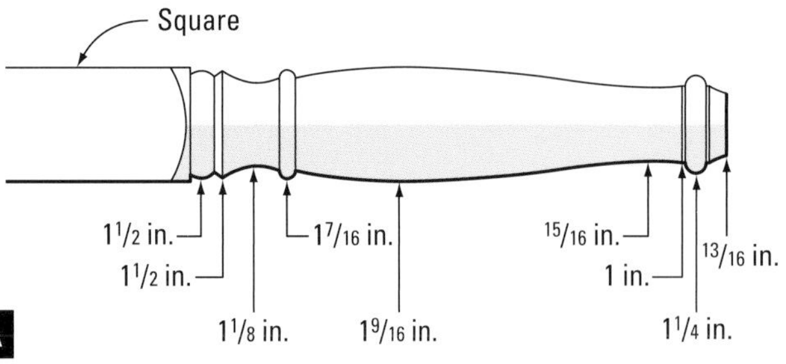

A

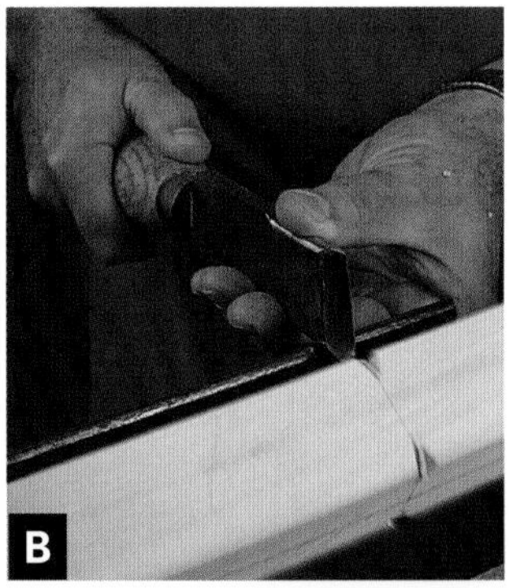
B

C

D

E

Turning a Tapered Leg

Because the leg used in this example has a square section for joinery, it's important to center the stock accurately in the lathe (**A**). Otherwise, the turned portion will be offset from the square portion.

Begin by turning the pommel with the point of a skew (**B**). First nick the corner; then cut from the right and the left. The pommel is complete when the cut from the skew runs the entire circumference (**C**).

Next, turn the leg round with a roughing gouge (**D**). Use the corner of the gouge to cut in the area adjacent to the pommel (**E**).

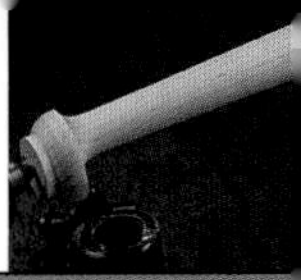

Once the leg is round, lay out the turning with a story stick (**F**). Next, shape the bead adjacent to the pommel. You'll need to use a skew to shape the bead in this tight spot.

The next step is to turn the cove and bead. Begin by cutting a fillet adjacent to the bead location (**G**). Then use a skew to remove the extra stock at the taper (**H**). Now, use a spindle gouge to shape the cove (**I**). Use a spring caliper to measure the final diameter of the cove. Most of the taper can be shaped with a gouge, but you'll need to use a skew to complete the taper as it approaches the bead. Finally, turn the bead and cove at the foot (**J**). Then sand the turning lightly to smooth it (**K**).

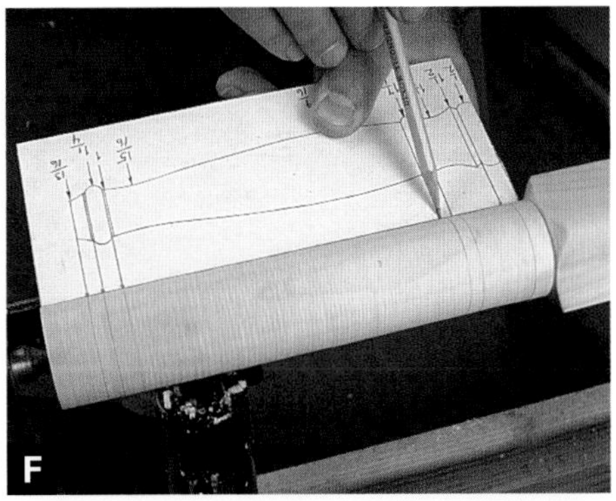

F

G

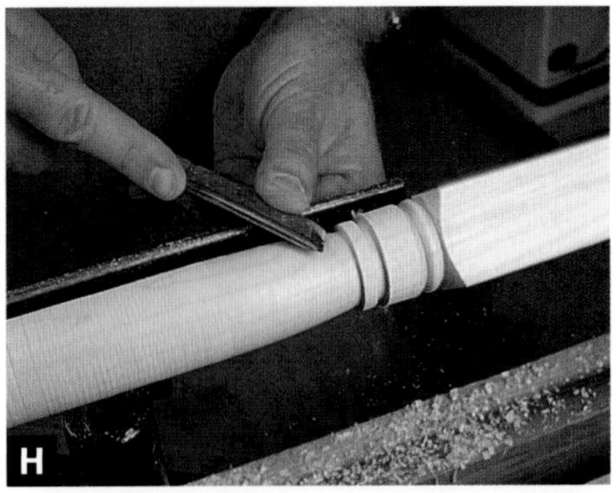

H

I

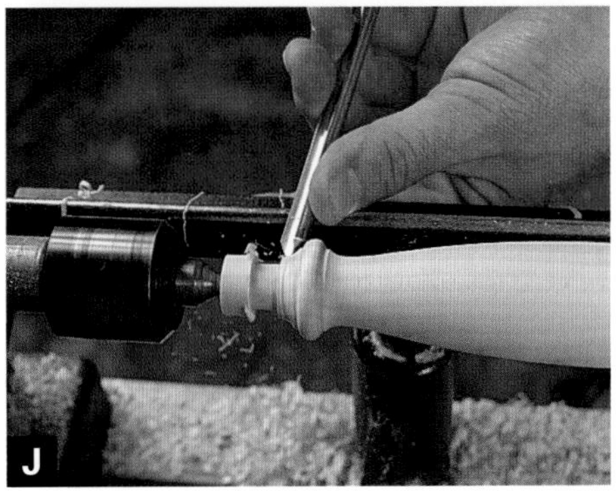

J

K

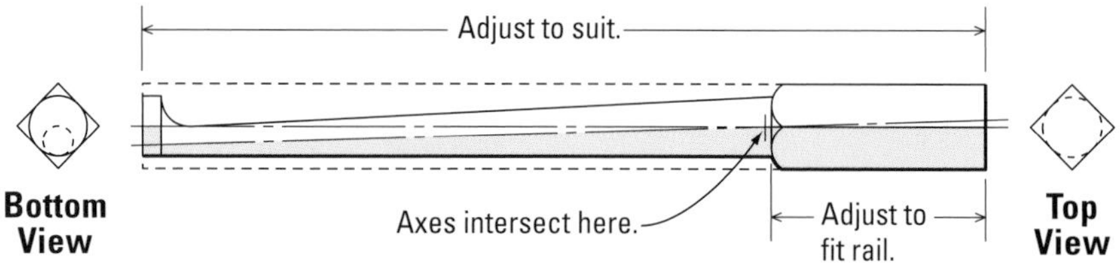

A

B

C

D

E

F

G

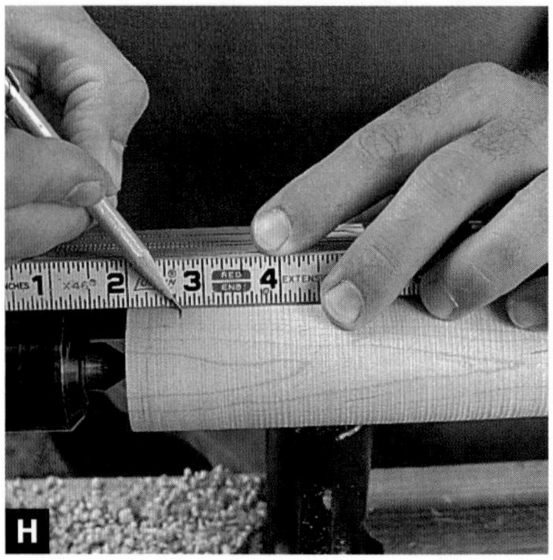

H

I

Turning an Offset Leg

The simple, yet attractive, offset leg is most often used on small tables. Unlike a true cabriole leg, this leg is turned in entirety, which makes it quick to produce. To make the leg, first turn the pommel with the stock centered. Then offset the turning in the lathe to turn the ankle and the taper of the leg. Finally, return the leg to center and turn the foot. Because two sets of points are used, the turning will have two axes. For the leg to have the correct appearance the axes should converge at the pommel (**A**).

Begin by locating the true center of the stock on each end of the workpiece; then locate the center for the ankle (**B**). Next, mount the leg in the lathe with the foot at the tailstock. This will avoid the risk of striking the drive center as you turn the foot. Now, turn the pommel with the point of a skew. First nick the corner (**C**); then cut from the left (**D**) and the right (**E**) until the point of the skew scores the entire perimeter (**F**). Afterward, turn the leg round below the pommel with a roughing gouge (**G**). Then mark a line to indicate the top of the foot (**H**). Don't turn the foot yet; otherwise you will cut away the center needed for turning the ankle.

The next step is to offset the stock in the lathe (**I**). Most of the offset occurs at the foot end of the stock. However, it's important to slightly offset the opposite end as well. Check the offset for accuracy before turning. When offset correctly, the two separate axes will converge at the pommel. Turn on the lathe and watch the spinning "ghost" of the leg to see where the axes converge. If necessary, stop the lathe and reposition the leg at the top slightly. Don't adjust the center location at the foot—otherwise you'll change the diameter of the ankle.

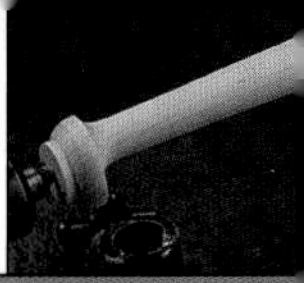

The next step is to turn the ankle. Before you begin, check the location of the tool rest. Position the rest as close as possible for the best support of the tool, but spin the work by hand to ensure that it clears the rest.

During the initial turning of the ankle, the gouge makes contact with the stock only once each revolution. Because of this, take light cuts to avoid having the stock grab the tool. Starting near the top of the foot, cut downward toward the ankle with a spindle gouge (**J**). Start with the gouge on edge, and roll it as you approach the bottom of the foot (**K**). Take several light cuts and then check the ankle size. When the cut encompasses the full perimeter, the ankle is complete.

Next, turn the tapered portion of the leg (**L**). If the leg vibrates, try wrapping one hand around it for support (**M**). The amount of stock to be removed diminishes as the taper ends at the pommel (**N**). Now, sand and smooth the taper before turning the foot (**O**).

To turn the foot, first reposition the turning on the true centers. Then turn the pad to diameter with a parting tool (**P**). Next, round the foot profile with a spindle gouge (**Q**). The technique is the same as that used when turning a bead. Sand the foot lightly to complete the turning (**R**).

> **WARNING Supporting slender stock with your hand works extremely well, especially on a taper where it may be difficult to mount a steady rest. But avoid wearing jewelry or long sleeves, and keep your fingers away from the tool rest where they may be pinched.**

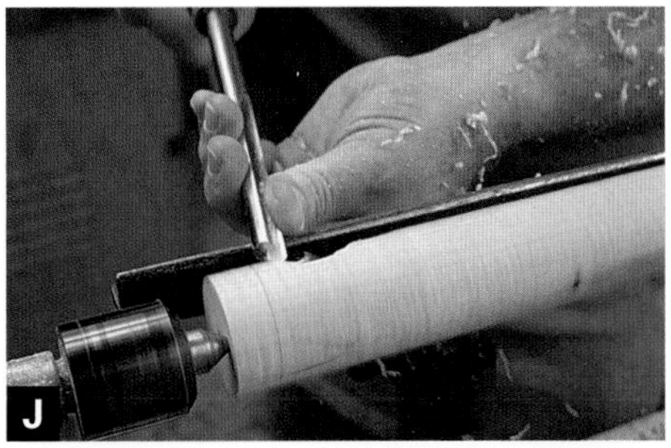

J

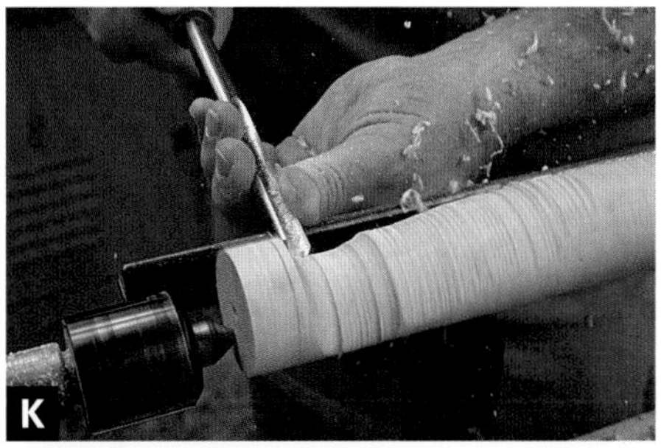

K

L

M

N

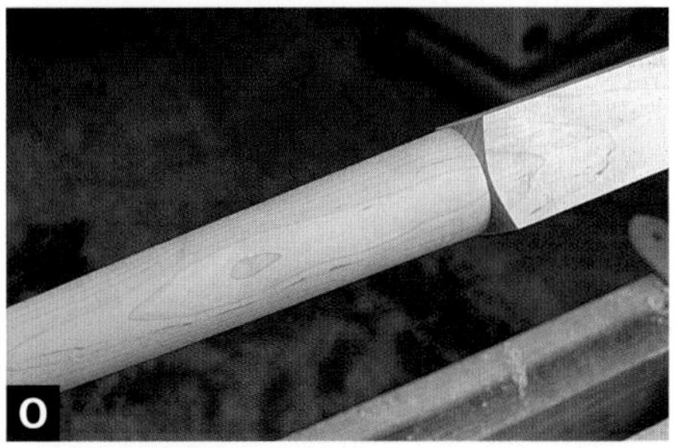

O

P

Q

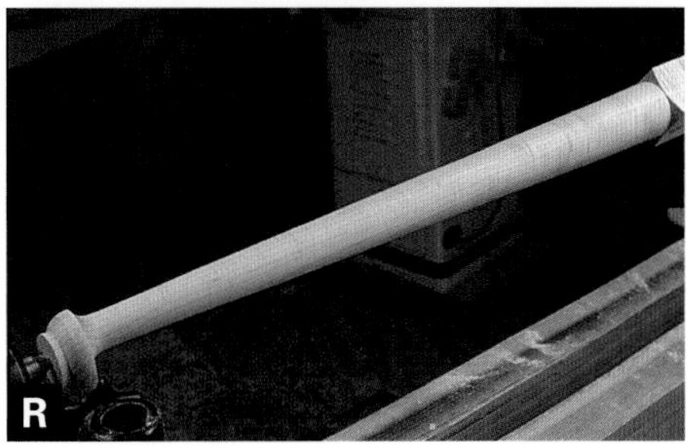

R

A

B

C

D

E

F

A Cabriole Leg

The cabriole leg is a beautiful example of compound curves. Although the shape appears complicated, it's relatively easy to create. In fact, most of the work is done on the bandsaw by sawing the contours of two adjacent faces of square stock. After sawing, the leg is further shaped and refined with hand tools.

Begin by sketching the leg onto ¼-in. plywood to make a pattern. When the sawing is completed, smooth the curves with a file. After selecting the stock, trace the contours of the pattern onto two adjacent faces of the leg blank (**A**). The pattern is oriented back to back rather than knee to knee. Next, cut the mortises while the leg is still square (**B**).

To avoid backing out of a long curve, begin sawing by making the short, straight cuts at the top of the knee and post block (**C**). Then saw the curves at the front (**D**) and back of the leg (**E**). After sawing the first face, use masking tape to reattach the offcut from the back of the leg and saw the second face (**F, G**).

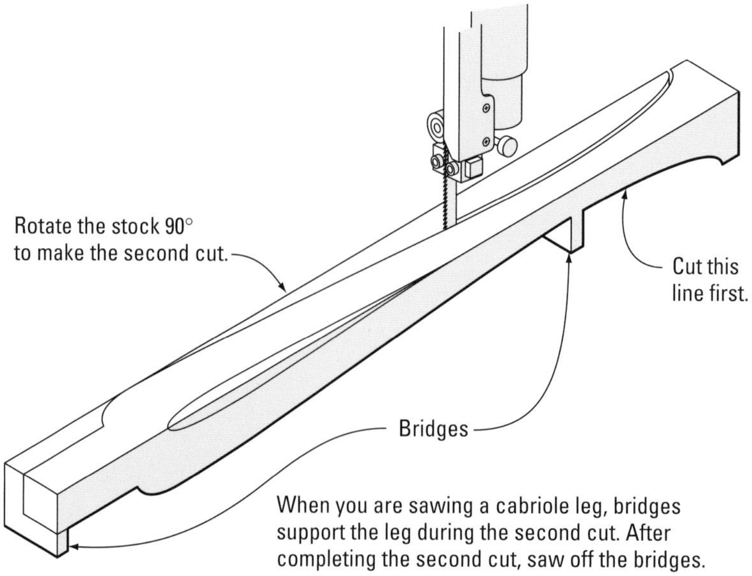

Rotate the stock 90°
to make the second cut.
Cut this
line first.
Bridges
When you are sawing a cabriole leg, bridges support the leg during the second cut. After completing the second cut, saw off the bridges.

G

To further shape and refine the curves of the leg, use a no. 49 Nicholson rasp. It reaches into the sharp curves where a spokeshave can't.

[TIP] To hold the leg secure while shaping, place it in a pipe clamp, which you can lock in the jaws of a bench vise.

Begin by shaping the front corner, creating a chamfer with the rasp (**H**). Then rasp the back corner in the same way (**I**). Finally, rasp the corners on each side (**J**). As you shape the leg with the rasp, examine the curves for irregularities. Holding the rasp askew, cuts away high spots quickly. Next, round each of the four corners (**K**). Depending on the style of the leg, the ankle may be round (or nearly so) while the rest of the leg remains square with rounded corners. To keep uniformity between matching pairs of legs, check the final ankle size with spring calipers (**L**).

Once the shaping is complete, smooth the leg—first with a file and then with a scraper (**M**). Now you're ready to carve the foot (**N**).

H

I

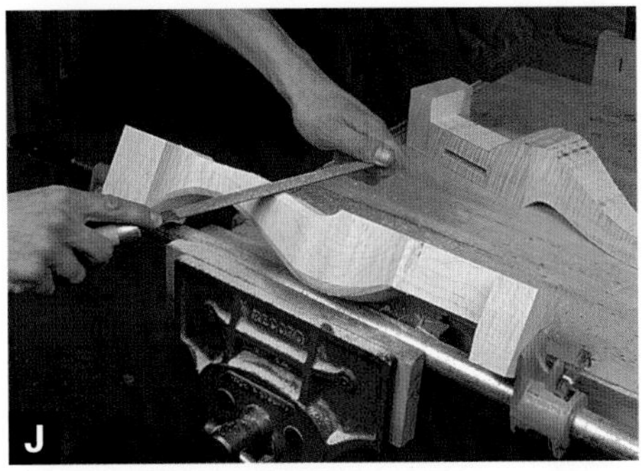
J

K

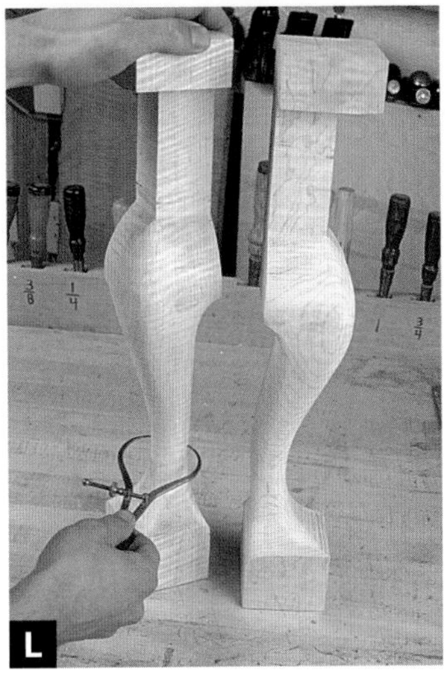
L

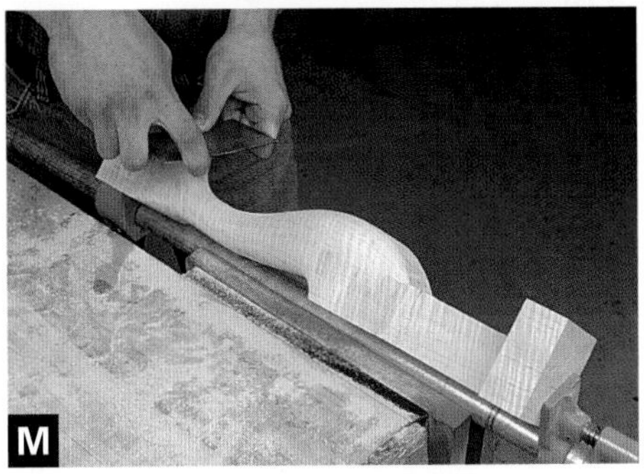
M

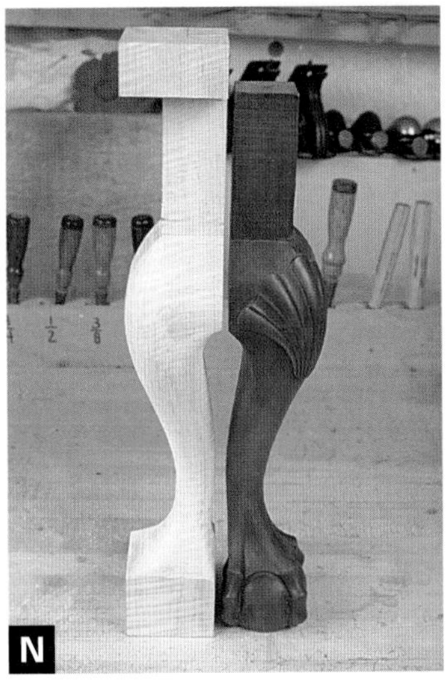
N

Tabletops

Scalloped Top

Dished Top

Rule Joint

➤ Scalloped Top (p. 38) ➤ Dished Top (p. 39) ➤ Rule Joint (p. 41)

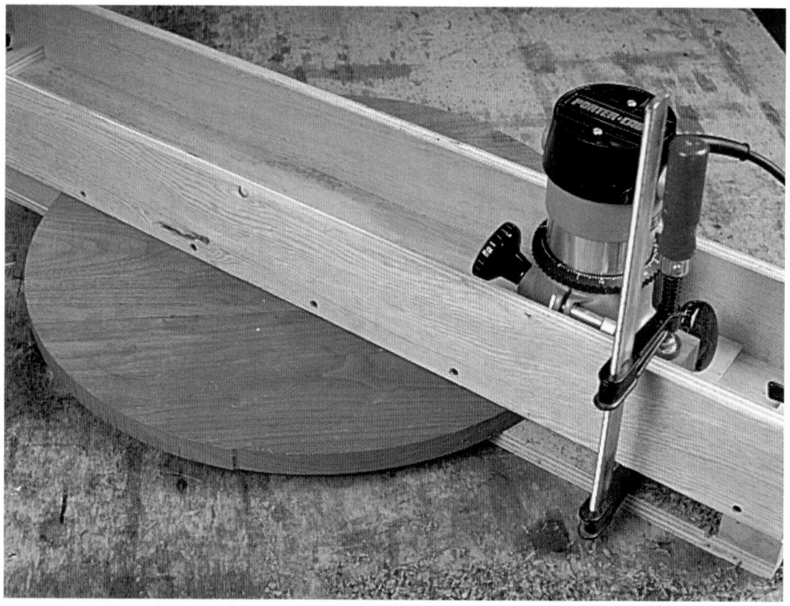

A dished tabletop can be shaped on a lathe, or more easily with a router mounted on a jig that suspends the router over the top. The lower edge is refined with handtools.

As with other 18th-century design details, tabletops reveal the tremendous diversity of period furniture makers. Judging from the surviving examples and estate inventories, tables were produced in mass quantity for every conceivable purpose. There were kitchen worktables, tables for both fine and casual dining, and tables for placing next to the bed. Also produced were numbers of specialty tables, candlestands for perching the light, tea tables for small social gatherings, and card tables with folding leaves and carved depressions for holding game pieces.

Tabletop design

Most tabletops from the period follow basic geometric shapes such as squares, rectangles, circles, and ellipses. However, other examples are quite unusual, such as the deeply scalloped tops on some Connecticut-dressing tables

and the protruding corners on porringer-top tea tables. Except perhaps for the most utilitarian worktables, edges were profiled with a simple molding both for decoration and for ease of use.

Some tops even have a raised molding profile along the edges. If the top were rectangular, a small, simple molding could be added to create a dished effect. However, round tops were turned to shape the rim and scoop out the center. The most elaborate were then scalloped and carved to created the piecrust table so popular in Philadelphia.

Many 18th-century tables had tops that tilted, folded, or leaves that dropped. Drop leaf tables had legs that would swing into position to support the leaf during use. These convertible tables were very efficient space-savers in the small homes of the period.

DRAWING AN ELLIPSE WITH TRAMMELS

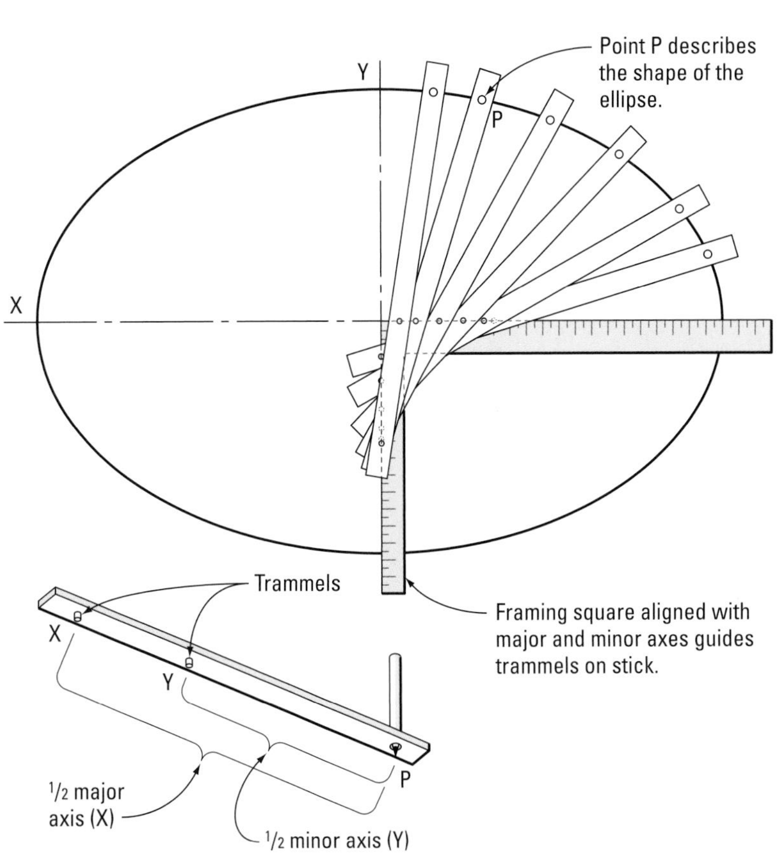

TABLE EDGES

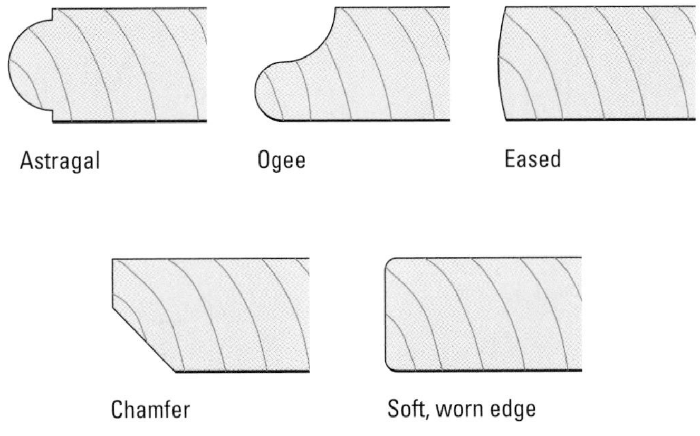

Scalloped Top on the Router

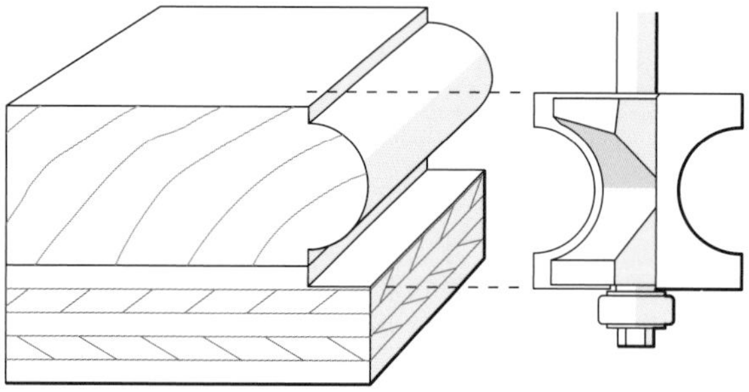

A Because the entire edge is removed, a template is needed when shaping this profile on a curved surface.

Anytime you shape a curved surface with a router, the rub bearing on the bit must follow a curve to guide the bit and limit the cutting depth. When only part of the edge is shaped, the portion that remains can serve to guide the bearing. However, when the entire edge is shaped, a template is needed to guide the cut (**A**).

After making the template, trace it onto the workpiece. Now saw the outline slightly proud of the line, which will provide extra stock to be removed by the router bit. If the top is large and your bandsaw is limited in size, you may opt to use a portable jigsaw (**B**). If so, clamp the work to the bench to keep it stationary while sawing.

Next, attach the template to the underside of the top with screws (**C**). The screw holes will later be hidden, but make certain that the screw doesn't penetrate the full thickness of the top.

Before shaping, set the bit height with an offcut from the top (**D**). Now you're ready to make the cut. To have complete control of routers and shapers, it's important always to feed in the opposite direction of the cutter rotation (**E**). When hand feeding a router, move it counterclockwise around the top's perimeter.

B

C

D

E

Dished Top

A dished tabletop has a molded rim that sets slightly above the rest of the table surface (**A**). The molding is small and refined and the effect is dramatic as it reflects light and casts shadows. The design is a classic one but the router technique for producing it is relatively new. The router is suspended over the top, which rotates on a hub. To use the technique you'll first have to build a jig.

[TIP] A one-board top looks best; but if you must use two boards, take care when matching the grain and color.

Begin by milling the stock for the top. Now draw the radius of the top (**B**). Next bandsaw the top perimeter and glue the hub to the center (**C**). If you sandwich a layer of heavy paper between the top and the hub, it is much easier to remove the hub after the process is complete.

After the glue has dried, mount the top into the jig (**D**). Before shaping the molding, it's necessary to true the edge of the top. A spiral straight bit cuts cleaner and with less chatter than an ordinary straight bit (**E**).

Once the bit is mounted, you're ready to begin. Never attempt to start the router when the bit is in contact with the stock. Instead, start the router, slide it along the rails until it touches the top, clamp the router in position, and rotate the top. Always rotate the top clockwise against the bit rotation (**F**).

(Text continues on p. 40)

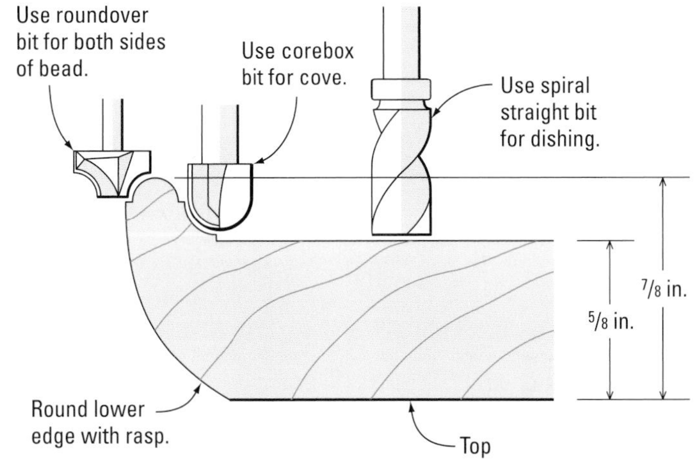

Use roundover bit for both sides of bead.
Use corebox bit for cove.
Use spiral straight bit for dishing.
7/8 in.
5/8 in.
Round lower edge with rasp.
Top

A

B

C

D

E

F

G

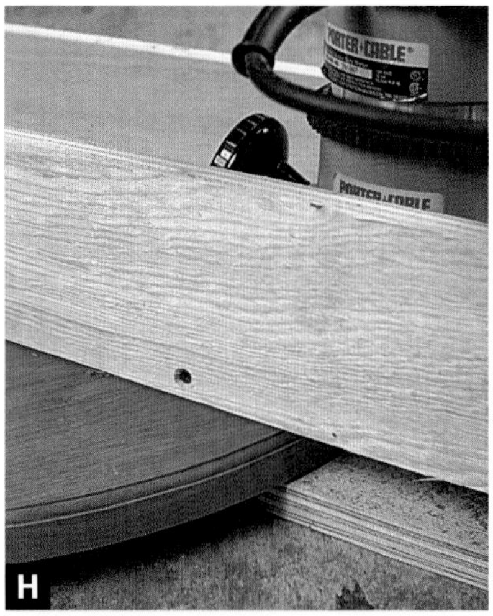

H

I

J

K

L

Next, switch to the roundover bit to create the bead. If you're not able to find a bit without a bearing it's easy to remove the bearing and grind away the bearing stud. To adjust the bit depth, use a block of plywood from the jig (**G**).

Shaping the molding is much the same as truing the perimeter: Start the router, clamp it in position, and rotate the top (**H**). To ensure that the molding isn't squeezed, begin from the outside edge and work inward (**I**). The molding is shaped in three steps: outside edge of bead; inside edge of bead; and cove, which is shaped with a bullnose bit.

Once the molding is complete, switch back to the straight bit to dish the top (**J**). This process goes quickly, because there is no careful positioning of the router as there was with the molding. If you have a helper, one of you can hold the router while the other rotates the top, which sidesteps the process of clamping the router for each cut.

With the router work completed, you're ready for the handwork. Clamp the top to the bench and scrape the surface smooth (**K**). Use care to avoid scarring the molding. After smoothing the top, the edge will need shaping along the underside to remove the square corner. This step also gives the top a thin, refined appearance. A rasp works well for this process, but first draw a line with a compass for use as a guide. Now secure the top in the vise and rasp the edge (**L**). Work the surface from the fillet at the bead to the layout line. When you're satisfied, smooth the edge with a file, scraper, and then sandpaper.

WARNING A dust collector is a must. Otherwise this process produces a choking cloud of fine dust and chips.

Making a Rule Joint

Rule joints are used for drop leaves on tables (**A**). A cove is cut on the lower edge of the leaf to mate with a thumbnail profile on the table edge. The result is both beautiful and functional. When the leaf is dropped, the two profiles mesh to create an attractive ovolo profile (**B**). Conventional wisdom is to locate the hinge barrel directly below the fillet. I prefer to position the barrel an additional 1/64 toward the edge to prevent the finish from wearing away each time the leaf is raised or lowered.

For this unique movable joint to function properly, it is important that the cove and thumbnail profiles match.

You can cut the profiles with molding planes if you are fortunate enough to have a matching pair. Or you can shape the profiles with router bits. Choose a radius that will leave a ¼ in. fillet; anything heavier tends to look clumsy. For the example in these photos, I'm using ½ in. radius bits with a ¾ in. top and leaf thickness. Also, before you jump in to this process, you'll need special drop leaf hinges; one leaf is longer than the other.

After shaping the cove and thumbnail, mark the hinge position with a knife (**C**). Next, mortise for the hinge thickness. I speed this up with a small router and a straight bit (**D**). After squaring the mortise with a chisel, cut a recess for the hinge barrel and fasten the hinges in place (**E**). Photo (**F**) shows leaf in position.

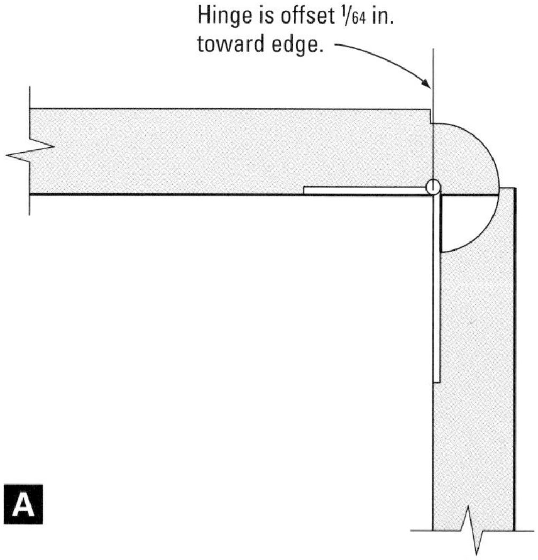
Hinge is offset 1/64 in. toward edge.
A

B

C

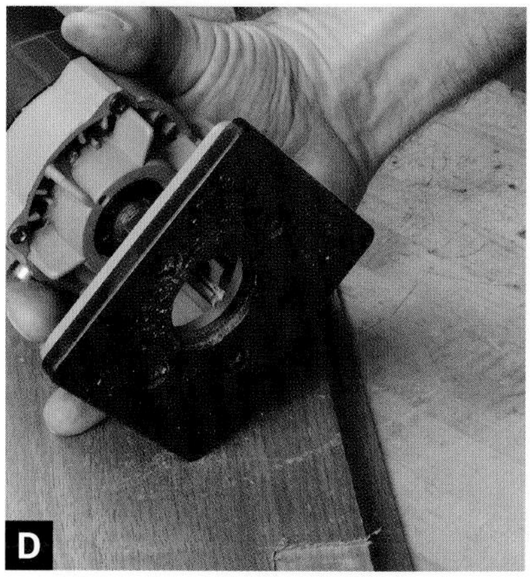
D

E

F

Feet

Pad Foot

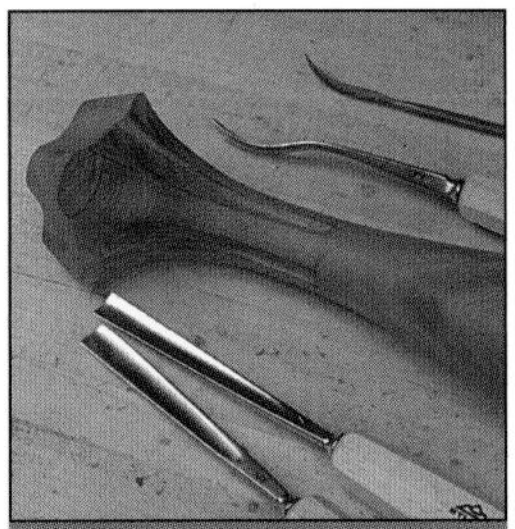

Trifid Foot

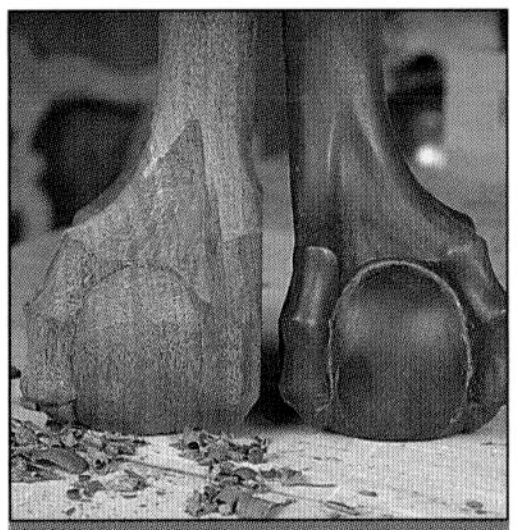

Ball and Claw Foot

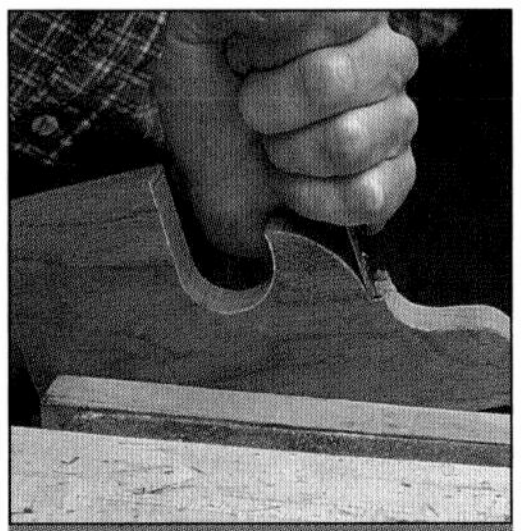

Flat Base

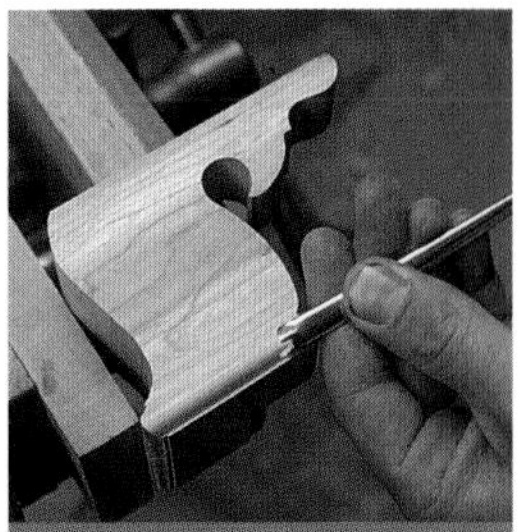

Ogee Feet

The simple elegance of the pad foot is shown in this 18th-century-style desk. The bottom of the pad is easily turned on a lathe.

CABRIOLE LEGS CAN TERMINATE in a wide variety of foot styles. Probably the most common is the pad foot, which is quickly and easily turned on a lathe. However, even pad feet can be far from ordinary. For example, those produced in Virginia are unusual looking thin disks resting on a thick platform. The spoon foot is the form that is most familiar and often reproduced.

Various forms of carved feet were also popular during the 18th century. The slipper foot is a slender, somewhat elongated version of a pad foot. And the trifid, or three-toed, foot was extremely popular in 18th-century Pennsylvania. A study of surviving example reveals enormous variation from thick and clumsy to highly refined and elegant.

Today, nothing symbolizes 18th-century furniture more than the claw-and-ball foot. It is said to have come to America from

China, where it represented a dragon's claw clutching a pearl. Once it migrated to the colonies, it became a symbol of wealth and status. A closer study of colonial furniture reveals regional differences more than any other style of foot. For example, Philadelphia feet appear tense, powerful, and perhaps the most realistic. New York feet appear somewhat boxy while feet from Newport have long undercut talons that grasp a nearly perfectly spherical ball.

The ogee bracket foot is a versatile element used to create bases for case pieces. Often used in high style pieces, it is more elegant and sinuous than a flat base.

Bracket feet

While it is possible to see short cabriole legs on desks and other casework, bracket feet were probably more common—and for good reason. While a short, stubby cabriole leg can appear as underdeveloped appendixes, the bracket foot appears strong and understated.

The bracket foot takes two forms; the flat bracket and the ogee bracket. Although neither example is difficult to construct, shaping the face of the ogee foot is somewhat more time-consuming. Both types of bracket feet are "capped" with a simple molding profile such as a cove or an ogee. The molding provides a transition to the case and visually ties the feet to the case as well as to each other.

REGIONAL VARIATIONS ON THE BALL AND CLAW FOOT

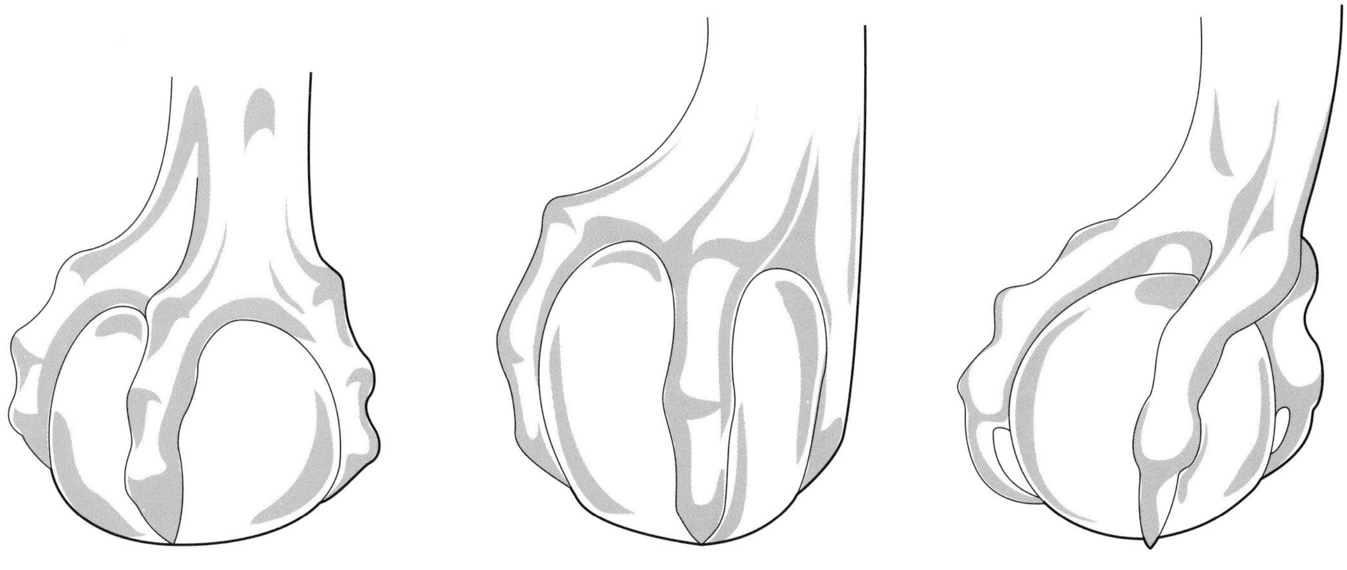

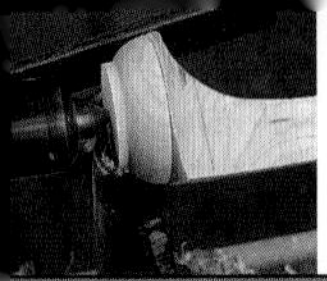

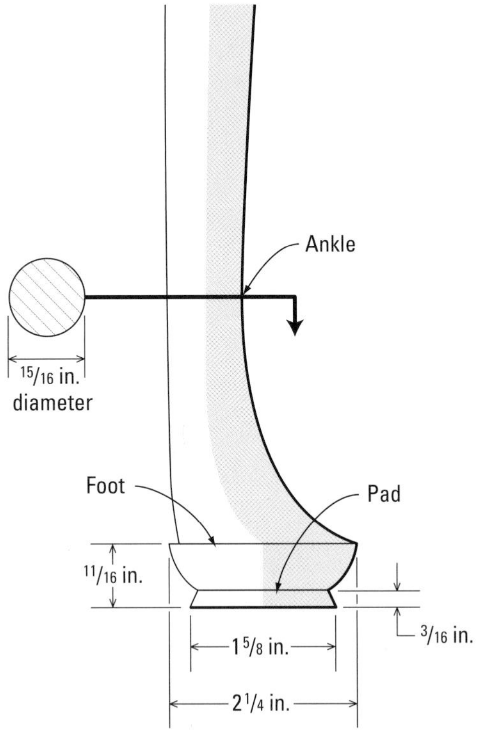

A Adjust dimensions to fit leg proportions.

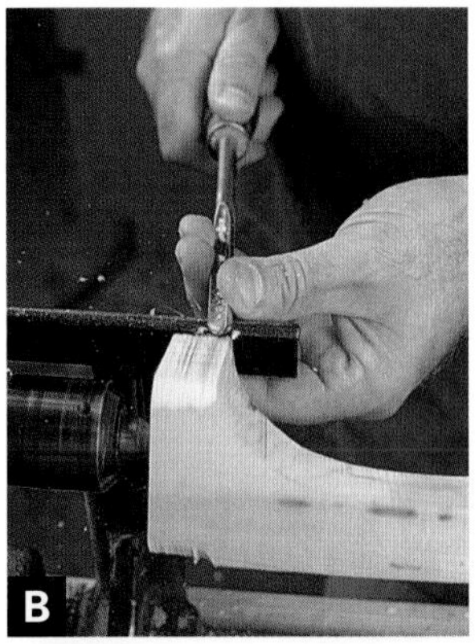

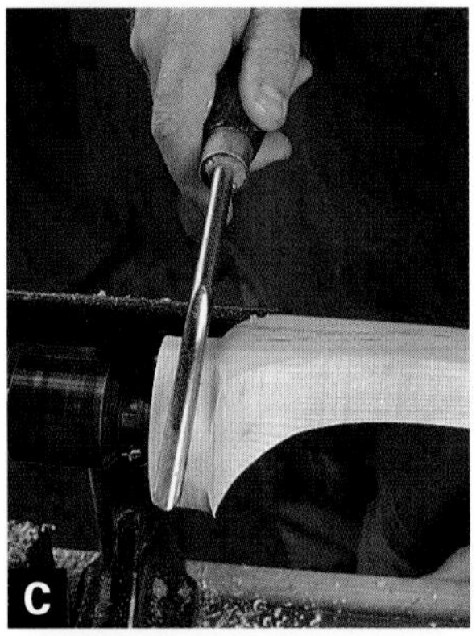

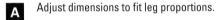

Turning a Pad Foot

The pad foot was the most common form of foot used on 18th-century cabriole legs (**A**). It's quite easy to turn, and the entire process takes just a few minutes. You'll need to use a slow lathe speed, because the asymmetrical leg spins off balance.

Begin by bandsawing the leg. Next, locate the centers and mount the leg in the lathe with the foot at the tailstock. This avoids the possibility of the gouge coming in contact with the drive center. Now, turn the foot round with a spindle gouge (**B**); the roughing gouge is too large and awkward for this cut. As you round the foot, use care to avoid cutting the ankle, which would spoil the curve of the leg.

As the work progresses, you can check for roundness by laying the shank of the gouge on top of the spinning foot (**C**). Once the foot is round, cut a small V at the top of the foot to indicate the height (**D**). Next, turn the pad to diameter with a parting tool and gauge it with a caliper (**E**).

The last step is to shape the foot. This step is identical to rolling a bead with a spindle gouge. For the first pass, start at the corner and round the foot to the pad (**F**). Remember, as you turn the foot, roll the gouge, lift the handle, and pivot the handle (**G**). To avoid chatter, it's a good idea to turn the foot in two or three passes. The final pass should be from the V to the pad to create a continuous curve (**H**).

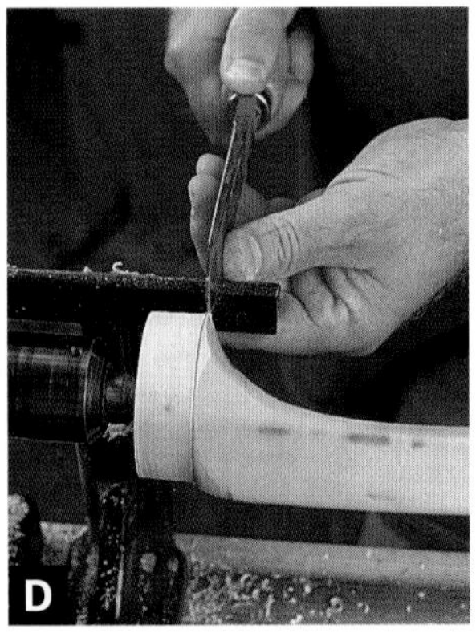

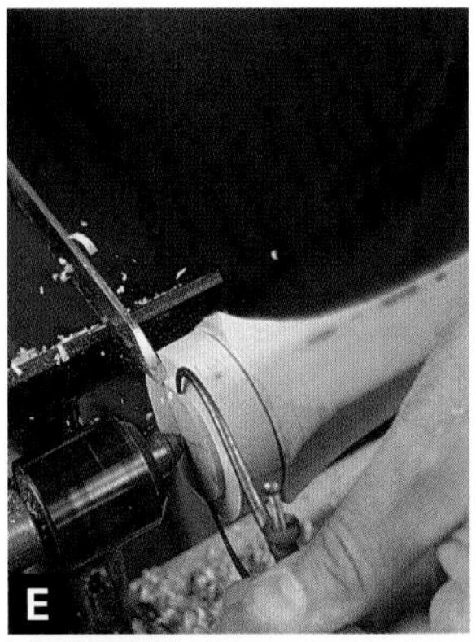

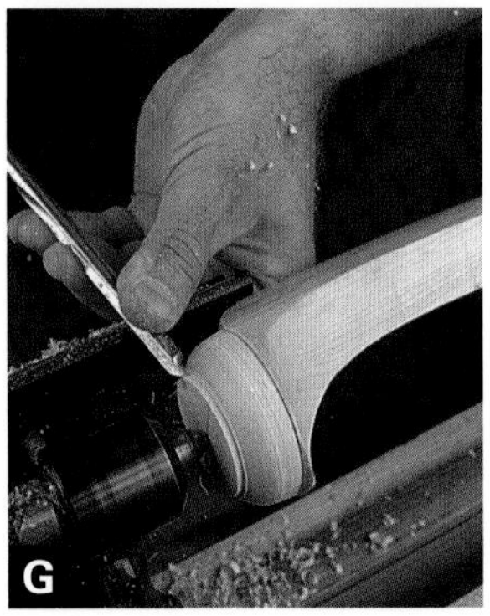

Carving a Trifid Foot

The trifid, or three-toe, foot is a simple, yet elegant carved foot commonly found on period furniture from Pennsylvania and the Delaware Valley. Begin by bandsawing and shaping the leg.

Next, make a pattern for the bottom of the foot to serve as a guide while carving. Heavy cardboard works well for the pattern; simply incise the outline with gouges that match the curves. Then position the pattern on the base of the foot and trace the outline (**A**).

To begin carving, secure the leg in a pipe clamp that is mounted in a vise. For consistency, use the same gouges for carving that you used for incising the pattern. Carve the profile of the toes starting at the top of the foot and working toward the base (**B**). As you carve, maintain the angles on the edge of the foot that were established earlier when bandsawing. Invert the gouge to carve the convex area (**C, D**). Afterward, smooth and blend the areas with a small file (**E**).

The next step is to carve the stocking. Begin with layout. First locate the height of the stocking with a compass (**F**). Used as a divider, the compass ensures that this measurement is consistent from one foot to the next.

(Text continues on p. 46)

A

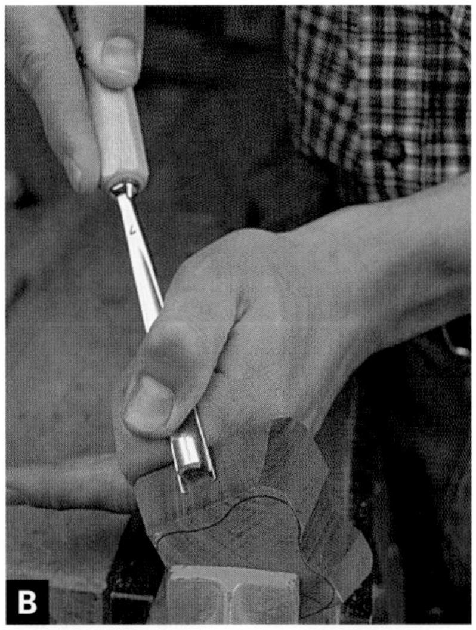

B

C

D

E

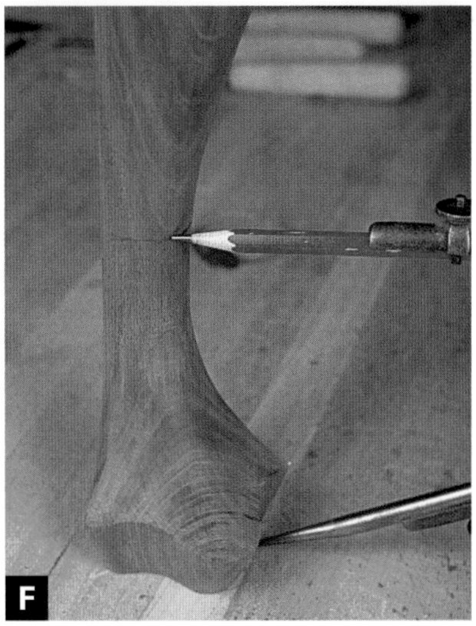

F

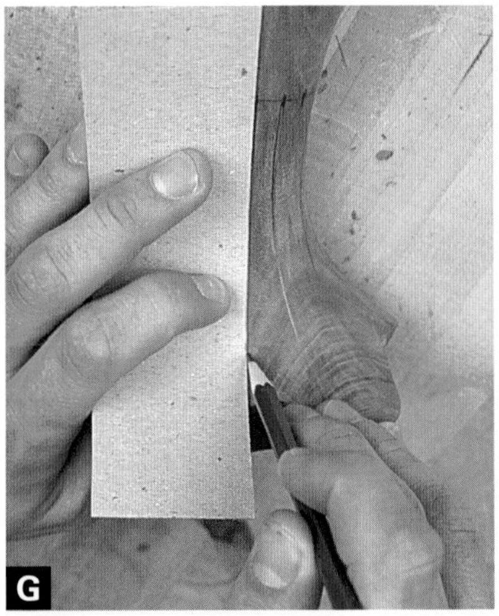
G

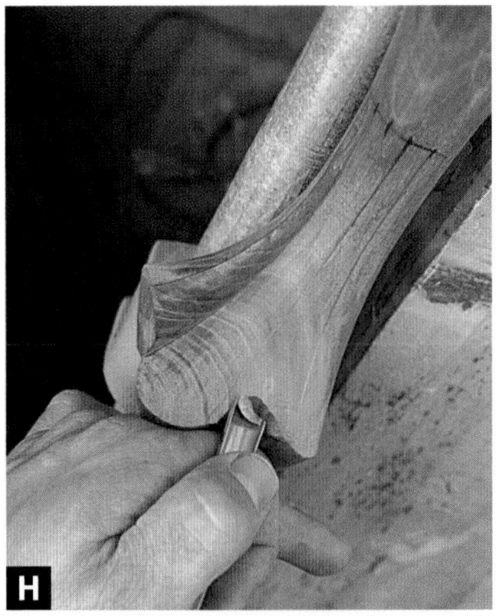
H

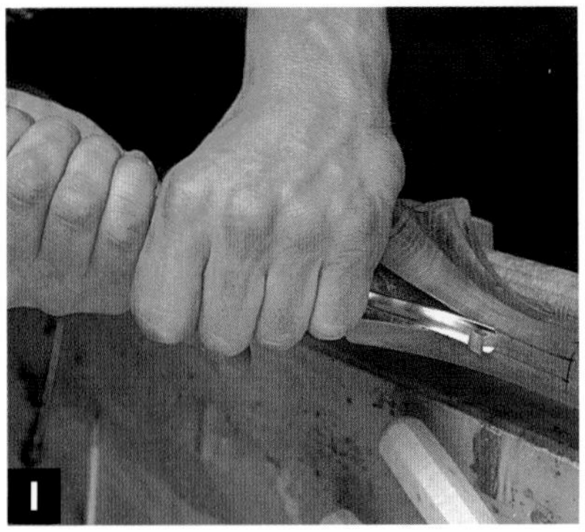
I

J

K

To outline the concave areas that form the stocking, flex a straightedge into the curve and trace it from toe to ankle (**G**). Now you're ready for the next stage of carving.

Beginning at the toe, scoop out the wood between the toes with a no. 5 gouge (**H**). As you near the sharp curve at the ankle the gouge will have a natural tendency to dig in (**I**). At this point, switch to a narrow spoon gouge and carve a little farther until the gouge begins to lift the grain. This is a sign that the grain direction has changed; switch directions and carve from the top of the stocking to this transition point and blend the two areas where they meet (**J**).

After carving, the stockings will be somewhat faceted from the gouges. But sanding this area would spoil the sharp ridges that outline the stocking. Instead, use a small bent file, otherwise known as a riffler (**K**). This unique tool will allow you to preserve the details as you smooth the surface.

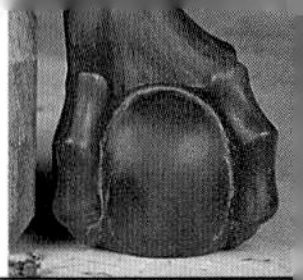

Carving a Ball and Claw Foot

The ball and claw foot is a classic design that has become an icon of Colonial American furniture. It first emerged during the mid-eighteenth century and quickly became popular as a sign of wealth and status. The foot shown here (**A**) is modeled after Pennsylvania examples. It features tense, powerful claws gripping a slightly flattened ball.

Begin by bandsawing the leg and shaping the contours with a rasp and file. Shaping the leg first ensures that the contours of the leg and foot blend together.

The next step is layout. Start by marking diagonal lines from the corners to locate the center of the foot. Next, draw a circle with a compass to serve as a guide when carving the ball (**B**). To outline the claws, draw a pair of parallel lines 5/16 in. from each centerline (**C**). Then extend each line upward to the ankle where the lines converge (**D**). Finally, mark the apex of the ball on each of the four faces.

With the layout complete (**E**), you're ready to begin carving. The first stage involves roughing in the contours of the ball. As the ball is shaped, the corners of the block are further exposed to be later formed into the claws. My favorite tool for carving the ball is an old 3/8-in. socket firmer chisel about 12 in. long. The extended length of this tool provides leverage beyond that of a standard carving gouge for quick removal of stock. Later on, after the contours of the ball are roughed in, further refine the ball and remove the facets with a no. 2 gouge. Start by carving from the apex of the ball downward toward the circle on the underside of the foot (**F**). Next, change directions and carve from the apex toward the top (**G**)

(Text continues on p. 48)

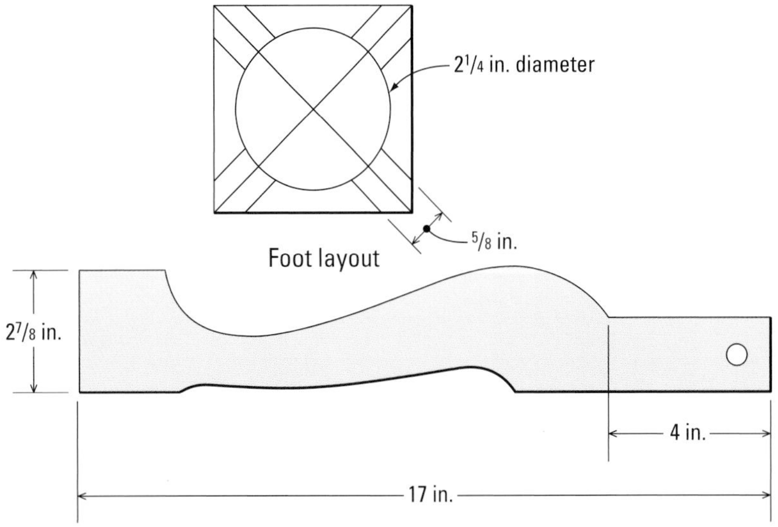

A

B

C

D

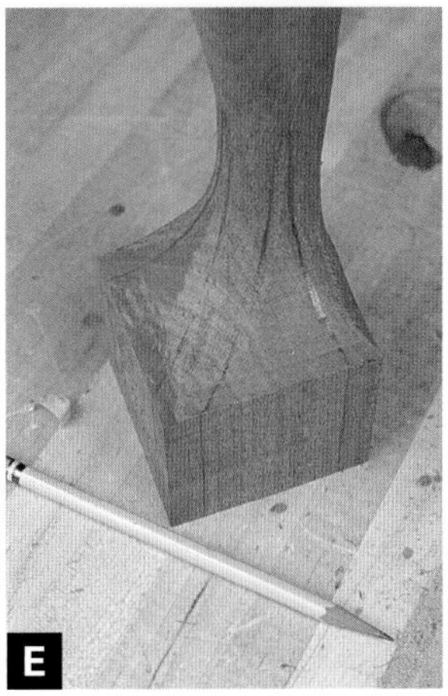
E

F

G

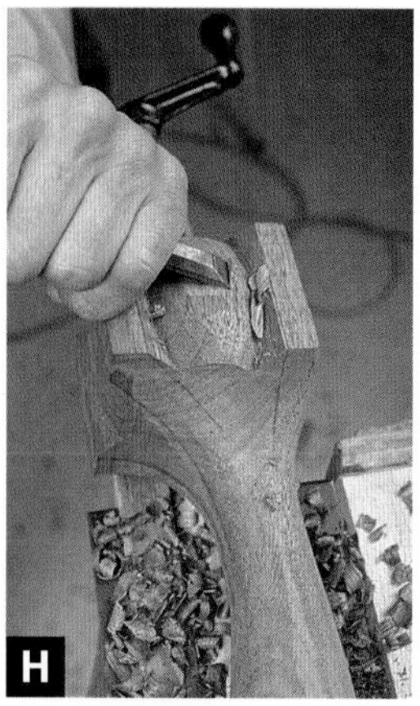
H

I

J

K

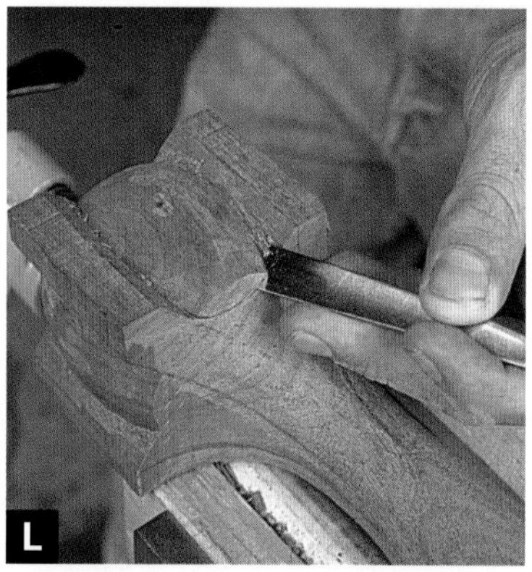
L

M

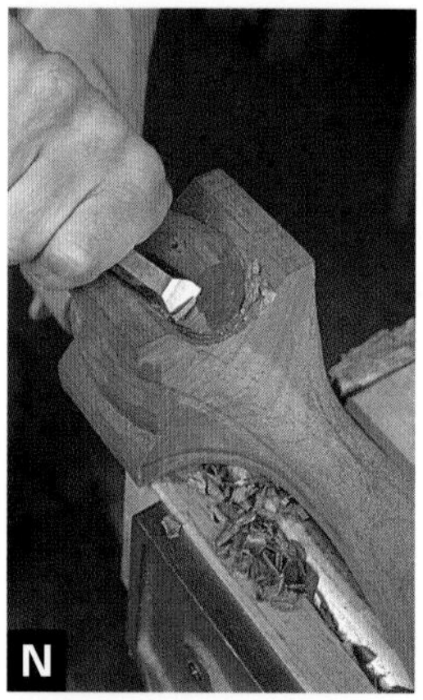
N

O

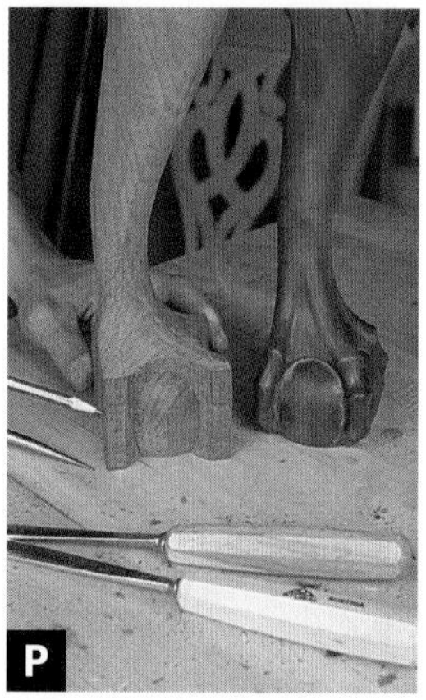
P

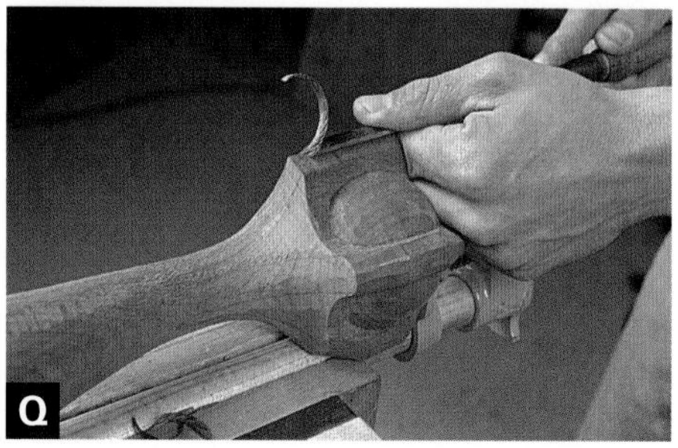
Q

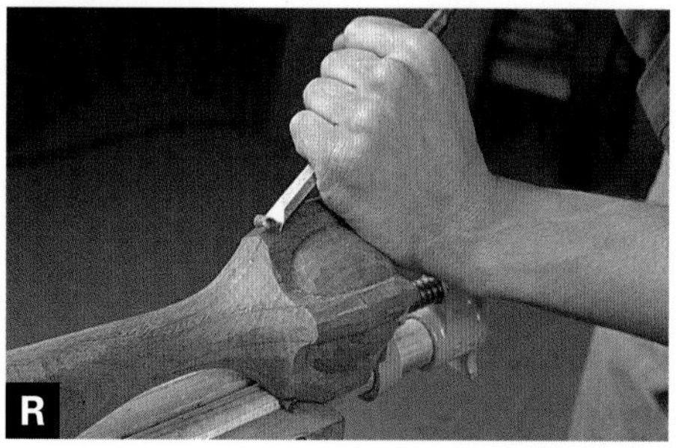
R

Compare the curvature of the top to that at the bottom and keep the two alike. Add additional curvature to the ball by carving across the grain from the apex toward the claw (**H**).

At the back of the foot, begin carving by outlining the curve at the top of the ball with a no. 5 gouge. Aim the gouge toward the ball's center and tap it lightly with a mallet (**I**). Repeat the process several times to form an arc. Afterward, carve the face of the ball downward toward the arc (**J**). Just as on the front, carve from the apex of the ball in every direction, and the ball will begin to emerge from the block (**K**).

Next, turn your attention to the front. Outline the web with a no. 5 gouge (**L**). Then use the corner of the chisel to remove stock at this area (**M**). With each cut, the ball will further emerge and the web will begin to form. Also, the height of the ball will shorten as it becomes round and fully formed (**N**).

Once all four surfaces of the ball begin to take shape, it becomes easier to visualize the overall form. Work your way around the ball once more and refine it so that the four surfaces become one sphere (**O**). Then you're ready to begin roughing in the claws.

Before carving the claws, use compass as a divider to lay out the location of each knuckle (**P**). Next, begin roughing in the claws by first removing the corners (**Q**). Then carve the excess block away so that the claws bend at the knuckles to follow the contours of the ball (**R**). Afterward, check the knuckle spacing with dividers and make any necessary adjustments (**S**).

With the claws contoured to follow the ball, the next step is to refine them (**T**). Using a no. 5 gouge, cut across the grain to hollow the space between each knuckle. This gives the knuckles a more lifelike appearance.

Next, use a no. 7 gouge to remove the excess stock at the web (**U**). This area is tough end grain, so keep the gouge sharp for greatest control. As you pare the excess stock away at the web, the claws at the top of the ball will begin to form (**V**). Continue to contour the web until you reach the ankle. At this point, the web diminishes as it blends into the curves of the ankle.

At the sides the claws flex inward at the second knuckle to follow the contour of the ball. Remove stock at the back of the claw to yield this effect (**W**).

Now carve the talons. Curve the surfaces of the talon with a no. 5 gouge and taper them to a blunt point (**X**). Next, add further refinement to the web by hollowing the corners adjacent to each claw with a no. 7 gouge (**Y**). Finally, smooth all of the surfaces. A no. 2 gouge will remove facets on the surface of the ball left by the chisel (**Z**). Afterward, smooth the ball with a file (**AA**). A short bent file known as a riffler is useful for smoothing the concave surface of the web (**BB**). Final smoothing is done with 240-grit sandpaper.

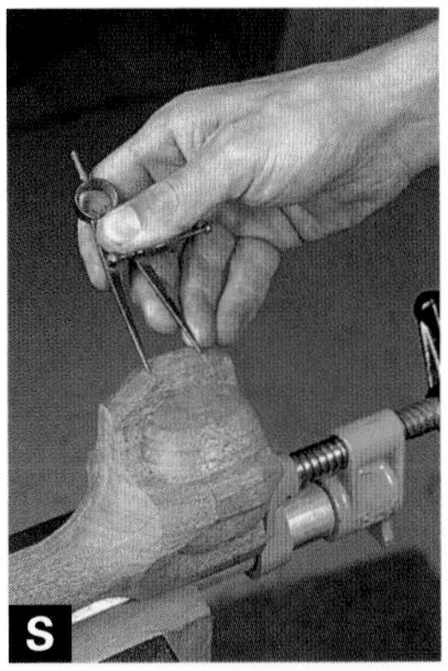
S

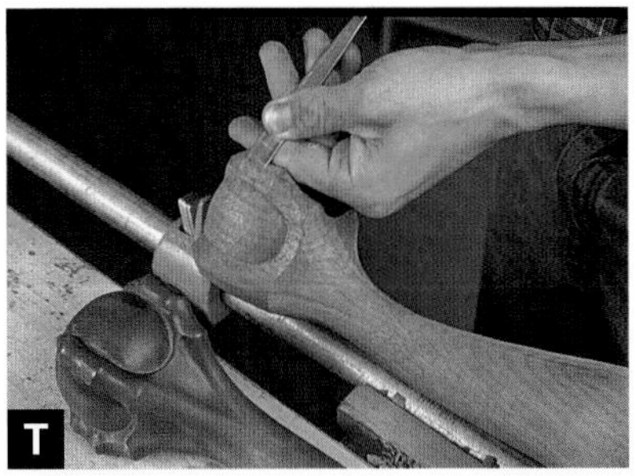
T

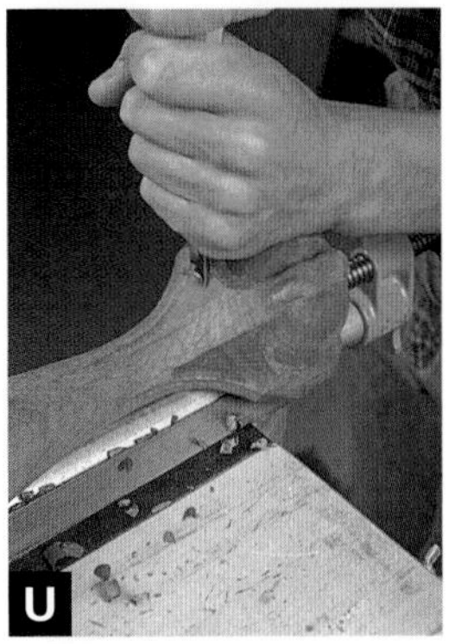
U

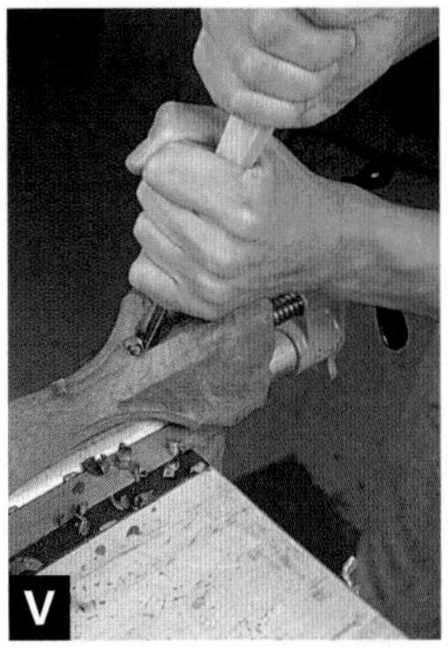
V

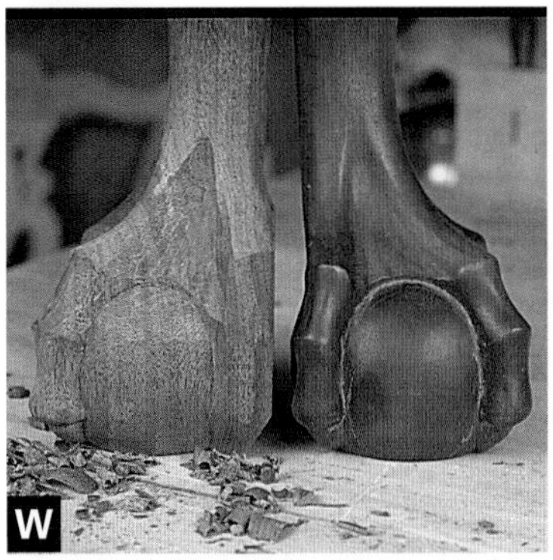
W

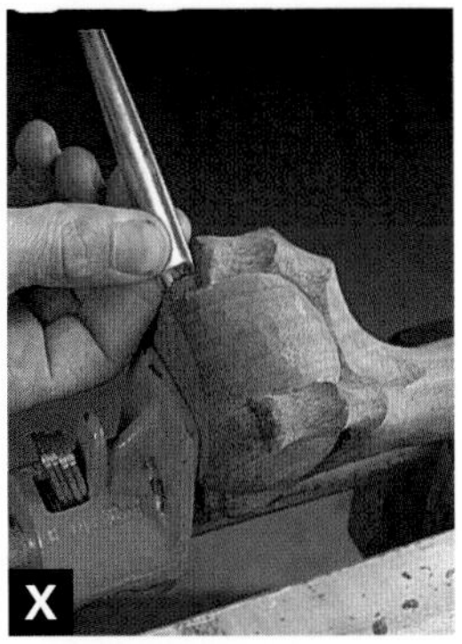
X

Y

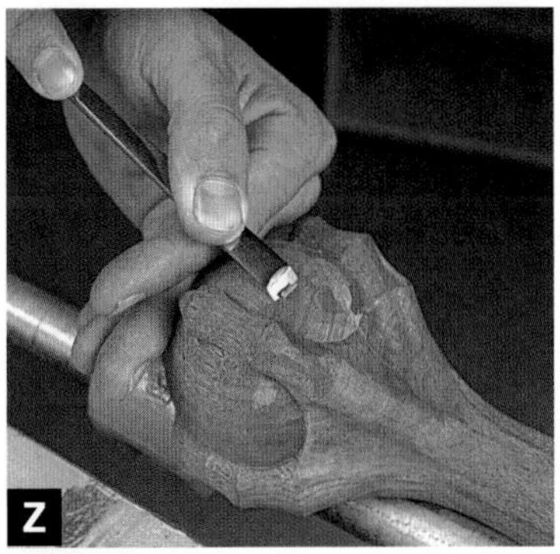
Z

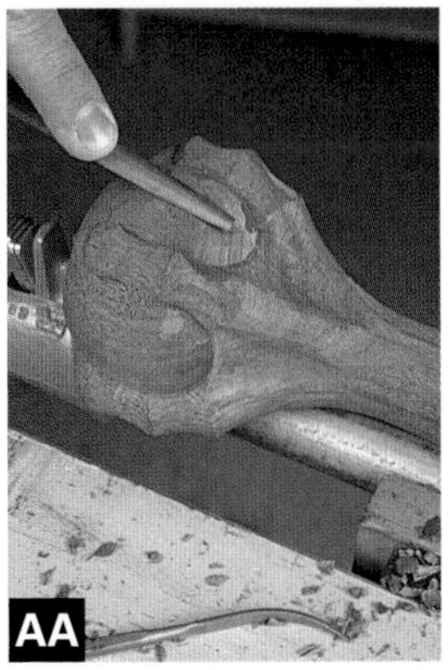
AA

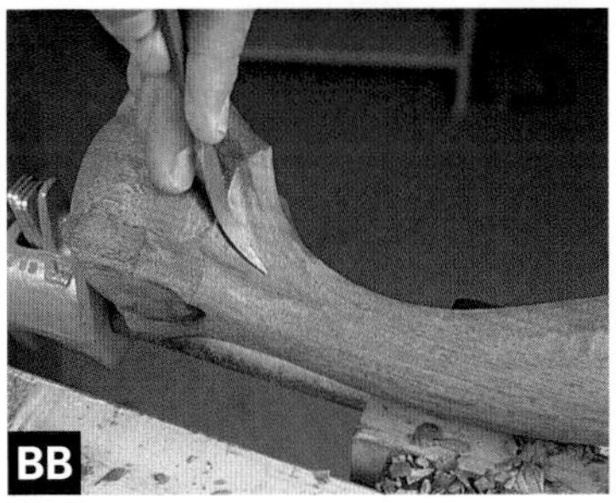
BB

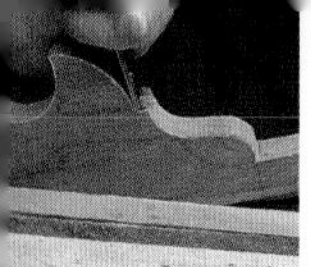

A

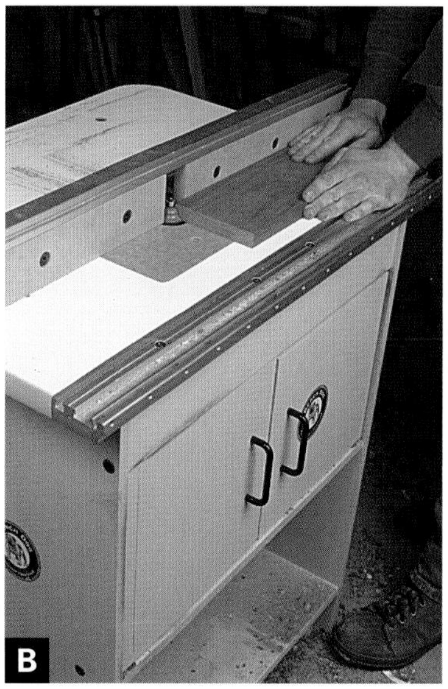

B

C

D

VARIATION

Cutting a Flat Base on the Bandsaw

Bandsawing should always begin with a pattern. This allows you to work out proportions and create smooth, flowing curves.

Begin by carefully tracing the pattern onto the stock (**A**). If there are slight imperfections in the wood, you can often orient the pattern to locate them in areas of offcuts.

The example for this technique is two bracket feet joined by molding. Shape the molding before bandsawing, while the straight reference edges are still intact (**B**). The long, straight section that spans the feet is difficult to cut with a bandsaw. Instead, make a stop cut on the table saw. The stop block prevents kickback (**C**), and a second cut from the opposite face will reach into the corners (**D**).

VARIATION You can get a straighter line between the bracket feet if you use the table saw instead of the bandsaw. It's called a stop cut, and the way to do it safely is with a stop block clamped to the fence or table.

Before bandsawing, mount a blade that will turn the tightest contour without binding. Then plan the cutting sequence to avoid trapping the blade (**E**). Backing out of the turn is a sure way to pull the blade off the wheels (**F**).

You can avoid tedious cleanup of the surface by carefully sawing to the layout line (**G**). When the bandsawing is complete, smooth the curves with a spindle sander (**H**) and clean up the intersections with a chisel for a crisp, defined look (**I**).

E

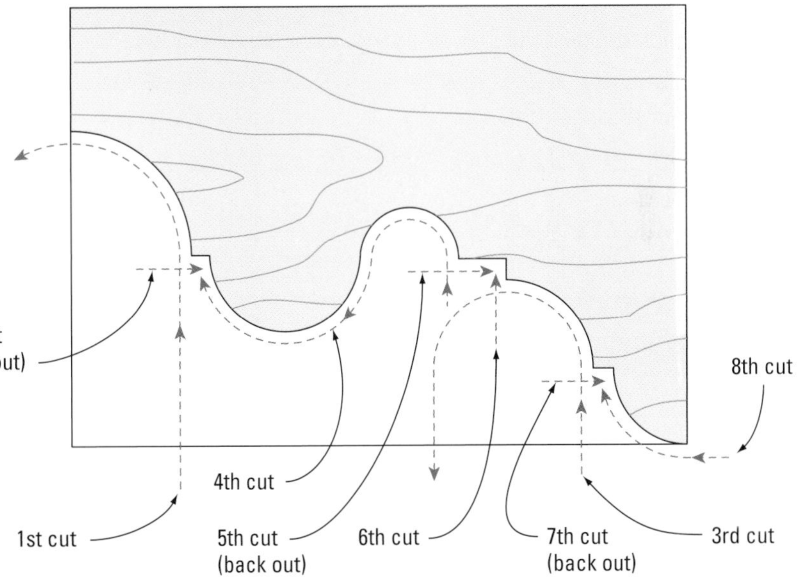

F

G

H

I

Shaping Ogee Feet on the Bandsaw

The curves of ogee bracket feet give a sculptural effect to chests, desks, and other forms of casework. Making them on the bandsaw is a four-step process of cutting the joints, sawing the bracket outline, assembling the feet, and bandsawing the ogee contour in the face (**A**). For the last step you'll need to construct a simple stand to support the foot during sawing.

[TIP] Because it's strong and doesn't require milling, ¼-in. plywood makes an excellent spline. Plywood is always less than the specified thickness, though, so cut the spline groove to fit the plywood.

First mill the stock to size and cut the joinery. The front feet are joined with a miter and spline. However, the back feet are designed to fit flush with the back of the case so they are joined with a half-blind dovetail (**B**). Begin by cutting the miter on the table saw (**C**). Then cut the groove for the

The first step in building an ogee bracket foot is making a pattern. The order in which you make the cuts is important.

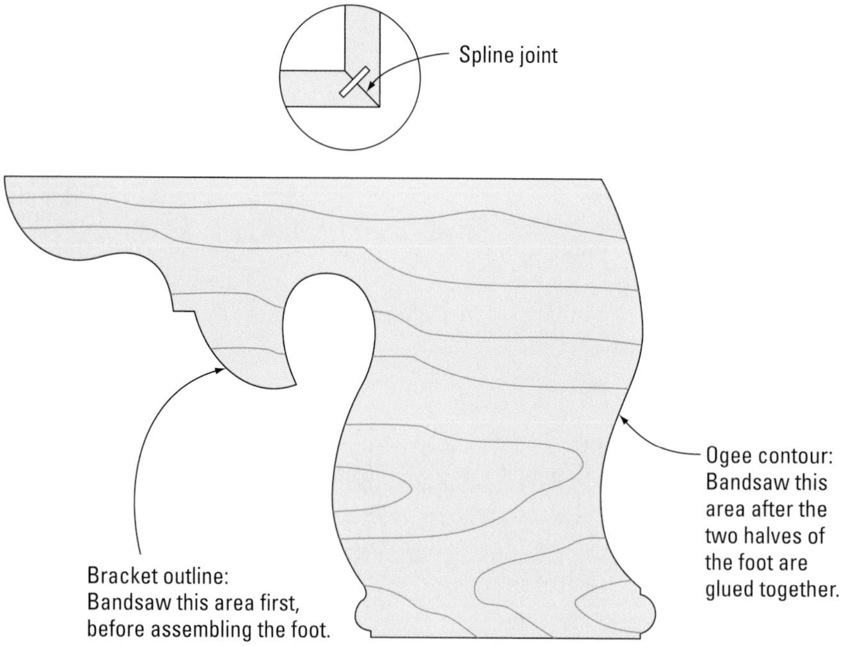

Spline joint
Ogee contour: Bandsaw this area after the two halves of the foot are glued together.
Bracket outline: Bandsaw this area first, before assembling the foot.

A

B

C

D

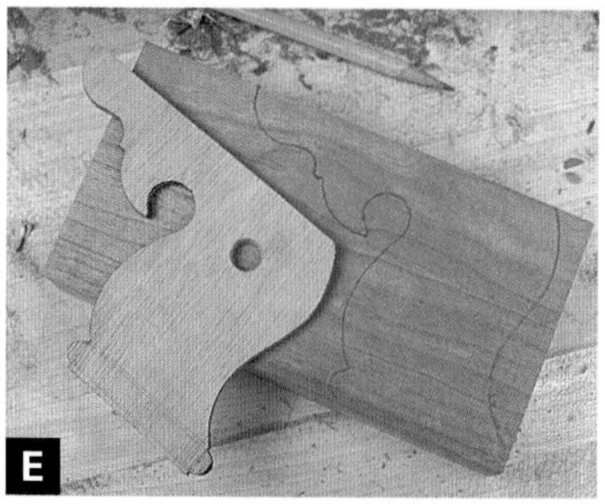
E

F

spline (**D**). Once the joinery is cut and fit, trace the foot pattern onto the face of each foot (**E**).

[TIP] Before sawing intricate scrollwork, save time by drilling segments that are circular.

When sawing the tight curves of the bracket, drill areas that form part of a circle (**F**). Next, carefully bandsaw the remainder of the bracket outline (**G**).

Now you're ready to assemble the feet. I've found that four small clamps work well to hold the miter joint tight while the glue sets. The spline keeps the two halves from sliding out of alignment when clamp pressure is applied (**H**).

First, you'll need to build a support stand to hold the foot in position during sawing (**I**). Keep it simple: Use four boards joined with dadoes, glue,

(Text continues on p. 54)

When bandsawing curves, you can save time and ensure accuracy by using a drill to form the parts of the curve that are true circles.

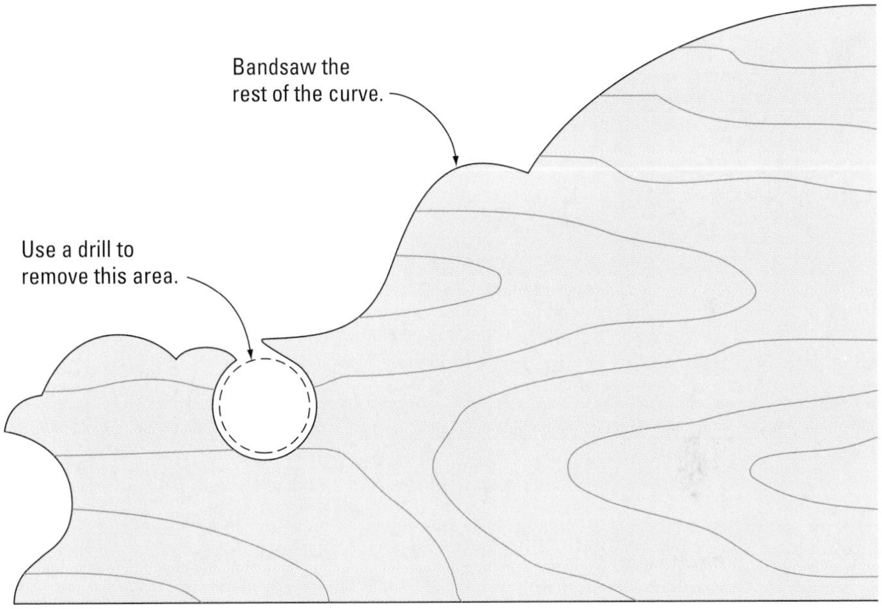

Bandsaw the rest of the curve.
Use a drill to remove this area.

TIP

G

H

When bandsawing an ogee contour in a bracket foot, make sure the foot is securely supported slightly above the table so that it is parallel to the blade.

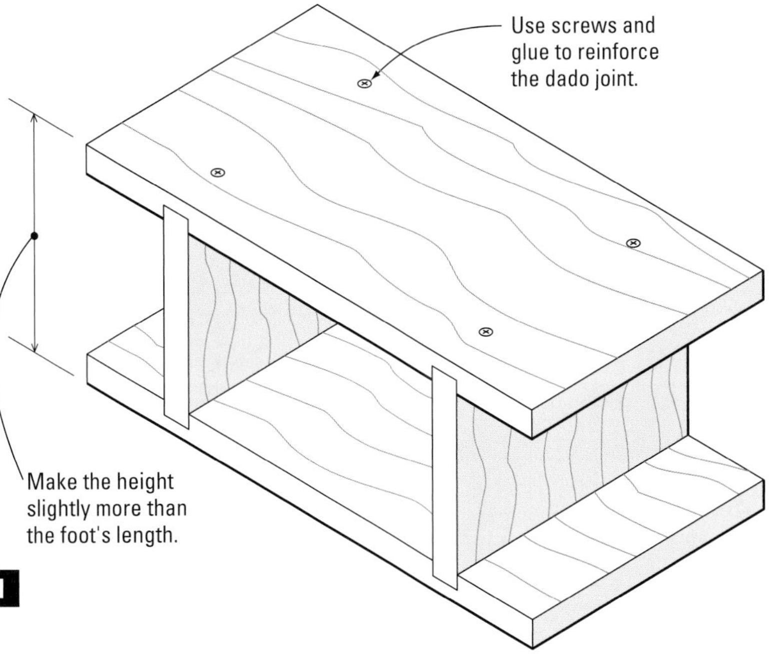

Use screws and glue to reinforce the dado joint.
Make the height slightly more than the foot's length.

I

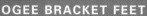

J

L

K

M

N

and screws. For the best results, you'll want to build the stand as short as possible—just high enough so that the bracket foot clears the bandsaw table. This will enable you to keep the upper saw guide positioned low for the best blade support.

The next step is to bandsaw the ogee contour in the face. Secure the foot to the support stand with a small clamp while sawing (**J**). After sawing the first face, the outline for the second face is revealed in the miter (**K**). Afterward, work the surfaces with hand tools to remove the saw marks. A rabbet plane works well for shaping the fillets that flank the bead (**L**). To shape the bead, use a carving gouge (**M**); smooth the ogee contour with a file (**N**). Complete the smoothing process by using a scraper and sandpaper.

Ogee Bracket Feet on the Table Saw

Another method for shaping ogee feet uses the table saw to create the ogee contour. It involves cutting a cove on a long strip and mitering short lengths of the strip to create feet.

The first step is to mill a strip of lumber long enough for all four feet. Next, the concave portion is created by cutting a cove with the table saw (**A**). To shape the convex area, begin by beveling the strip (**B**). Then use a block plane to complete the contour (**C**).

When you're satisfied with the ogee profile, miter the two halves of the foot (**D**) and cut a groove for the spline (**E**). Next, bandsaw the bracket outline into the face of each foot (**F**). After gluing the two halves together (**G**), smooth and refine each foot with files before scraping and sanding (**H**).

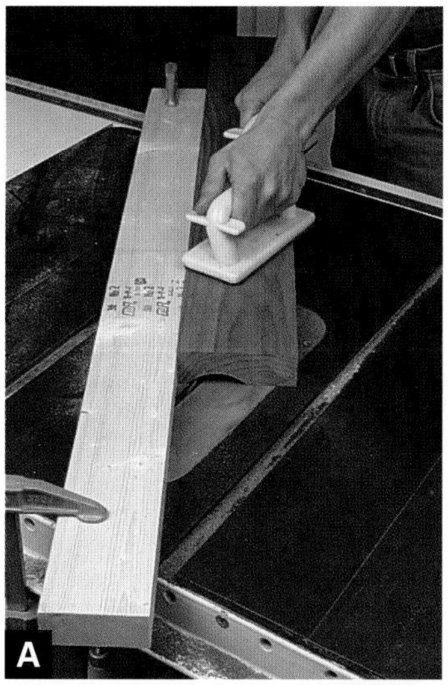
A

B

C

D

E

F

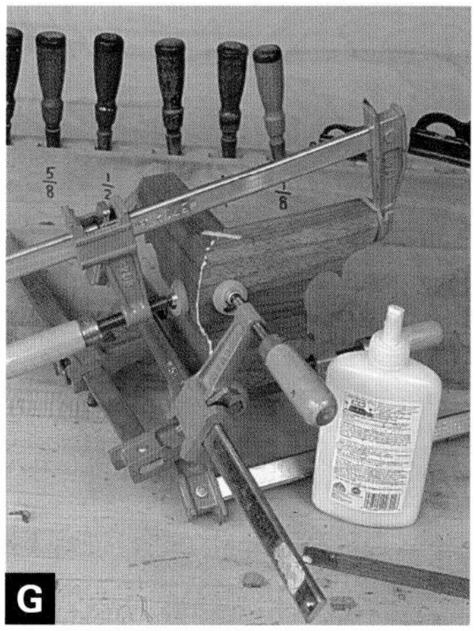
G

H

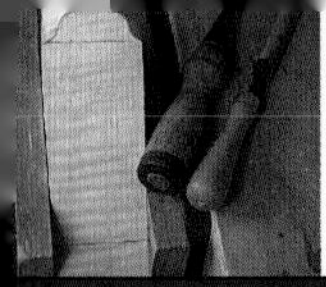

Bedposts

Bedposts

Unlike most contemporary beds, most period beds had tall posts. Rooms were heated with a fireplace, and much of the heat escaped through the chimney. Tall post beds, along with their heavy drapery, provided a room within a room in an effort to provide extra warmth and privacy. It was only natural for the most wealthy gentry to order highly ornate turned and carved bedposts. Surprisingly, even the most ornate beds have plain, tapered posts at the headboard where the posts were hidden as the drapery was drawn and tied back. For those who would not go to the expense of a turned and carved bed, the tapered pencil posts were a simple, if not elegant, option.

Today, the posts are easy to shape—either with hand tools or with a router table or shaper.

Laying out and cutting posts

Obviously, posts are important structural elements, unlike purely aesthetic elements such as moldings or carvings. So from a design standpoint a bedpost must have sufficient dimension for adequate joinery. So, to avoid creating a heavy, utilitarian look, the remainder of the post can be reduced in size and shaped to enhance its appearance.

A typical bedpost has slender proportions; the post is commonly 2½ in. square by 80 in. tall. A short portion of the post is left square to accommodate the bed rail mortise-and-tenon joinery. Above the rails the taper begins and gradually reduces in size until it reaches the top. The top of the post is typically 1 in. across.

You can make an octagonal taper several ways: by hand, with a router, or with a shaper. The first method involves using a drawknife and plane, and is a quiet and enjoyable method. Laying out the taper in preparation for handwork is quick and precise with a sparmaker's jig. This special marking gauge uses two wooden dowels, which follow the edges of the post to guide the pins as they scratch the outline.

See *"Pencil Bedpost with hand tools"* on p. 61.

If you prefer using your router table or shaper, you'll need to build the jig in drawing. The base supports the four-sided taper

Mortising the headboard into the taper can be tricky, but accurate layout is the key. The rails attach to the flat part of the post and joined with bed bolts for strength and portability.

TYPICAL PENCIL-POST DESIGN

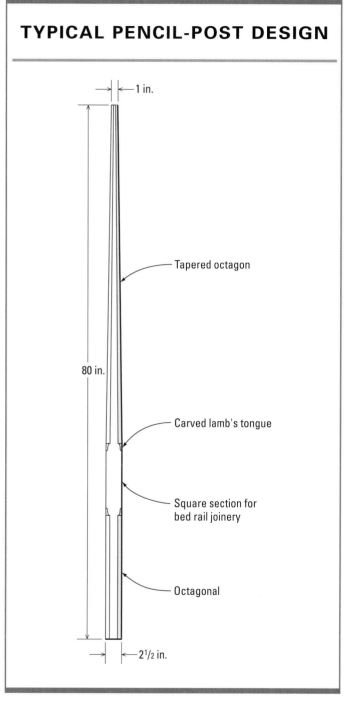

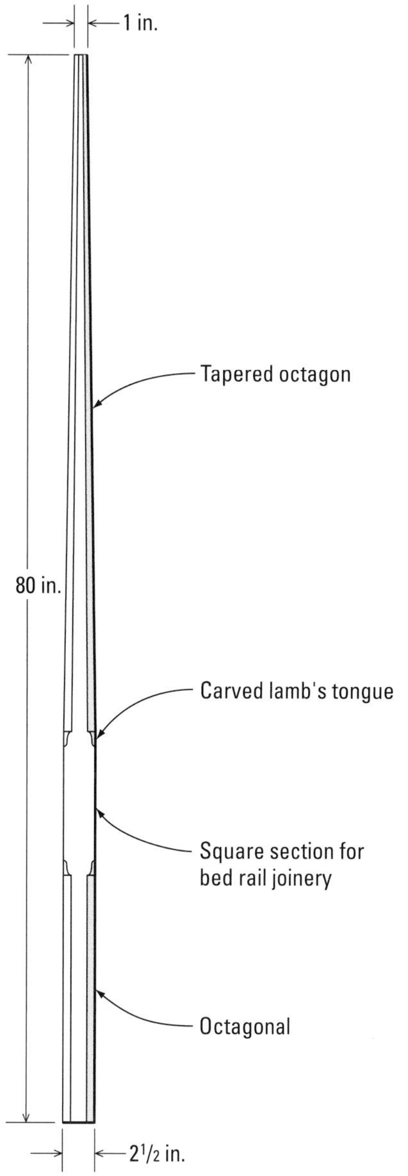

JIG FOR SHAPING OCTAGONAL TAPERS WITH ROUTER TABLE OR SHAPER

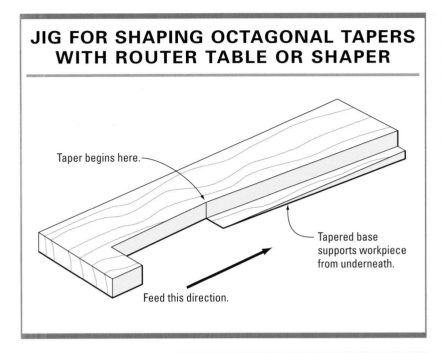

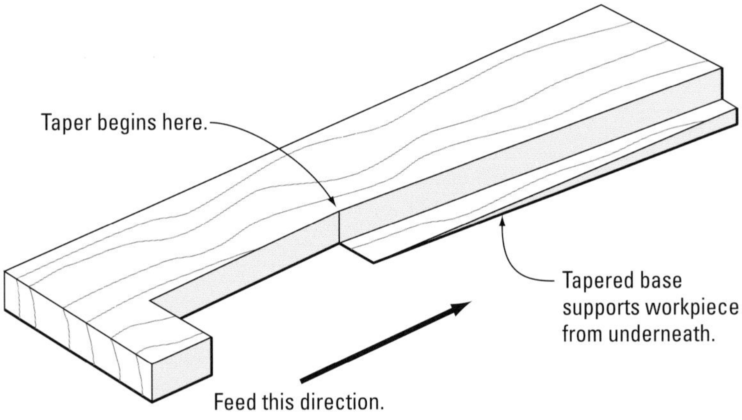
Taper begins here.
Tapered base supports workpiece from underneath.
Feed this direction.

DETERMINING THE TAPER

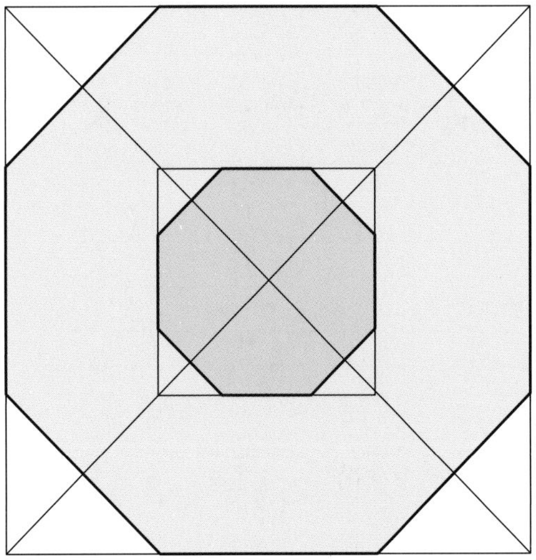

Before building the jig, lay out the octagon at each end of the taper.

as the work passes a chamfer router bit or shaper cutterhead. To determine the degree of taper on the base, draw a pair of octagons. The first represents the start of the taper; the second represents the end. Cut the tapered base on the bandsaw and attach it under the plywood frame of the jig.

Octagonal Bedpost on the Router Table or Shaper

Begin by milling the post square and drawing an octagon on one end. Next, mount a router bit or shaper cutter. If you're using a shaper, mount the cutterhead to cut from underneath the stock for safety (**A**).

The final step in the setup is to adjust the fence and cutter height. Your drawing on the end of the post makes it easy. Just position the post adjacent to the cutter and lock the fence and cutter height.

Now you're ready for the cut (**B**). If you're creating a stop chamfer, clamp a stop block to the outfeed fence or make a mark on the fence or table to align with a mark on the stock (**C**).

A

B

C

A

B

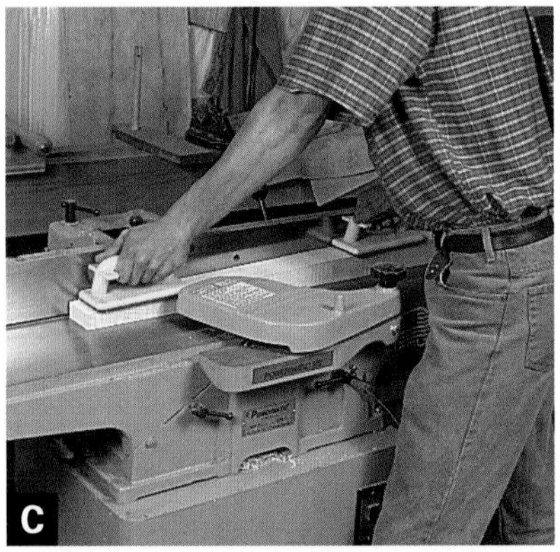
C

D

E

F

G

H

Pencil Bedpost on the Router Table or Shaper

Before shaping a tapered octagon, always begin by drawing two full-size octagons. The first represents the start of the taper; the second drawing represents the end.

Next, lay out a four-sided taper on the stock (**A**) and cut the four tapers using your favorite method (**B**). Now you're ready to chamfer the corners to create the eight-sided taper. But first smooth away the saw marks with a handplane or jointer (**C**).

To chamfer the corners, first build a jig to support the stock during the cut. Next, mount a chamfer cutterhead or bit on your shaper or router table (**D**). Adjust the bit height for the full depth of cut according to the drawing you made earlier (**E**). The jig will raise and support the small end of the stock to create the necessary amount of chamfer at each end (**F**).

Position the work in the jig with the trailing end of the stock resting firmly against the stop. Now feed the workpiece and jig past the cutterhead to cut the tapered chamfer (**G**). When you reach the end of the taper, stop and make a mark on the table or fence (**H**). This gives you a reference point when cutting the three remaining chamfers.

Pencil Bedpost with Hand Tools

You don't need a router or shaper to create elegant octagonal tapers; as with any woodworking process, there's a way to achieve the same results with hand tools (**A**).

If you're unfamiliar with using hand tools, creating octagonal tapered bedposts by hand is a great way to get started.

Begin by shaping a four-sided taper using any of the previous methods. Next, lay out the chamfered corners. This step may seem complicated, but it's easy when you take a few minutes to build a spar-maker's gauge (**B**). If you keep the gauge's dowels against the stock, the pins will mark a perfect taper (**C**).

To remove the excess stock, use a drawknife, which will enable you to take large, controlled cuts (**D**). As for any hand tool, sharpness is a key to control. Once you've gotten close to the layout lines, finish the surface with a plane, taking the stock to the layout line (**E**).

Finally, carve a bevel at the termination of the cut to create a stop (**F**).

A

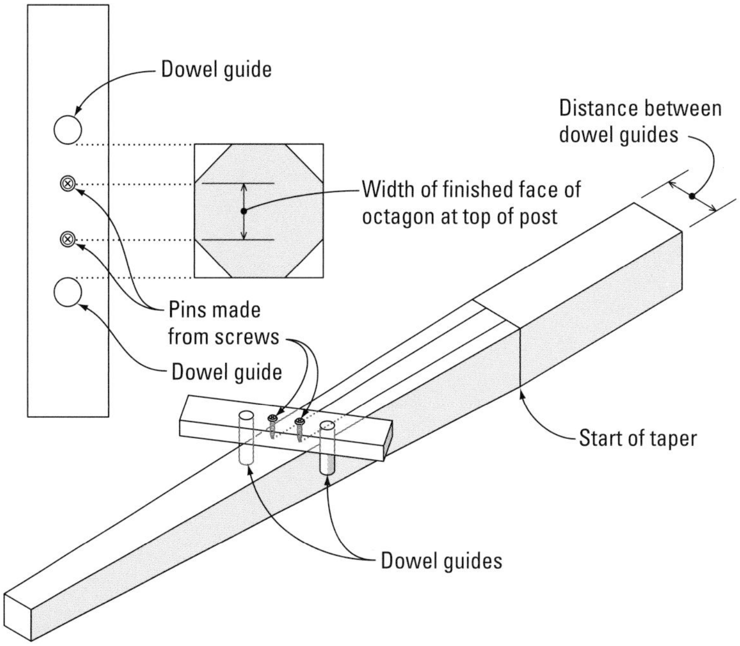

B

C

D

E

F

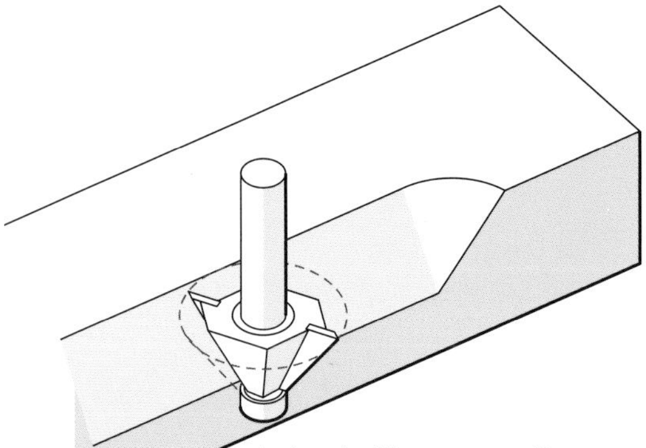

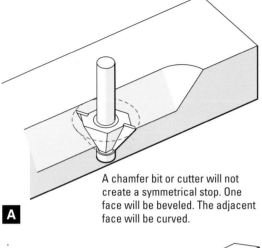

A chamfer bit or cutter will not create a symmetrical stop. One face will be beveled. The adjacent face will be curved.

A

B

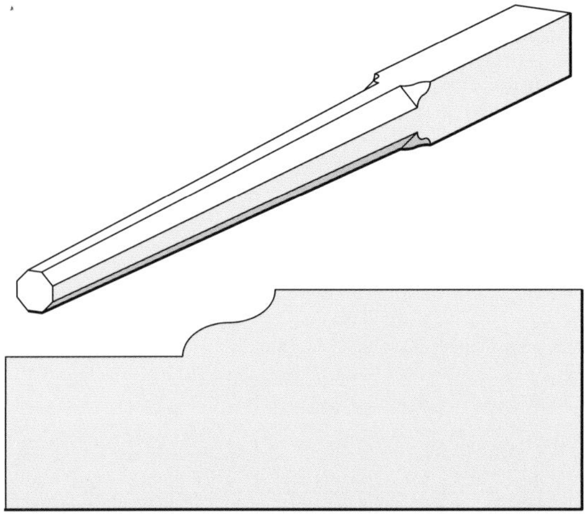

C Before carving, make a pattern for tracing the lamb's tongue onto the post.

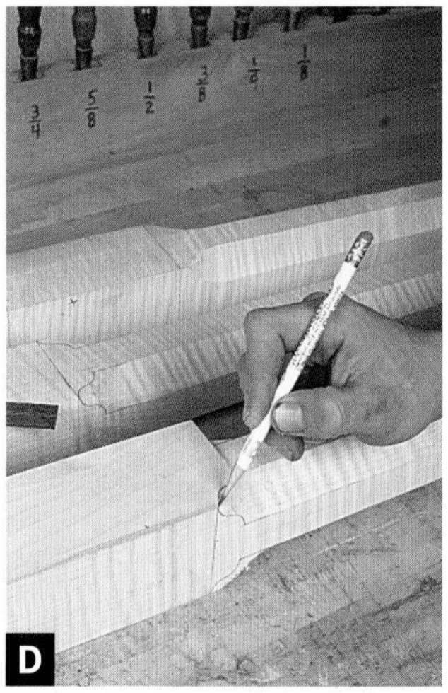

D

E

F

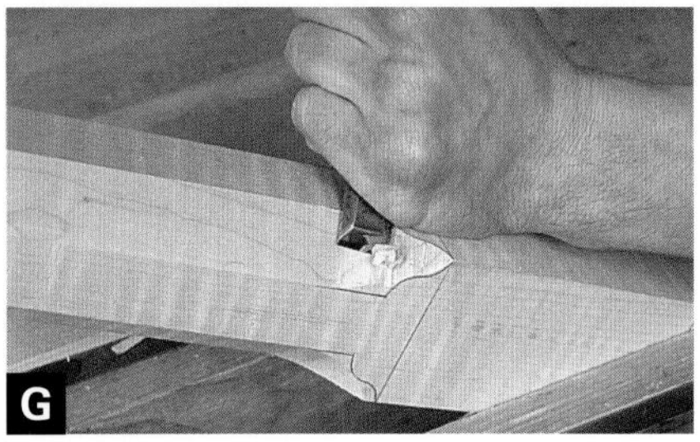

G

H

Carving a Lamb's Tongue

When creating an octagonal taper with a router or shaper, the cutter will leave the end asymmetrical (**A**). Because the tool cuts in a spinning motion, one face will be an arc, the other a bevel.

To create visual unity, you'll probably prefer to finish the detail by hand. One option is simply to make both surfaces either curved or beveled. Either choice is attractive, and each creates a more contemporary look.

Another more traditional approach is to carve an ogee at the end of the taper (**B**). This detail is, obviously, a bit more time consuming. But the unique effect is worth the effort because of the distinction it adds to the piece.

To carve a lamb's tongue on a post, begin by drawing the design along the edge of thin plywood to make a pattern (**C**). After bandsawing and smoothing the curves with a file, trace the pattern onto the post (**D**).

Start shaping the lamb's tongue by removing the excess stock with a chisel, bevel down, and then bevel up (**E**). The convex segment of the lamb's tongue intersects the post at a crisp inside corner (**F**). If the grain is running in a reverse direction, cut across the grain to prevent tearout (**G**). To finish the detail, smooth it with a file (**H**).

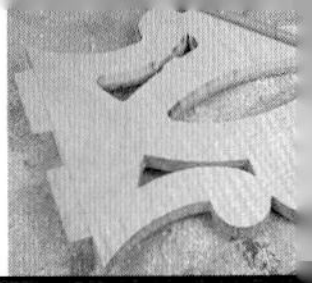

Chairs

Splats

Arm and Post

Chair Legs

Chair Shoe

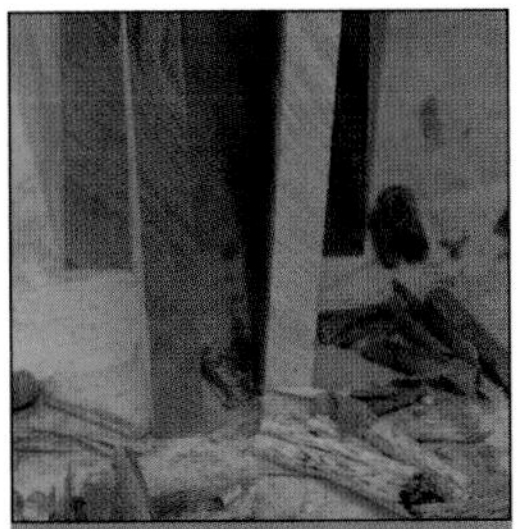

Side Rails

CHAIRS ARE AMONG THE most elegant forms of 18th-century furniture. But the unusual angles and flowing compound curves that give chairs their grace and beauty also make them a challenge to build. Fortunately, many period chairs share a common framework and construction methods. So once you've constructed one type of chair, you will find that other types are variations along the same theme. Although there are regional differences, such as the through rear tenon on many Pennsylvania chairs, most differences are in the proportions and the aesthetic design details. Let's take a look at some commonly shared chair details.

Backs

Early chairs of the period had straight backs. But once the Queen Anne style gained popularity, the straight lines of William-and-Mary gave way to the reverse curve. Later, as furniture evolved into the Chippendale Era, the bow back became favored. Finally, design came full circle, as it often does, and the straight back was once again popular.

Splats

Splats were the classic, solid vase-shaped form during much of the first half of the century. As furniture became more elaborate, the splats were pierced and often carved. One important detail is the bevel along the edges of the splat. This small detail gives the

COMMONLY SHARED CHAIR DETAILS

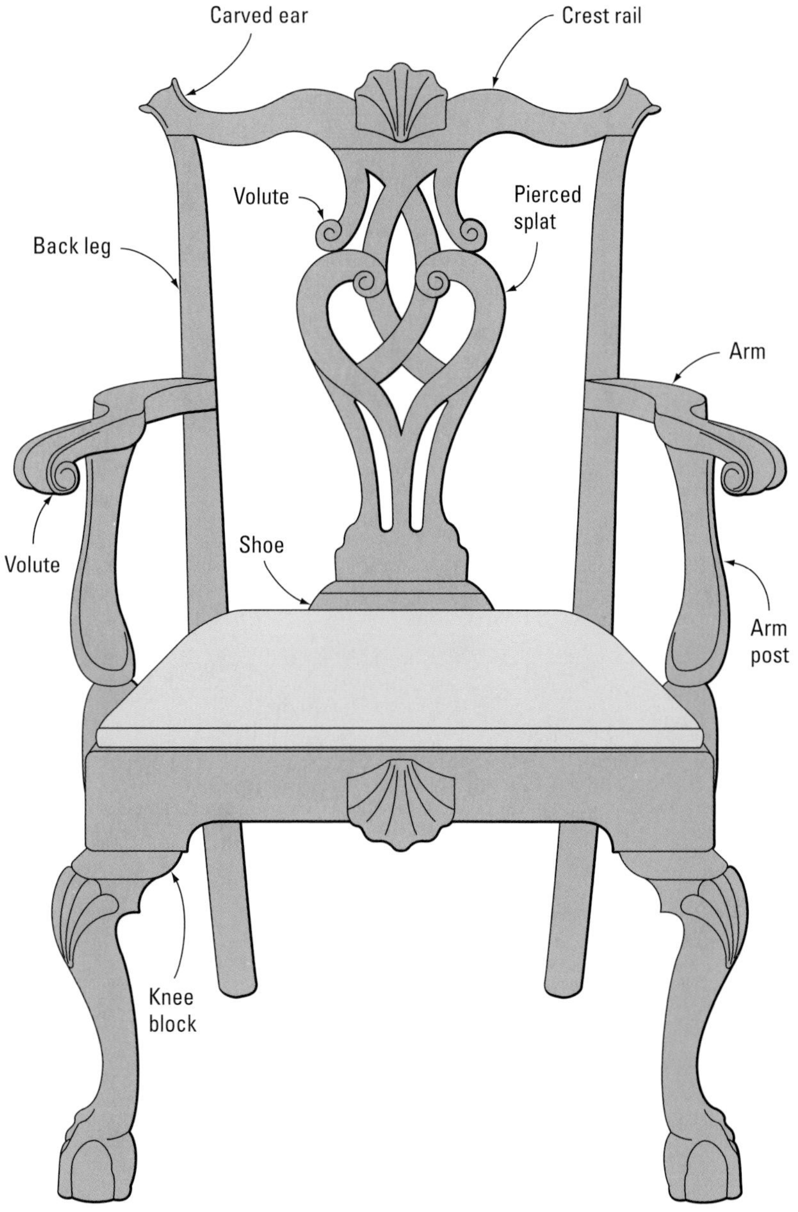

splat lightness and allows the viewer's eye to see the true profile at the front of the splat without distraction from the back edge. Later on, splats gave way to pierced and carved ladder rungs and eventually to elaborately inlaid Federal shields.

Joinery

Mortise-and-tenon joinery was the predominant method for constructing the framework of a chair. The joints were often strengthened with wooden pins and, in the case of many Pennsylvania chairs, the side seat rail tenon goes through the back leg post.

Of all the joints in the chair, the tenon at the back of the side seat rail is most complicated to layout and cut. Because of the compound angle involved, it is best to derive the layout from fully developed drawings of the seat and back.

Armchairs

Period armchairs are not simply sidechairs with arms added. Instead, they are wider and deeper than a matching sidechair. As you might expect, the frame members of an armchair, such as the legs, splat and crest rail, are larger, too, in order to keep with the heavier proportions in the seat.

When developing an armchair, designing an attractive arm and support can be a challenge. Although separate pieces, the completed arm and post should appear as one flowing, sculptural unit. The post is first joined to the arm with a tusk tenon, which doubles the glue surface area. Then the two are bandsawed, shaped, sculpted, and finally carved. The result of this tremendous amount of work is worth the effort; the arms

NEST PARTS TO SAVE LUMBER

Let's face it, sawing curves is wasteful. But one way to avoid needlessly wasting excessive stock is to nest parts together. When I select stock for chair legs, I look for pieces wide enough for at least two or three legs. This has the added advantage of getting a consistent grain and color match for the parts.

You can reduce waste substantially by nesting parts together. Here, I've used a plywood pattern to draw two nested sets of Chippendale chair rear legs on one wide board.

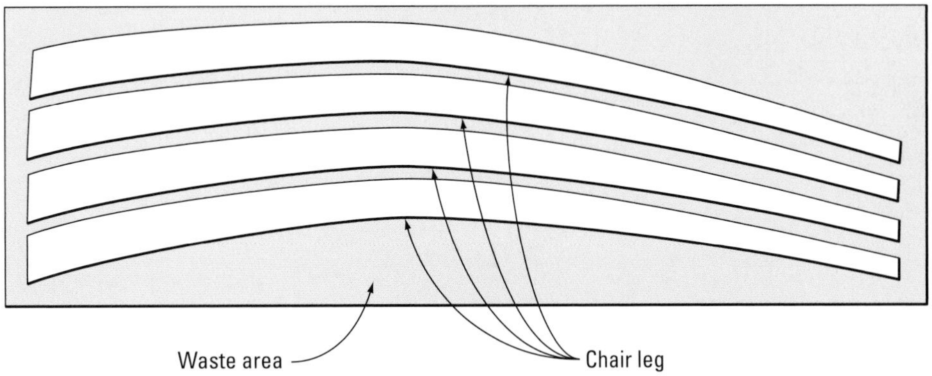

provide a sculptural addition to the chair, not to mention the degree of support and comfort that they add.

Legs

The front legs of 18th-century chairs were often highly decorated, using the cabriole leg and the ball and claw foot in my period styles. The rear legs were quite simple, but have a fluid shape in keeping with the overall design of the chair. When making a set of chairs, it makes sense to maximize the available stock by nesting parts.

See *"Cabriole Leg "*and *"Ball and Claw Foot"* on pp. 34 and 47 for information.

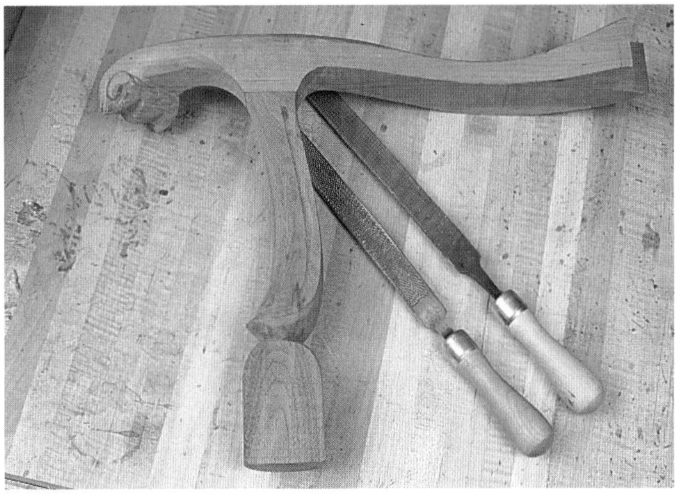

The arm and post are cut and shaped as separate units, then sculpted and carved to create a unified appearance.

A

B

C

D

Resawing a Splat

Resawing is the process of ripping a board through its thickness. By resawing a shallow curve, you can create wide, curved panels such as chair backs.

Begin by selecting stock thick enough for the curve. To create a curve that is free of dead spots, it's best if the stock is thick enough to bury the blade throughout the entire cut.

I prefer a wide (1 in. or more) blade with a coarse, variable pitch (**A**). If your saw won't tension a wide blade, select a ⅜ in. variable pitch blade and tension it as much as possible. Also check the table for squareness to the blade before you begin.

Bandsaw the convex face first by carefully sawing freehand to the layout line (**B**). Then remove the saw marks with a spokeshave.

By skewing the spokeshave, you can avoid tearout in most instances (**C**). Otherwise, switch to a scraper (**D**).

To resaw the second face, use a point fence (**E**). This simple device is a great aid for keeping the two cuts parallel and the work of uniform thickness. Clamp the fence so that the point is positioned parallel to the teeth of the blade. Before making the cut, scribe a layout line parallel to the first fence. As you saw, follow the line precisely, making sure the work is in contact with the fence (**F**).

When smoothing the concave face, work with the grain, from the ends to the middle, to reduce tearout (**G**).

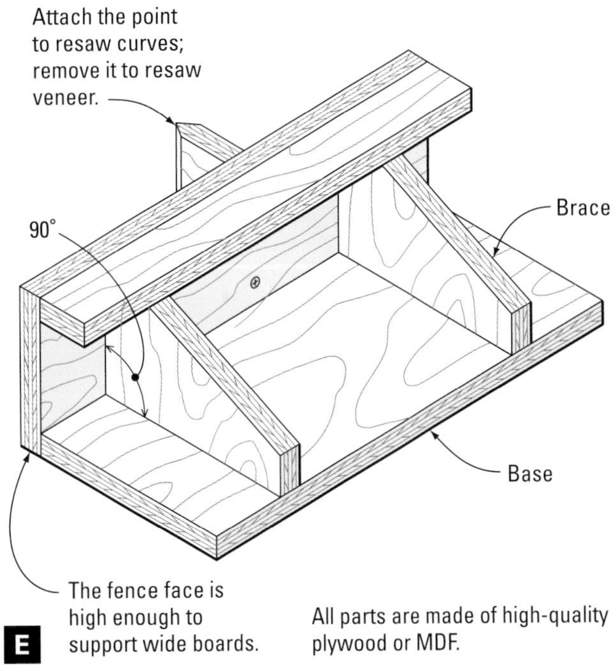
Attach the point to resaw curves; remove it to resaw veneer.
90°
Brace
Base
The fence face is high enough to support wide boards.
All parts are made of high-quality plywood or MDF.

E

F

G

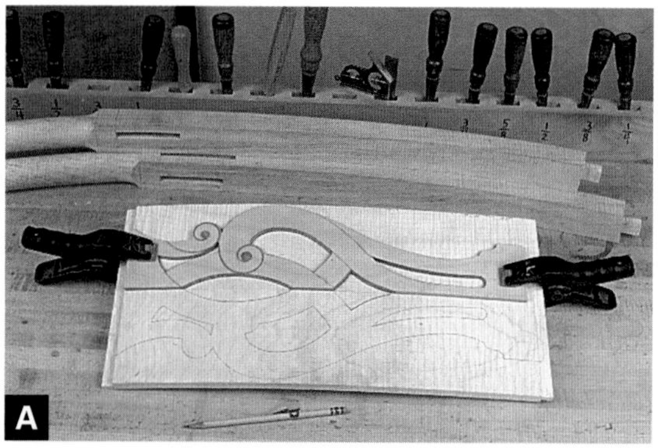
A

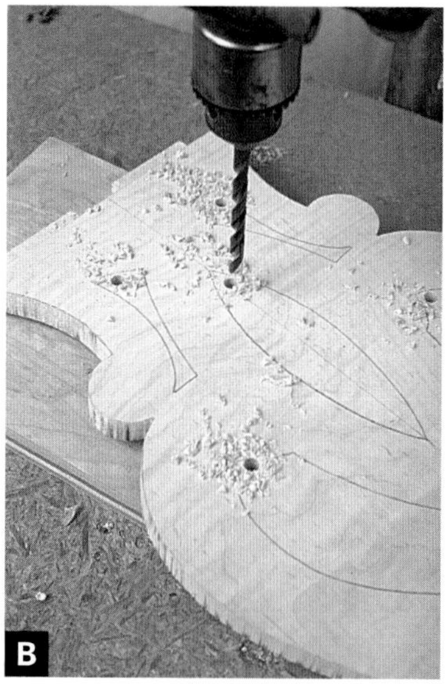
B

C

Scrollsawing Interior of a Splat

The scrollsaw is the tool of choice for interior cuts. (A jigsaw can also be used, but it won't be as accurate and will require more cleanup with a file and sandpaper.) The blade of a scrollsaw can be unclamped at one end and threaded through a hole in the workpiece. Because the blade is clamped securely at each end, the cut is precise with minimal flex.

As an example of this process, I'm using a curved chair back. When tracing the pattern, it's necessary to flex it so it conforms to the curve of the work. You can hold it in position with clamps while tracing the outline (**A**).

Next, drill a small hole at each interior cutout for threading the blade (**B**). When sawing, take your time and follow the layout lines closely; this greatly reduces the amount of tedious cleanup later (**C**).

To create the illusion of thinness and delicacy, scrollwork is sometimes beveled on the edges. It's time-consuming work, but the refined appearance is worth the effort.

See *"Beveling Splat Edges"* at p. 69.

VARIATION You can also use a coping saw or fretsaw to cut interior curves by loosening the blade and freeing it so that you can enter the work through the drill hole.

Beveling Splat Edges

Beveling the edges of curves is a centuries-old technique for making the stock appear thinner than it actually is. This detail creates an illusion of lightness without sacrificing strength.The difficulty is that the work of beveling all those tight, interconnected curves is extremely tedious.

To help speed the process, first bevel the edges with a modified router bit. Beginning with an inexpensive high-speed steel router bit (**A**), grind away most of the steel to create a chamfer bit with a 15-degree angle (**B**).

Next, mount the bit in a laminate trimmer, which is really a small router (**C**). The small base will easily follow the curved surface of the splat, and the small-diameter pilot on the bit reaches into the corners (**D**). Before beginning the cut, adjust the depth so that the pilot of the bit just grazes the edges of the surface.

After routing, you will still need to carve the corners (**E**) and complete the bevel. But much of the tedious handwork has been eliminated.

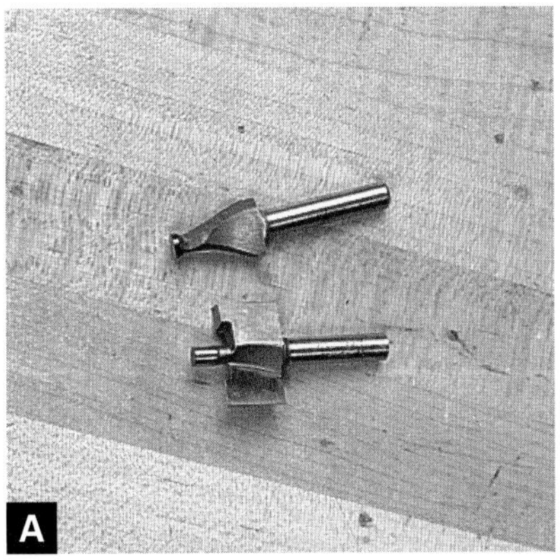

A

C

B

D

E

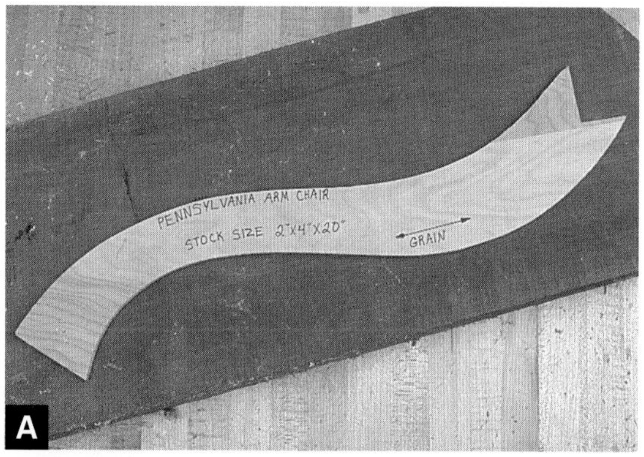

A

Making an Arm and Post

The following techniques are useful for creating furniture (especially chairs) that is composed of flowing, sculptural curves. As an example, I'm going to use an arm and post from a chair.

As with any bandsawn component, it's important to begin by sketching the design and creating patterns (**A**). This provides an objective starting point for logical progression. After milling the stock to size, trace the arm pattern (**B**) and bandsaw the outline of the arm (**C**). It makes sense to saw the contour before cutting the mortise for the post; the convex curve of the arm works as a reference point for the joint.

After bandsawing the arm, lay out (**D**) and cut the mortise (**E**). Next, lay out the curves of the arms and the tenons (**F**). Then cut the tenons on the post while the stock is still square (**G**), because square surfaces are best when cutting joints on the table saw (**H**).

B

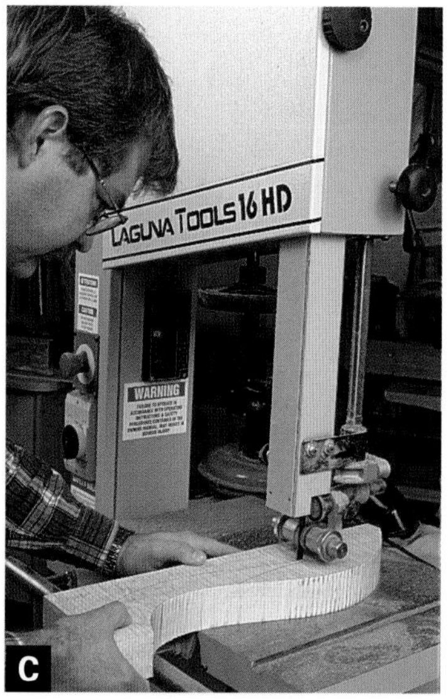

C

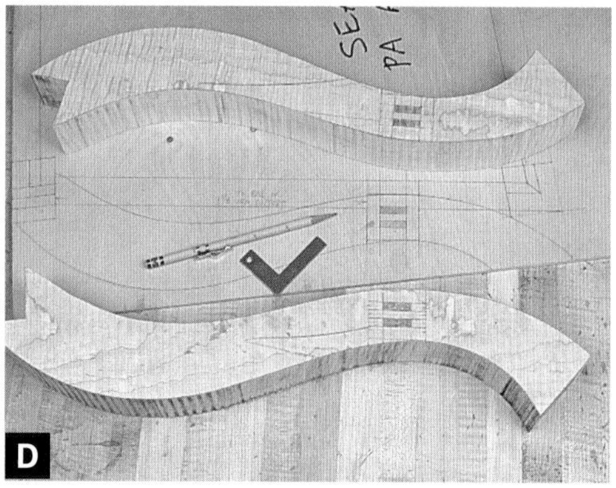
D

E

F

Next bandsaw the post—first the front (**I**) and then the side. Save the offcuts from the first series of cuts and tape them back into position with double-sided tape for sawing the adjacent surface (**J**).

Next bandsaw the curves on the top and bottom of the arm. Because the arm is asymmetrical, it's important to plan the cutting sequence carefully to avoid a miscut and spoiling the arm. More specifically, as the arm curves, the profile is simultaneously stretched and compressed.

After tracing the patterns (**K**), saw a relief cut at the base of the knuckle. When starting the cut, it's necessary to raise the back end of the arm so that the layout line is parallel to the blade (**L**). Next, cut from the post joint to the cut you

(Text continues on p. 72)

G

H

I

J

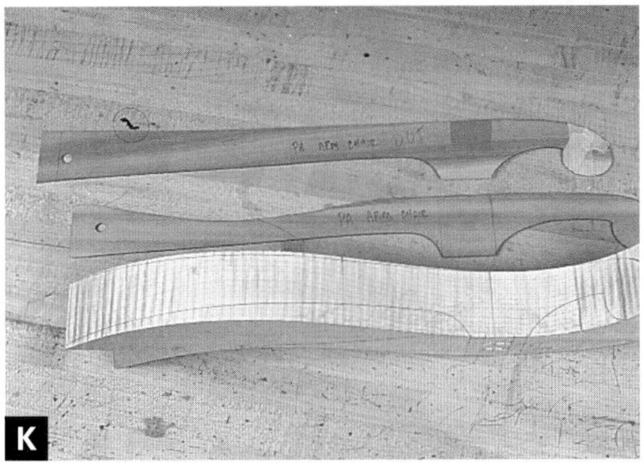
K

L

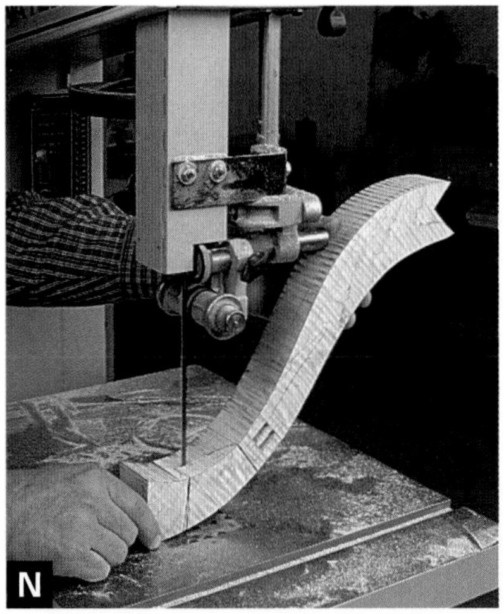

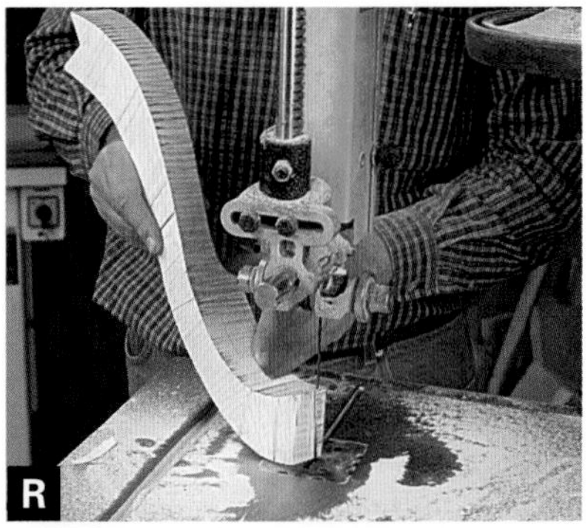

made at the knuckle (**M**). After making the turn, lift the arm again as the blade approaches the junction (**N**).

The next cut begins at the post joint (**O**) and continues to the back end of the arm. Afterward, make the simple, shallow relief cut on the top of the arm (**P**).

Finally, remove the square corners from the knuckle. Starting with the top, lift the arm so that the work is parallel to the blade (**Q**) and make a full turn to the bottom of the arm (**R**). Now the arm is ready for shaping (**S**).

Shaping the arm is a process of refining the curves with the appropriate tools to match the contour. Begin by smoothing the outside edges of the arm with a spokeshave (**T**). A carving gouge works well for the curve of the knuckle (**U**).

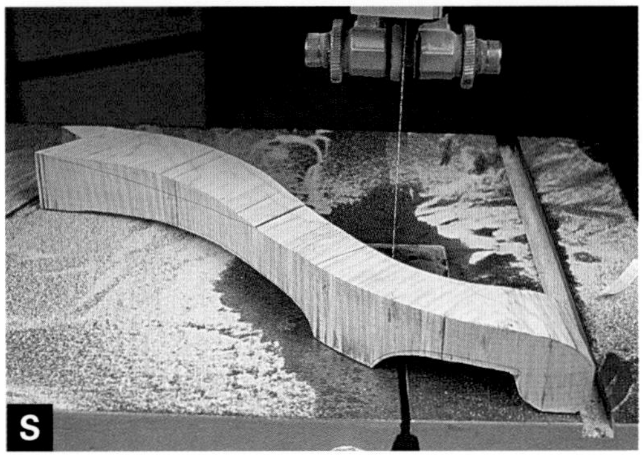

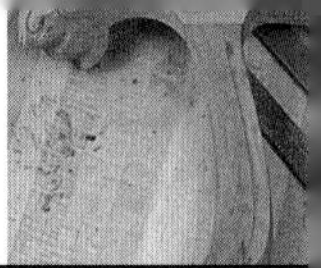

Beginning underneath the arm, round the knuckle so that the curve flows continually to the top. A gouge is also used to remove excess wood behind the knuckle (**V**). For the subtle curves on the top (**W**) and bottom (**X**) of the arm, use a rasp to further shape and refine. The inside curve on top of the arm is dished out (**Y**) with the rasp, and the contour is blended with the rest of the arm.

The front and back corners of the post are rounded, while the side corners remain relatively sharp. Secure the work in a clamp that is mounted in the vise. Beginning with a long, firm chisel, remove the excess stock (**Z**). Next, round the corner to blend the two surfaces into one flowing contour. As you're shaping, alternate between pushing (**AA**) and pulling (**BB**) the rasp to follow the grain and blend the curves effectively.

Once the major portion of the shaping is completed, dry assemble the arm and post and blend the area around the joint (**CC**). At this stage, the knuckle is ready for carving.

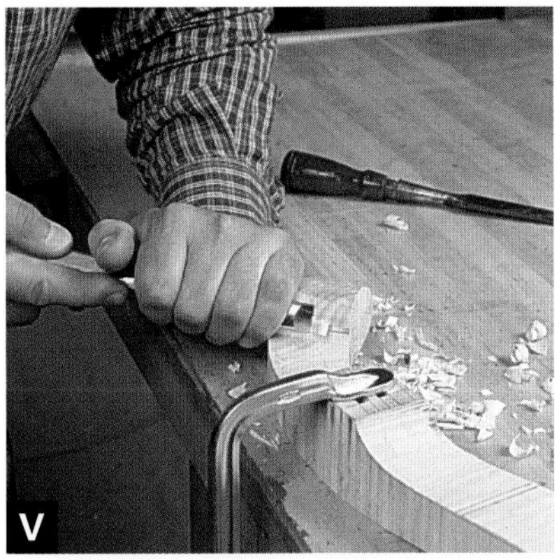

V

W

X

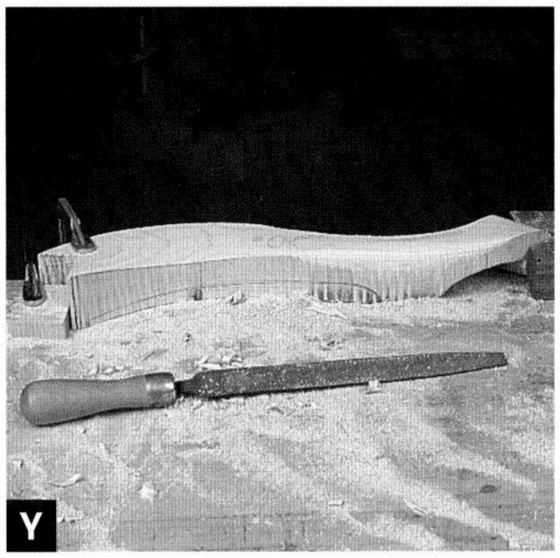

Y

Z

AA

BB

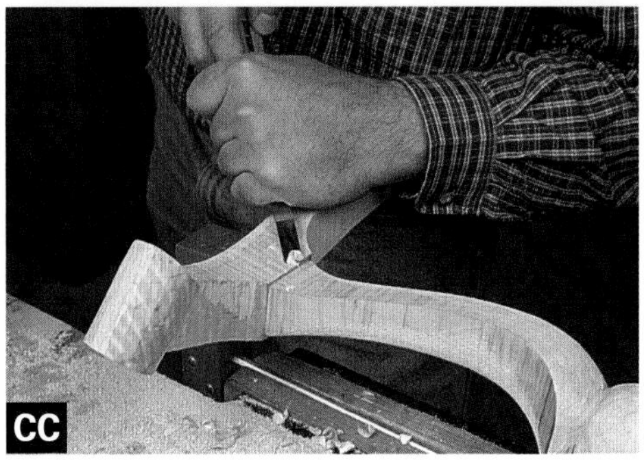

CC

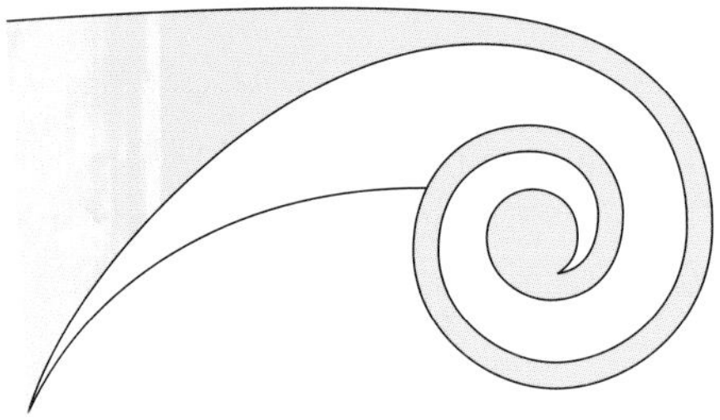
A

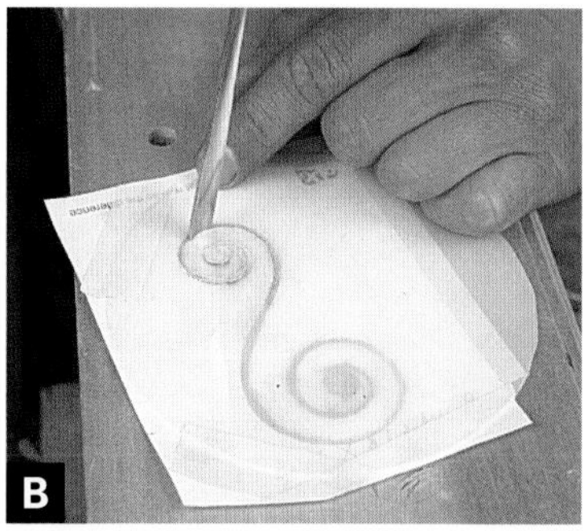
B

C

D

E

F

G

H

I

Carving a Volute

A volute is a spiral (**A**). It's used as embellishment on the ends of arms and the back of chairs—among other areas—to create the appearance of a scroll. As the volute unwinds, the curve naturally broadens. This beautiful effect is easily created by using a series of gouges.

Begin by drawing the volute. Although it would be easy if the volute fit within a mathematical framework, it seldom does. Instead, the volute must fit within the area of the workpiece on which it will be carved. For this example, I've connected volutes of two sizes to create a sample carving block.

Whether found on furniture or architecture, volutes are typically carved in pairs. As you might imagine, drawing accurate pairs of volutes can be time consuming. So for ease of duplication, I prefer to make a plastic template. First draw the design on paper; then position a transparent plastic sheet over the drawing and incise the outline to form a template (**B**). Next, trace the template onto the stock (**C**) and begin carving (**D**).

Beginning with the center hub, incise the outline of the volute with the same series of gouges that you used to incise the template (**E**). As the curves become broader, use wider gouges with less sweep (**F**). A typical series of cuts would begin with a no. 7, progress to a no. 5, and end with a no. 3 gouge. Incise the volute to a depth of ⅛ in.

Next, make a second series of cuts that intersect the first cut at a shallow angle (**G**). Each time you make a cut, a small chip of wood should be released. This will have the effect of creating a raised spiral ridge (**H**). After this procedure is followed around the entire spiral, a series of facets will remain. Use a no. 3 gouge and take sweeping cuts around the volute to remove the facets (**I**).

Bandsawing Chair Legs

Although you can bandsaw a broad curve with a narrow blade, it requires more concentration and effort because a narrow blade has a natural tendency to wander in the cut. I prefer to use a wide blade (**A**), because it naturally follows the broad curves of components such as chair rockers. After mounting the blade, trace the pattern onto the stock (**B**). Then carefully follow the layout line (**C**).

Use a compass plane to smooth the surface after sawing (**D**). The flexible sole will adapt to both convex and concave surfaces (**E**). Clamp the matching pairs of stock together to check for square (**F**). If you don't have a compass plane, a spokeshave can be used to clean up the surface.

A

B

C

D

E

F

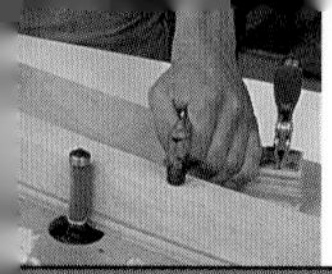

Flush Trimming Chair Legs on the Router Table

Bandsaws don't create a finished surface; so after sawing curves, the saw marks must be removed. Without a doubt, the router is the most versatile tool for template shaping. It cuts curves, flush cuts, creates molded profiles, and shapes into tight corners. A template-guided straight bit will do the job quickly and efficiently. For this example, I'm using the rear leg of a chair. A pair of toggle clamps secures the leg in the template, which is equipped with two edges: one for the leg's face and the other for the leg's back (**A**).

To the shank of the bit, add a bearing that will follow the template (**B**). After bandsawing the leg heavy of the layout line, position the leg in the template for the first cut (**C**). The order that you complete the cuts is important, because the template is designed to remove equal amounts for each of the two cuts. Cutting out of order means that the first cut will be too heavy. In addition, if you cut out of sequence there will not be sufficient stock for removal during the second cut. Start the cut with the bearing in contact with the extended portion of the template base (**D**). This will give you a smooth entry into the cut. Feed the stock at a steady rate and listen to the machine to determine if you're feeding the stock too quickly (**E**). Afterward, reposition the leg and make the second cut (**F**).

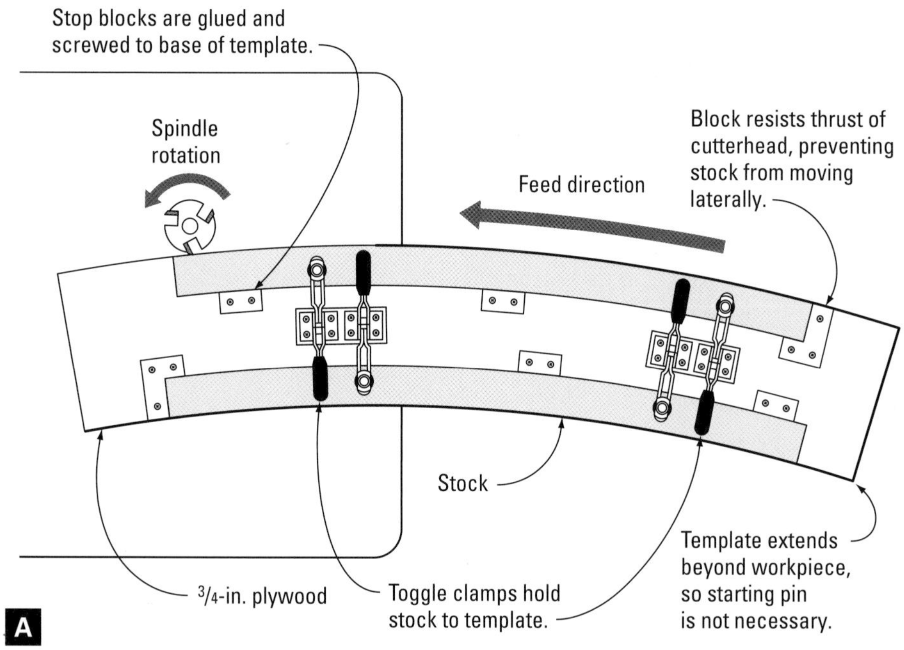
Stop blocks are glued and screwed to base of template.
Spindle rotation
Feed direction
Block resists thrust of cutterhead, preventing stock from moving laterally.
Stock
Template extends beyond workpiece, so starting pin is not necessary.
3/4-in. plywood
Toggle clamps hold stock to template.

A

B

PA ARM CHAIR
FIRST CUT!!

C

D

E

F

Chamfering Chair Legs

When shaping a chamfer on a curved surface, the bearing on the router bit registers against the stock to limit the cutting depth. Any roughness or void in the surface will be re-created in the chamfer as the bearing rolls over the surface.

Begin by smoothing the curved surface. The bandsaw marks can be cut away with a spokeshave or compass plane. Another option is to flush trim the surface with a template and flush-trimming bit.

The next step is to mount a chamfer bit in the router table and adjust the height for a light cut, no more than 1/8 in. You'll also need a fulcrum to pivot the work into the spinning bit. Otherwise the stock could kick back violently. The fulcrum can be a pin or block; for the greatest mechanical advantage, it should be located as close as possible to the bit.

To make the cut, position the workpiece against the fulcrum and pivot it into the spinning bit (**A**). Once contact is made with the bearing, begin feeding the workpiece (**B**).

When making a stopped cut on a curved surface, it will be necessary to begin two of the cuts in the middle. Position the workpiece against the fulcrum and aim the start of the cut for the outer cutting circle of the bit (**C**). If you come up short of the line, don't back up! Instead, pull the work away and try again.

A

B

C

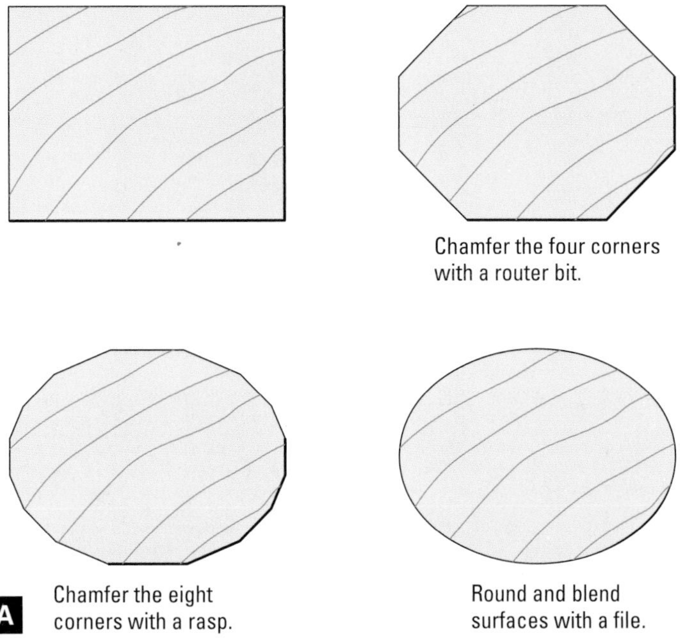

Chamfer the four corners
with a router bit.
Chamfer the eight
corners with a rasp.
Round and blend
surfaces with a file.

A

Rounding a Simple Curved Leg

This method of rounding is useful when the leg is rectangular in section rather than square. When rounded, a rectangular leg becomes elliptical. By shaping it, you effectively lighten the look and add refinement without a loss of strength (**A**).

To make the process more efficient, first remove the excess stock with a chamfer router bit (**B**). Next, mark a centerline as a guide while shaping (**C**). Then clamp the leg in a vise and shape the leg with a rasp in the direction of the grain (**D**). When the grain direction changes, reverse the rasp and pull it toward you (**E**). Work gradually to the centerline to create an elliptical contour (**F**). When you're satisfied with the overall shape, smooth the leg with a file (**G**), followed by a card scraper (**H**).

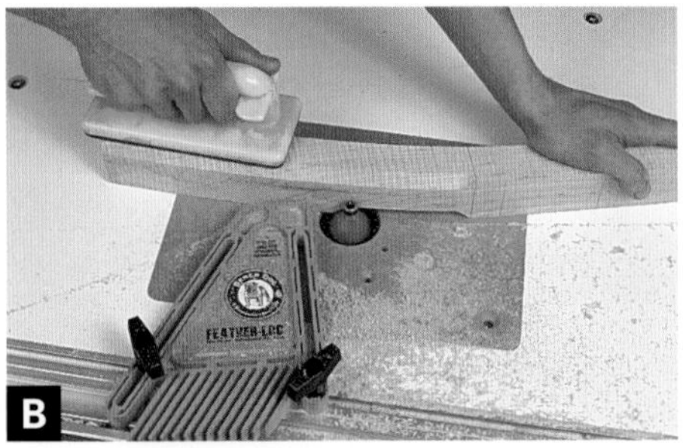

B

C

D

E

F

G

H

Making a Chair Shoe

When speaking of chairs, the shoe is a pedestal that is glued to the top edge of the back seat rail to provide a terminus for the splat. The top edge of the shoe is mortised to accept the backsplat tenons.

First, mill the stock to size. I always dimension the stock wide enough for two shoes; the wider size adds safety and stability as I cut the cove. If I'm making a single chair, I'll just set the extra shoe aside for a future chair.

Next, mark the width and depth of the cove on each end of the stock as an aid for setting the fence angle on the tablesaw. After cutting the cove (**A**), rip the shoe to the final width (**B**) Next, shape the thumbnail profile on the top edge of the shoe on the router table (**C**). Featherboards hold the stock in position and prevent it from tipping and spoiling the profile.

The next step is to bandsaw the long, curved profile on each end of the shoe. Because of the cove on the face, it is easiest to layout and saw the profile from the back. To stabilize the workpiece while bandsawing, I clamp it in the jaws of a wooden handscrew (**D**).

Finally, layout the mortises for the splat (**E**) and cut them with your favorite method (**F**), (**G**).

A

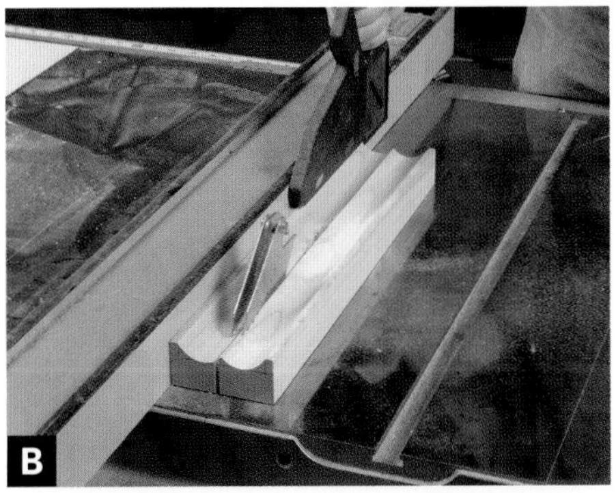
B

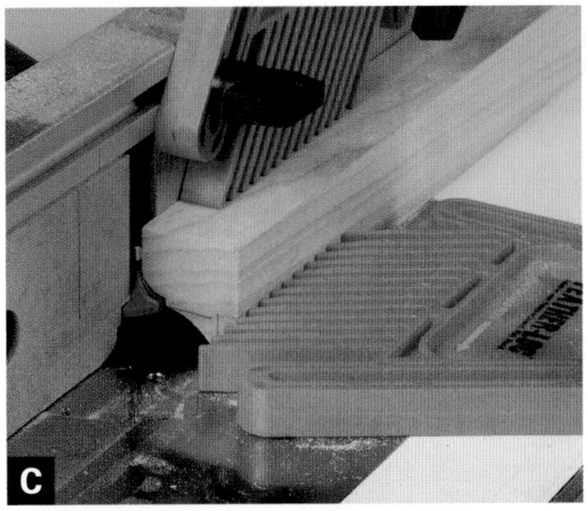
C

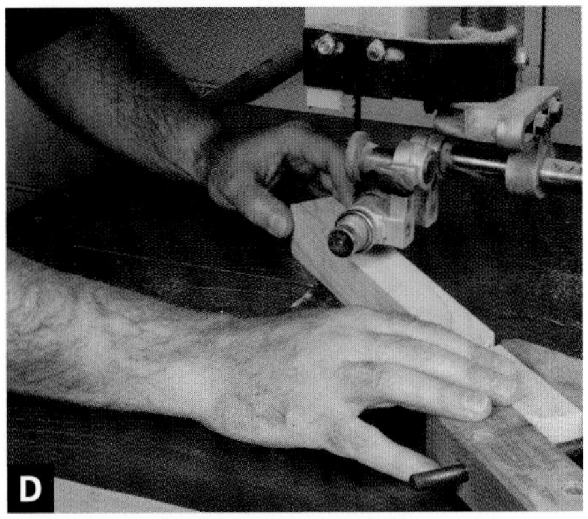
D

E

F

G

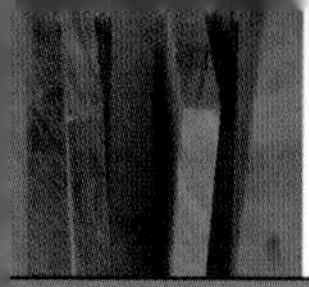

A

B

C

D

E

F

Chair Side Rail Tenons

Of all the tenons on a period chair, and there are a number of them, the side rail tenons are most complicated. This is because the angle of the back legs combines with the tapered seat frame to create a compound angle at the intersection of these members. To correctly layout the tenons, it is best to first create full-sized drawings of the chair back and seat.

First, layout the tenon shoulders, faces, and ends with a knife (**A**), (**B**). Next, saw the faces of the tenons and carefully follow the layout lines. For greatest accuracy, it is best to saw from each corner (**C**) and allow the two cuts to meet in the middle. Next, saw the tenon shoulder and then pare to the line with a chisel (**D**). The chisel edge will easily follow the knife line you created earlier (**E**). (**F**) shows the completed pair of tenons.

Carving a Shell

The first step is to draw and proportion the shell that you would like to carve. All carvings, including shells, can be varied in size and proportion to fit with the design of the furniture to which they're applied. The shell shown here (**A**) is a five-lobe example that I designed for a Pennsylvania armchair (**B**).

When you're satisfied with the drawing, make several photocopies of it. Next, glue a copy of the drawing to the stock for the shell (**C**). After carving, this shell will be glued to the front seat rail of the chair; it's important that the grain in the shell runs from side to side to coincide with the grain in the seat rail.

The next step is to select the gouges for carving. The sweep, or curvature, of the gouge should closely follow the outline that you sketched earlier. For the lobes on this shell, use a 14mm no. 7 gouge (**D**). For the area around the hinge, use a 25mm no. 5 gouge. Although the narrow gouge could be used for both, the wide gouge is more efficient and easily yields smooth, uninterrupted curves around the hinge.

The next step is to bandsaw the outline of the shell to remove the excess stock. It's important to saw approximately 1/16 in. from the line (**E**) because the final outline of the shell is created with carving tools.

Next, begin incising the perimeter of the shell with gouges (**F**). Be aware that the grain at the top center lobe has a tendency to split off. To avoid this problem, position the corner of the gouge beyond the stock when incising the concave areas that flank the center lobe (**G**). This will prevent the center lobe from

(Text continues on p. 82)

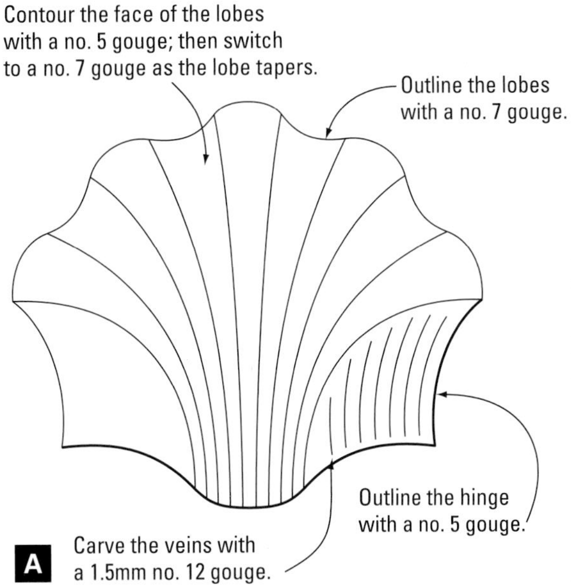

Contour the face of the lobes with a no. 5 gouge; then switch to a no. 7 gouge as the lobe tapers.
Outline the lobes with a no. 7 gouge.
Outline the hinge with a no. 5 gouge.
Carve the veins with a 1.5mm no. 12 gouge.

A

B

C

D

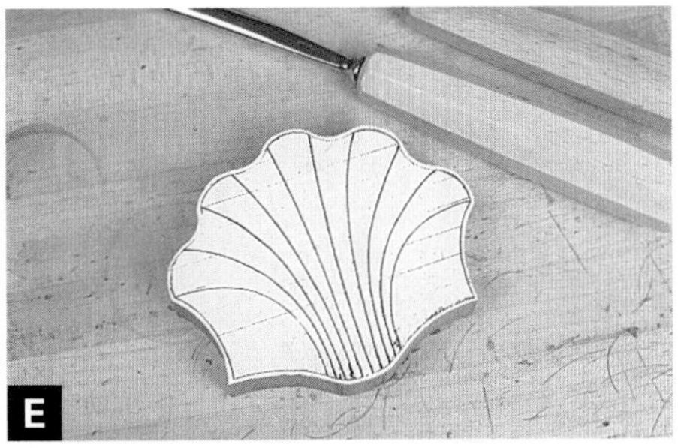
E

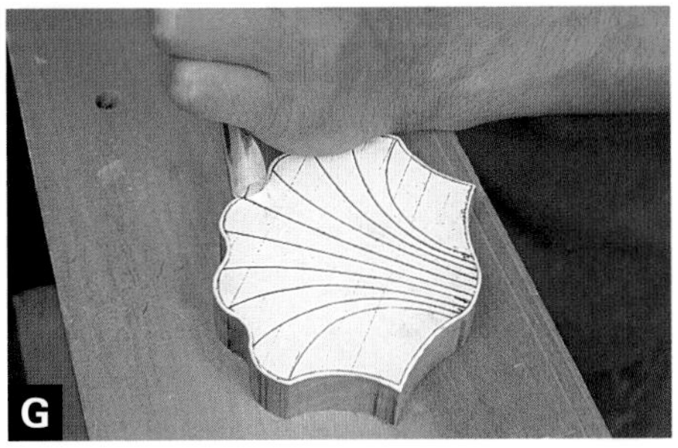
G

F

H

I

J

K

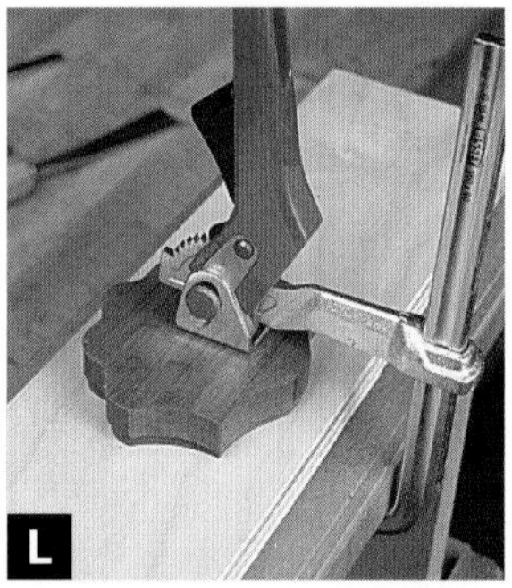
L

M

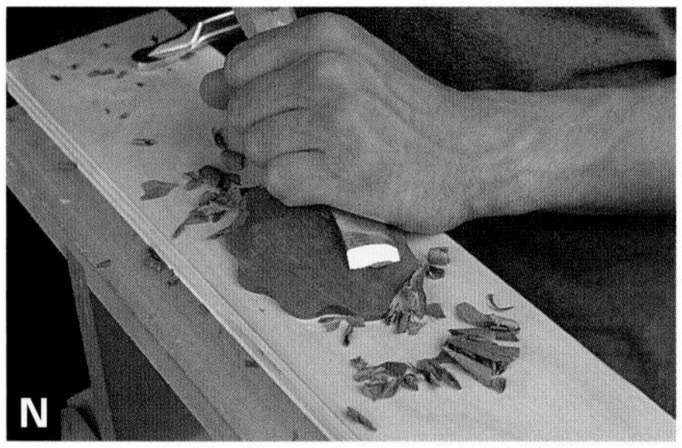
N

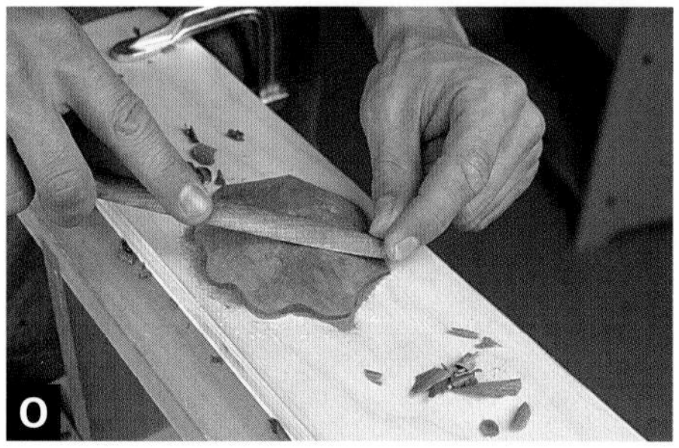
O

splitting (**H**). The entire outline will later be inverted to become the base of the shell, so it's not necessary to incise beyond $\frac{3}{16}$ in. deep (**I**).

When incising the outline of the shell, it's important to keep the cuts vertical. To achieve this, you'll need to angle the gouge away from the work for the concave cuts. This will compensate for the bevel on the edge of the tool. Also, concentrate on keeping the cuts interconnected and flowing uninterrupted around the shell.

When you're satisfied with the outline of the shell (**J**), you're ready to move on. The next step is to glue it face down to a short length of inexpensive stock. Afterward, the clamps are positioned on the scrap stock to give you full access to the shell for carving. Don't use a lot of glue; the shell must be pried up after carving. Besides, a small amount of glue is all that's necessary to hold it firmly (**K**). Clamp the shell to the board and allow the glue to thoroughly dry (**L**).

The next stage of the process is to contour the face of the shell. But first mark the high point of the contour. The point is centered left to right and slightly below center from top to bottom (**M**). Now select a 25mm no. 2 gouge for shaping the contour. The goal of this process is to produce sweeping curves from left to right and top to bottom (**N**). After paring the face of the shell, the only original surface remaining will be the high point that you marked earlier. Watch the grain direction and cut with the grain or across; you'll want to produce clean shavings, not splinters. Carve the surface down to the $\frac{3}{16}$-in. perimeter that you incised in the first step.

After carving the contour, you can remove any remaining facets with a smooth file (**O**). Avoid using sandpaper though—the abrasive grit will

settle in the pores of the wood and quickly dull your tools later in the process.

The next step is to draw the lobes as a guide for carving. Using your original drawing as a guide, locate the points of the lobes with dividers (**P**). Then divide the base of the shell into equal spaces (**Q**). Next, connect the points by sketching smooth, flowing curves (**R**). To achieve visual balance in the carving, spacing is important. Examine the curves closely and, if necessary, redraw any that need improvement.

Now you're ready for the next stage of carving. The first step in this stage is to incise the hinge area. Hold a 25mm no. 5 gouge nearly vertical to create a steep wall (**S**) and carve this area gradually until you reach the layout line (**T**). Finish the inside corner with a 6mm no. 7 gouge. Take long, sweeping cuts to blend the wall with the hinge area (**U**).

The next step is to outline the curves on the face of the shell with a V gouge. For greatest control, take several light cuts and progressively deepen the V. Also, as you carve the V's, watch the spacing and flow of the curves; if necessary, make corrections as you deepen the cuts (**V**).

Next, carve the convex lobes. Start by contouring the ends of the lobes with a 12mm no. 5 gouge (**W**). As the lobe tapers back, the curvature becomes tighter, so you'll need to switch to a 10mm no. 7 gouge; then a 6mm no. 7 gouge. Gradually, as the lobe reaches the apex of the shell, switch to a 4mm no. 7 gouge. Finally, the curve on the face of the lobe diminishes.

(Text continues on p. 84)

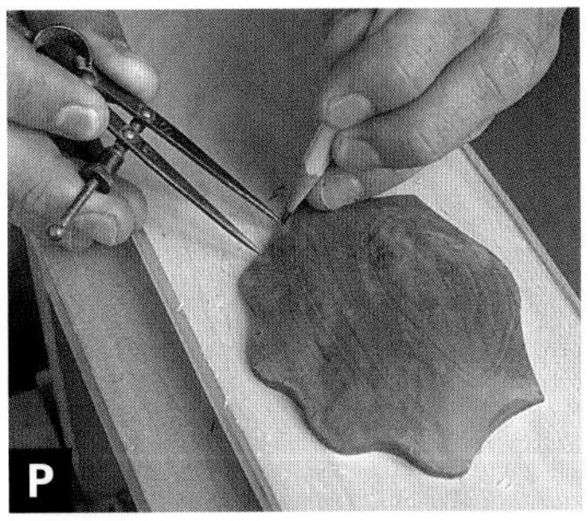
P

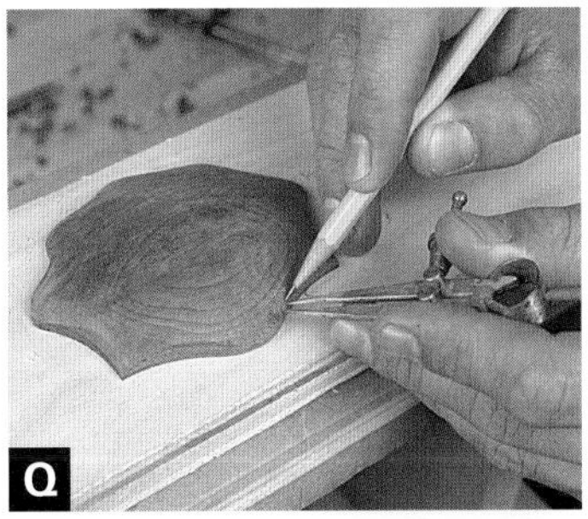
Q

R

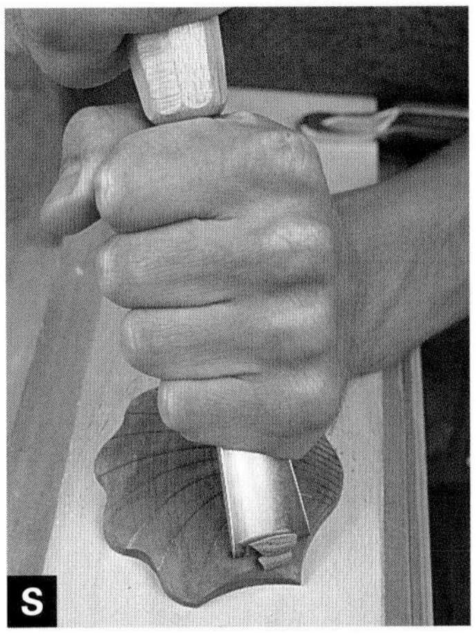
S

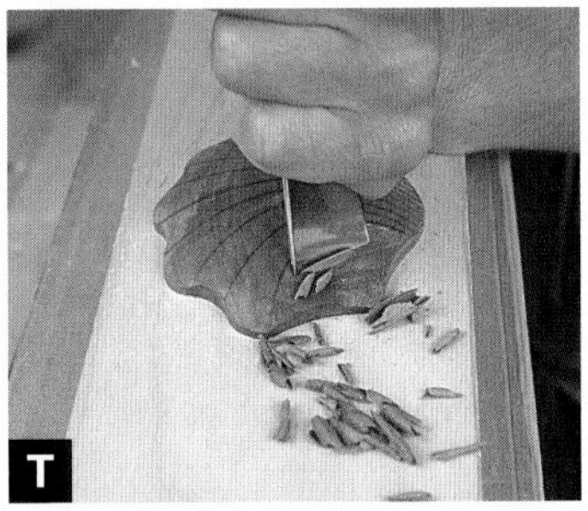
T

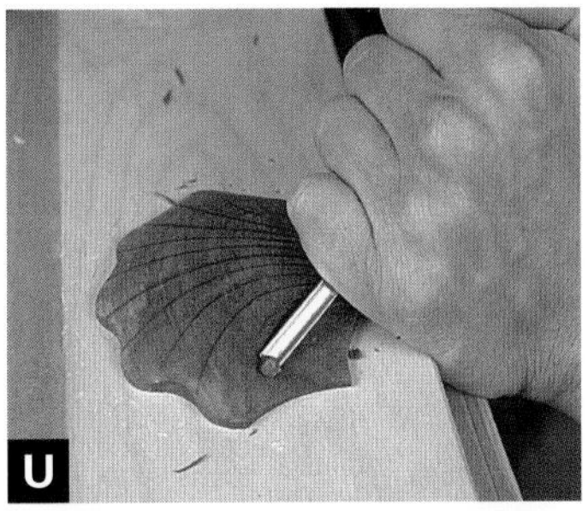
U

V

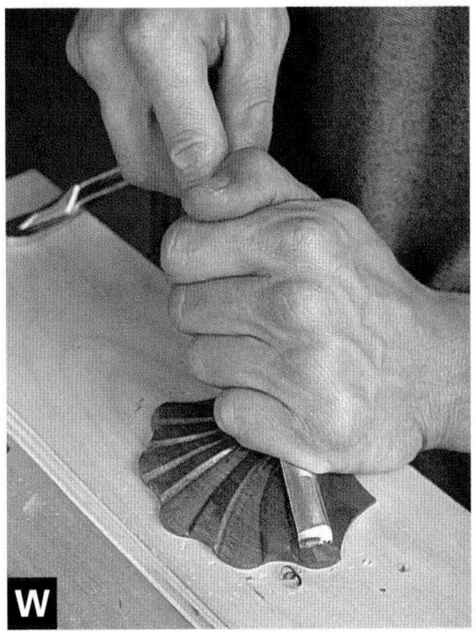
W

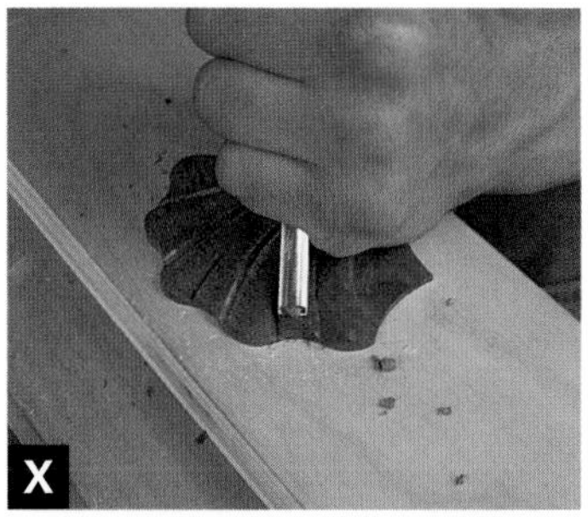

X

Y

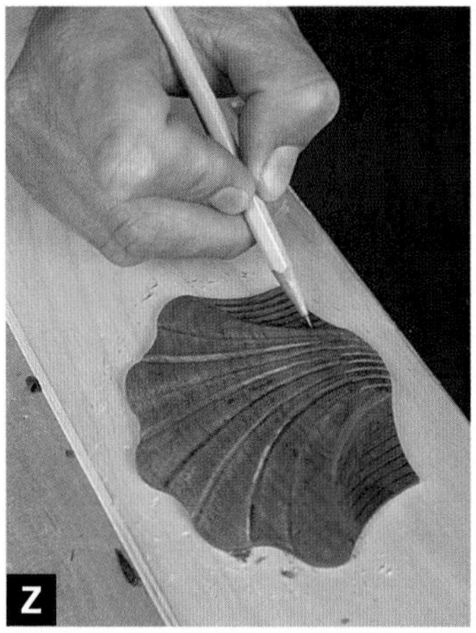

Z

AA

BB

Next, carve the concave rays between the lobes (**X**). Beginning with a 10mm no. 7 gouge, work back gradually; then switch to a 6mm no. 7 and, finally, a 4mm no. 7 gouge. As you carve the rays and lobes, use the gouges to blend the curves (**Y**). During the entire process, stop periodically and hone the gouges; sharpness is the key to accuracy and control.

The final step is to carve the veins into the surface of the hinge. These tiny U-shaped grooves break up the flat surface to add more interesting detail.

Starting at the outer edge, sketch each vein with a pencil (**Z**). Keep the spacing uniform and follow the curve at the edge of the hinge. Next, use a 1.5mm no. 11 gouge to carve the veins (**AA**).

The completed carving should be crisp, flowing, and full of visual details (**BB**). You can smooth the carving lightly with 240-grit sandpaper to blend the facets. But be careful not to spoil the sharp details.

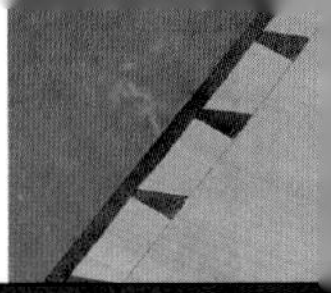

Casework

Dovetails

Template Shaped Components

Gooseneck Molding

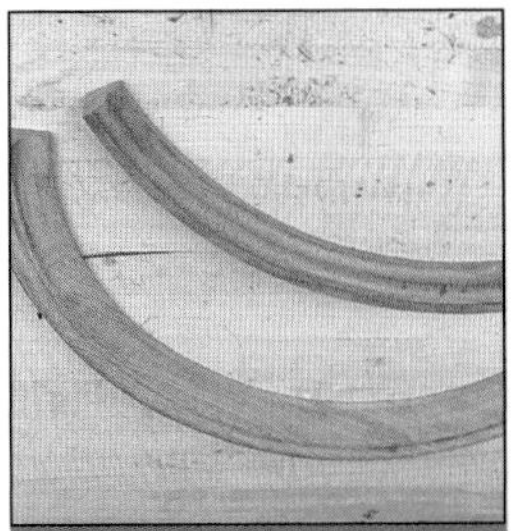

Arched Molding

Rosettes

Finials

Doors

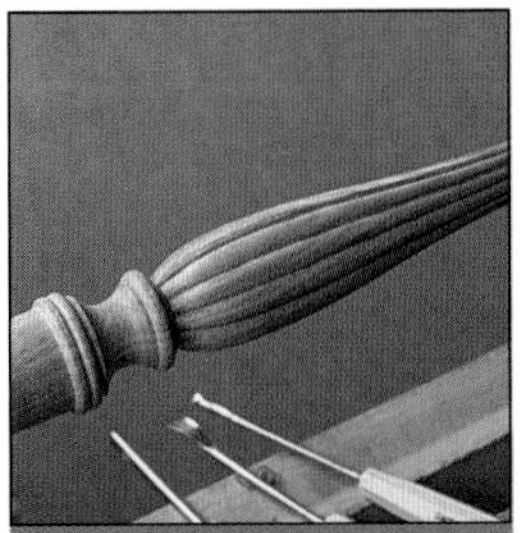

Flutes and Reeds

Base and Capital Molding

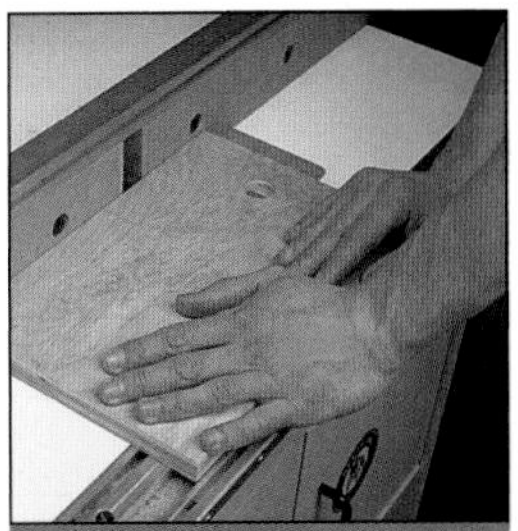

Candle-Slide

This tea caddy has the Golden Rectangle proportions of 1:1.618. The height equals 4 in. The length to the outside of the box equals 6½ in. (4 in. x 1.618 = 6.472 in., which rounds up to 6½ in.)

The small tombstone door of the gallery in this desk fits into the Golden Rectangle.

PERIOD CASEWORK CAN SEEM exceedingly complex. Yet, if you strip away the feet, moldings, curves, and other details from period casework, what remains is a dovetailed box. The drawers are just a series of boxes fit within the larger box. The key to building large, complex period casework is to divide the process into small, manageable steps. Once the box is constructed, the period details, such as tombstone doors, ogee feet, and complex moldings, are added to make the piece visually stimulating.

Proportioning casework

After years of studying period furniture, I am convinced that the craftsmen of the time used mathematical systems for proportioning. Two of the most common of such systems were ratios of whole numbers and the Golden Rectangle. With a ratio of 1:1.618, the basic geometric shape has been revered for centuries by architects, designers, and craftsmen as having perfect proportions. Some examples include the Parthenon and the credit cards you carry in your wallet. Amazingly, it is the only rectangle of which you can derive a square and the remaining space forms another Golden Rectangle.

The diminutive tea caddy is my reproduction of one that a client found years ago at an antique shop. A few quick measurements reveal that the front of the box fits within a Golden Rectangle, yet when viewed from the top, the box has a ratio of 2:1. During the 18th century even something this small and inexpensive was carefully proportioned.

Once a cabinet has been proportioned, the details within the case must be proportioned if the completed case is to be visually successful. For example, as the focal point of

ANATOMY OF A PENNSYLVANIA SECRETARY

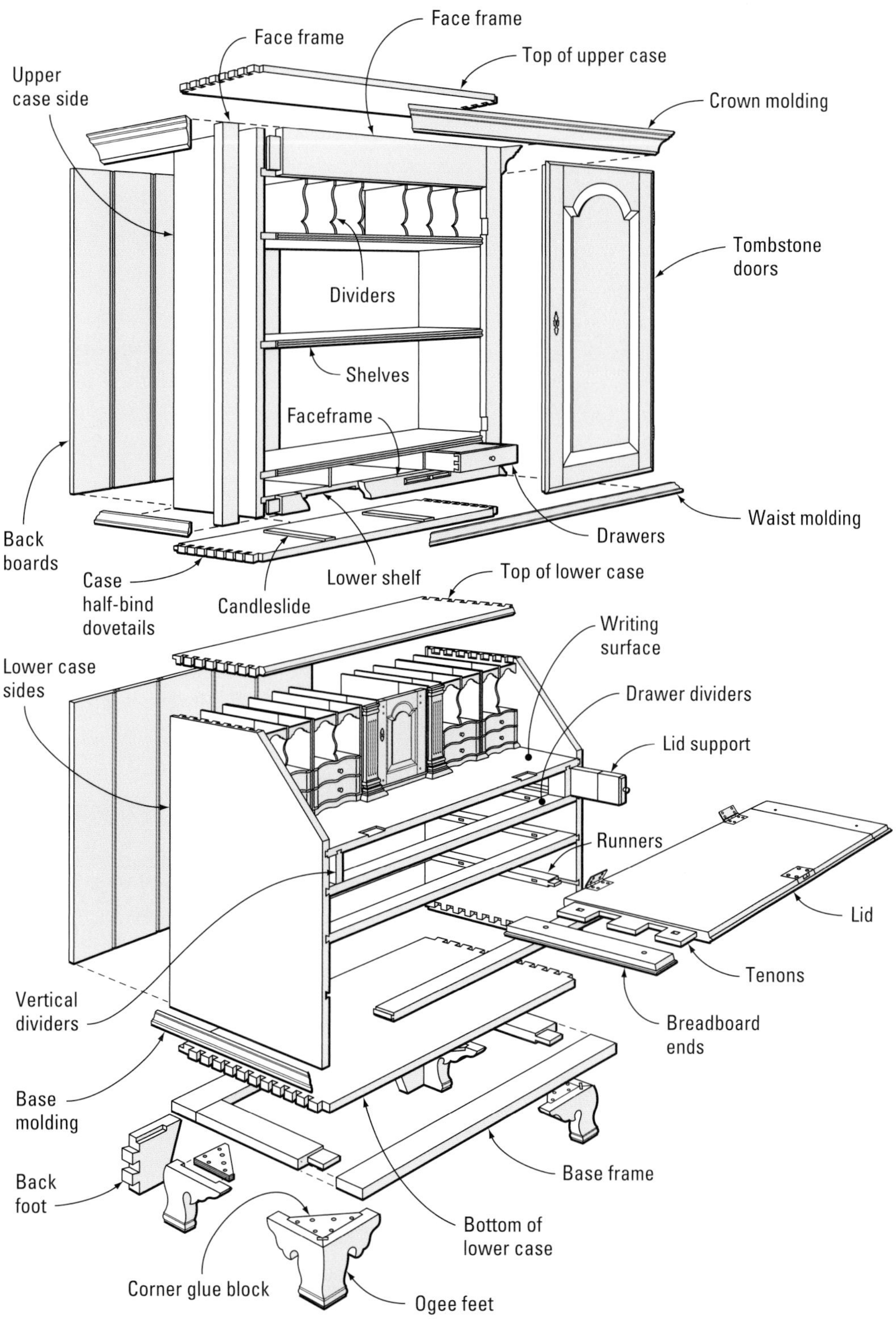
Face frame
Face frame
Top of upper case
Upper case side
Crown molding
Tombstone doors
Dividers
Shelves
Faceframe
Waist molding
Back boards
Drawers
Case half-bind dovetails
Lower shelf
Top of lower case
Candleslide
Writing surface
Lower case sides
Drawer dividers
Lid support
Runners
Lid
Tenons
Vertical dividers
Breadboard ends
Base molding
Base frame
Back foot
Bottom of lower case
Corner glue block
Ogee feet

MOLDINGS ON A CORNER CABINET

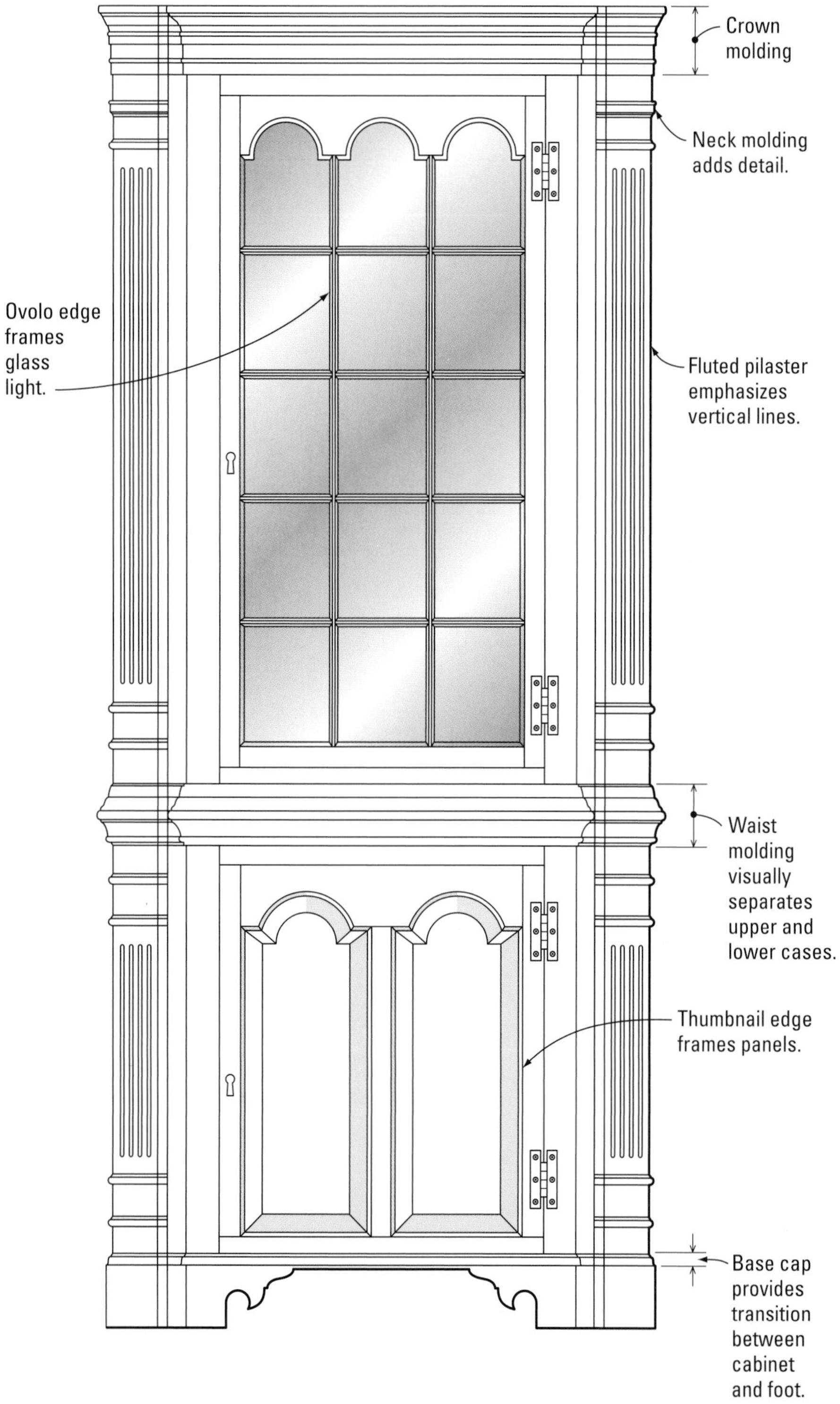
Crown molding
Neck molding adds detail.
Ovolo edge frames glass light.
Fluted pilaster emphasizes vertical lines.
Waist molding visually separates upper and lower cases.
Thumbnail edge frames panels.
Base cap provides transition between cabinet and foot.

the gallery in the small tombstone door fits perfectly within a Golden Rectangle.

Drawers look best if they graduate, that is they deepen as they progress. One sure method is to use the system of arithmetic progression. It works like this: A constant value X, is added each time to size the next drawer in the series. Using the drawer divider as X works well. For example, assuming a value of 7/8 in. for X, the first drawer measures 3 1/2 in., the next three measure 4 3/8 in., 5 1/4 in., and 6 1/8 in.

Finally, use proportioning systems as a guide and feel free to change dimensions as the design progresses. Your eye should always be the final judge.

Pediments

Although flat top case pieces are quite attractive, gooseneck pediments seem to command attention when you enter the room. As the graceful "S" curves rise toward the center of the pediment board, they often terminate in a turned and carved rosette. Crowning the pediment is a turned and carved finial. Often the finial is flanked by matching finials which are positioned on the lower corners of the pediment near the miter of the gooseneck molding.

When making a gooseneck pediment, it is always a good idea to start with a drawing to work out the dimensions and proportions. Once you have drawn the "S" curve, you can duplicate the parallel curve with the simple jig in the sidebar on p. 90.

The details of rosettes and finials should also be first worked out in a full-scale drawing, then a three-dimensional prototype. A prototype brings this type of work to life and is a great aid in determining the relationship of the various elements to each other, as well as to the rest of the pediment.

Casework joinery

Because of the myriad of joints used in period casework, reproducing period casework requires a mastery of joinery. The predominate joint was the half-blind dovetail. Unlike the through dovetail, the half-blind variation is exposed on only one face. This method not only prevents the joint from distracting from other more prominent details (a seemingly prevalent thought of the period), it is also prohibits seasonal movement from pushing on molding that may cover the area around the joint.

Because jigs cannot duplicate the myriad of variations of period dovetails, it is best to develop the skill to cutting them by hand. Although the skills may seem difficult to master, cutting dovetails is really just sawing and chiseling to a layout line. The key is accurate layout. It should be done with a knife and a marking gauge. These tools leave a crisp incision that is a great aid to sawing

The graceful curve of the gooseneck molding on this period clock calls attention to the flame finial in the center. Rosettes enhance the termination points.

PROPORTIONING DRAWERS

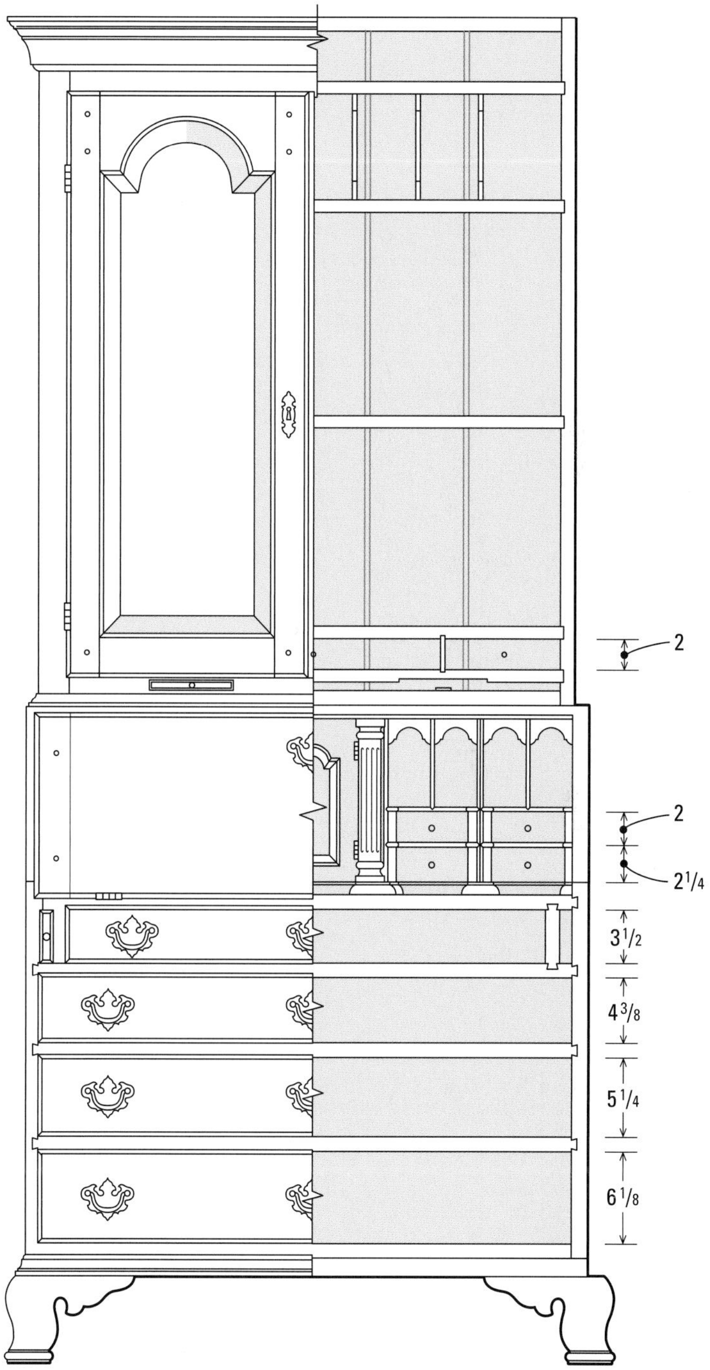

Arithmetic progress yields pleasing proportions in a series of drawers.

and chiseling. A pencil should be avoided. Pencil lines have thickness and create an indefinite layout line that is imprecise.

The ongoing argument of cutting pins or tails first is moot. The goal is always to produce a precise, tight-fitting dovetail joint that is authentic to the period. As with much of woodworking, there are several paths to reaching the goal.

The drawer dividers in large casework are typically joined to the case with a sliding dovetail. As you might expect, there are regional differences. For example, on some New England pieces, the dovetail is through so that the end of the divider can be seen on the sides of the case.

The desk gallery with its intricate arrangement of drawers and pigeonholes appears difficult to construct but is actually

MAKING A PATTERN FOR A GOOSENECK MOLDING

How do you draw two freeform curves that are absolutely parallel to each other? The answer is to use a disk to guide the pencil. The edge of the disk rolls along the edge of the first curve and guides the pencil for a parallel curve. You'll need to make the radius of the disk equal to the width of the molding. To ensure that the disk is a perfect circle, turn it on the lathe.

Begin by carefully sketching the freeform curve on thin plywood. Next, bandsaw the *negative* contour. Now tack the plywood over a second layer of plywood. Trace the negative pattern, then use the disk to draw a second line parallel to the first. The result is a perfect pattern.

After bandsawing the *negative* pattern of the curve, transfer it to a second sheet of plywood.

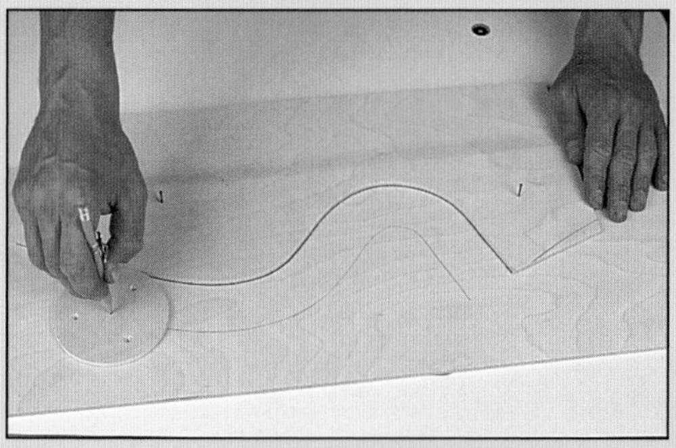

Use a disk equal in radius to the width of the molding to guide your pencil.

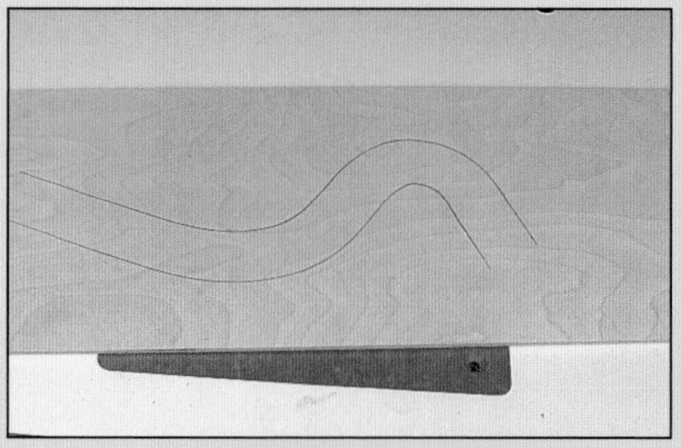

An accurate pattern results from cutting to the parallel line.

ANATOMY OF A DESK GALLERY

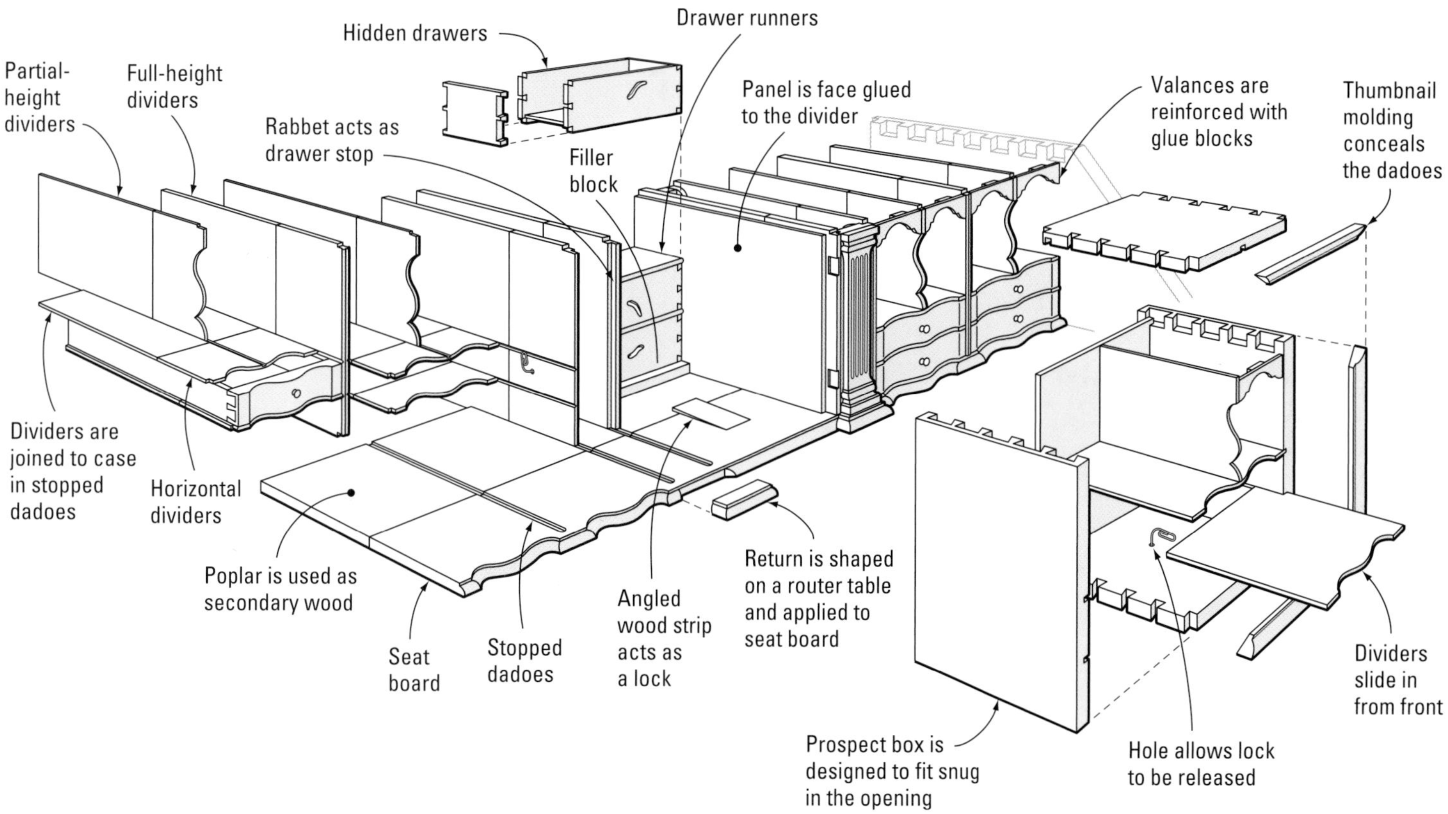

Hidden drawers
Drawer runners
Partial-height dividers
Full-height dividers
Rabbet acts as drawer stop
Filler block
Panel is face glued to the divider
Valances are reinforced with glue blocks
Thumbnail molding conceals the dadoes
Dividers are joined to case in stopped dadoes
Horizontal dividers
Poplar is used as secondary wood
Seat board
Stopped dadoes
Angled wood strip acts as a lock
Return is shaped on a router table and applied to seat board
Prospect box is designed to fit snug in the opening
Hole allows lock to be released
Dividers slide in from front

quite simple. The seat board provides a foundation for the thin partitions and dividers which are fitted into shallow grooves. To yield a finished appearance, the front of each groove is terminated with a vee joint.

Doors

Period doors can vary tremendously in design but fall primarily into the categories of frame-and-panel, solid stock, or divided light. All doors look best as vertical rectangles rather than a square. Square doors can be divided into two vertical panels for a more pleasing appearance A common theme in period doors is the so-called tombstone arch. After shaping the tombstone panel with power tools, the corners flanking the arch must be carved by hand.

Doors made from a solid plank are usually narrow such as the clock waist door or the prospect door of a desk gallery. Solid doors are often embellished with figured stock or veneer, carved shells, or inlay.

Sash doors allow display of the contents of a cabinet. The delicate bars, or mullions, that divide the panes of glass are joined with tiny mortise and tenon joints. Old or reproduction glass looks much more authentic

VARIATIONS ON THE TOMBSTONE PANEL

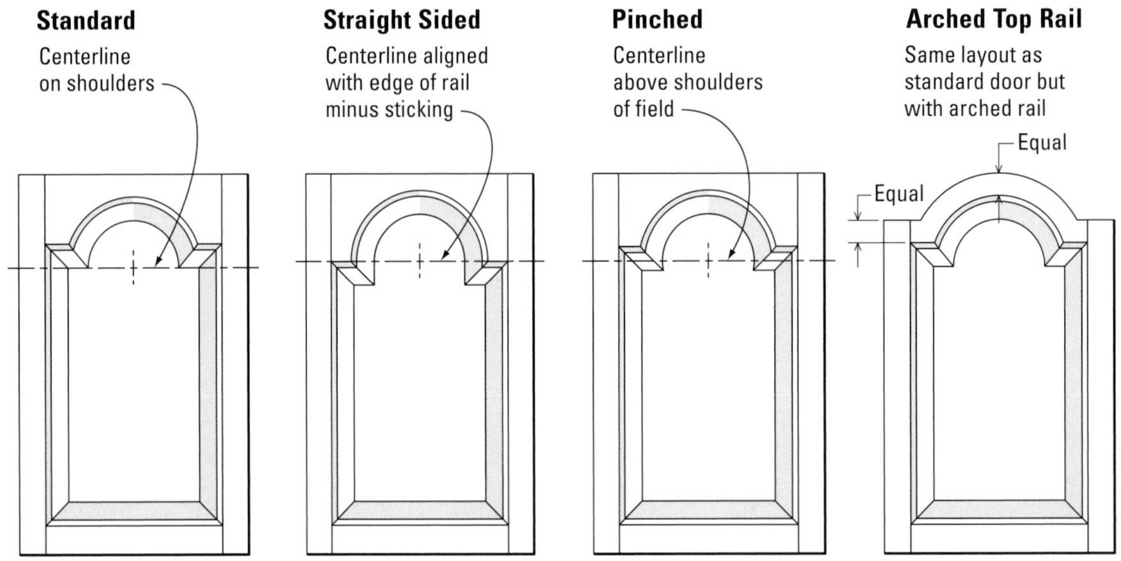

SASH DOOR ANATOMY

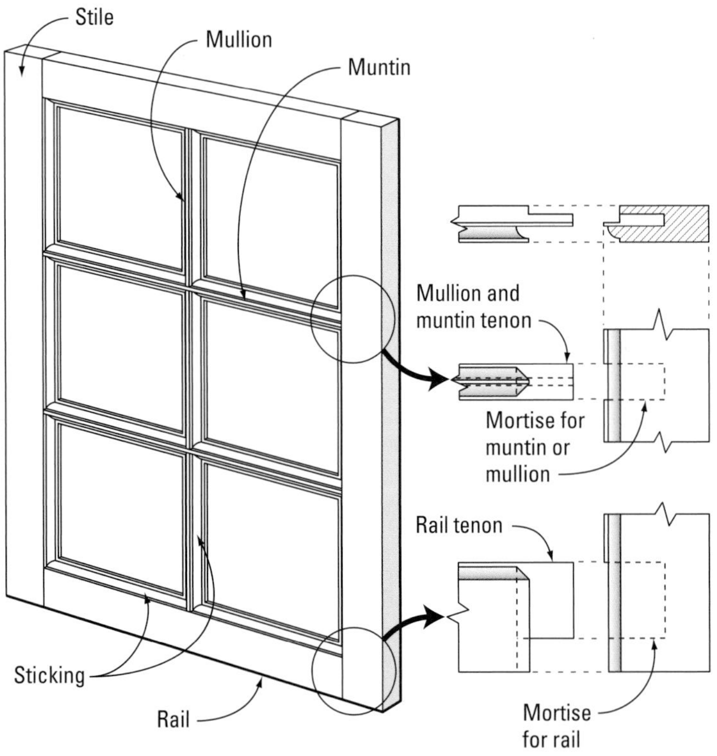

than flat new panes. After installation, the glass is held in place with glazing putty.

Lipped doors and drawers are rabbeted along the edges. The "lip" that remains after rabbetting is shaped with a small, simple thumbnail profile. Lipped doors can be a bit fussy to install; a special offset hinge is required, and the rabbet on the hinged edge of the door is reduced to prevent binding. Double doors that meet in the middle require a false cabinet stile, which is really just an extension of the right stile of the left door.

Some of the most unusual door and drawer construction is encountered in the galleries of slant-front desks of the period. Most 18th-century desks feature a small, flush-fitting door in the center of the gallery. The door can be a hinged plank of figured stock, a carved panel, or a diminutive frame-and-panel complete with a carved tombstone arch. The door is often flanked by a pair of tall, narrow document drawers. Though sometimes dovetailed, the document drawers are usually just joined together with small cut nails. The drawer fronts are often embellished with flat columns, called pilasters, which clearly portray the close ties between furniture and architecture of the period. The desk gallery is also an ideal place for hidden compartments. Many 18th-century desks feature drawers with false backs or bottoms and hidden boxes for concealing valuables.

Period drawers are almost always dovetailed, half-blind in the front and through in the back. The bottoms are solid stock and the edges of the bottom are beveled to slide into grooves in the drawer front and sides. Drawers and doors can be mounted flush or lipped. The gap around a flush door or drawer should be small and uniform which requires careful hand-fitting with planes after assembly.

LIPPED DOORS WITH THUMBNAIL PROFILE

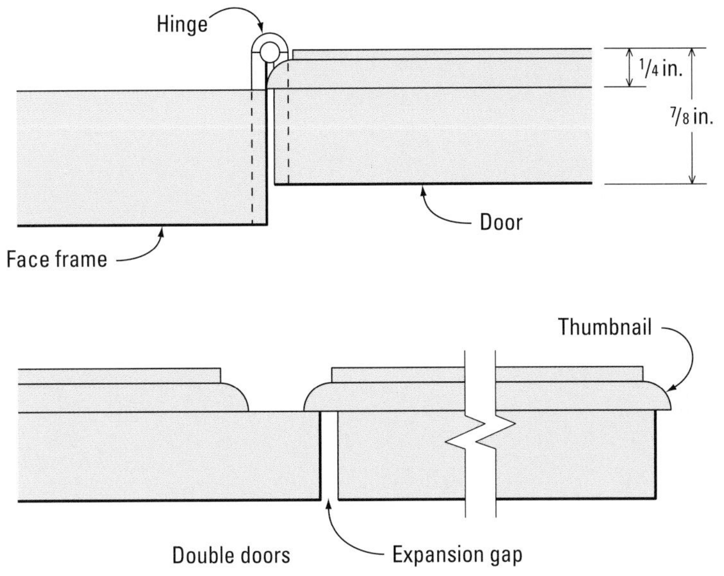

LIPPED DRAWER FRONT WITH LAYOUT HALF-BLIND DOVETAIL

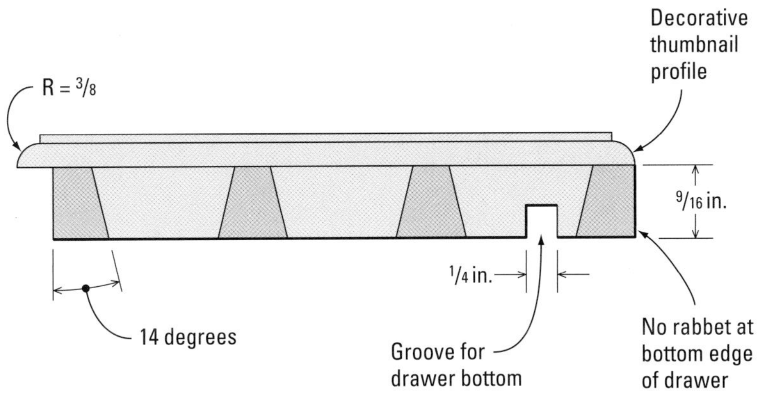

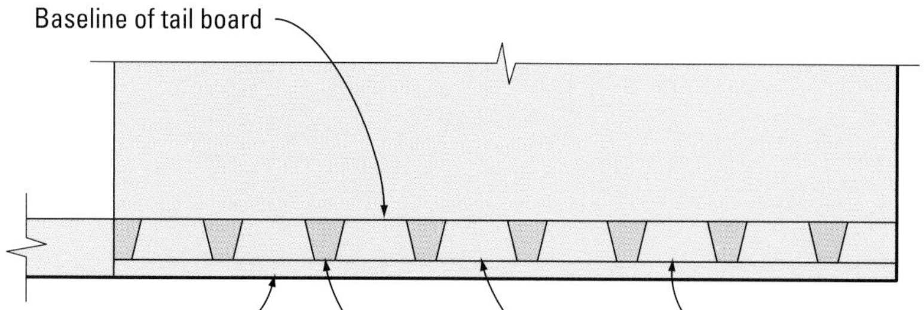

A

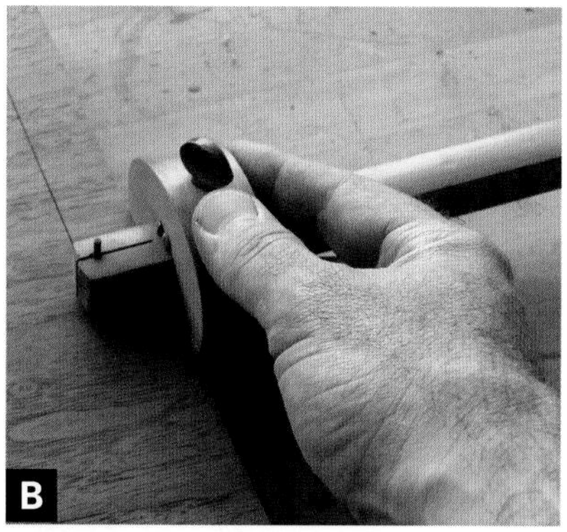
B

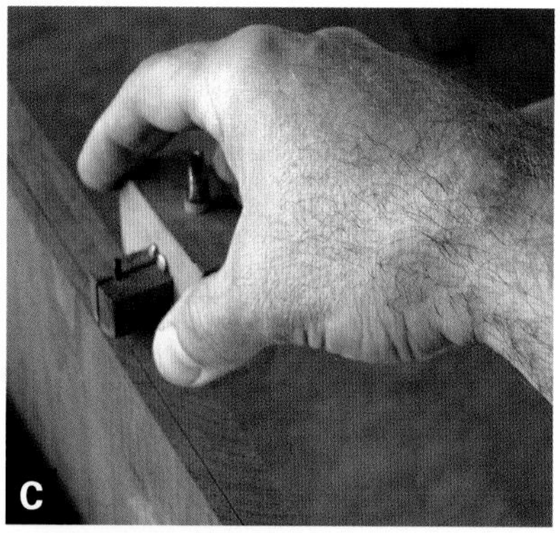
C

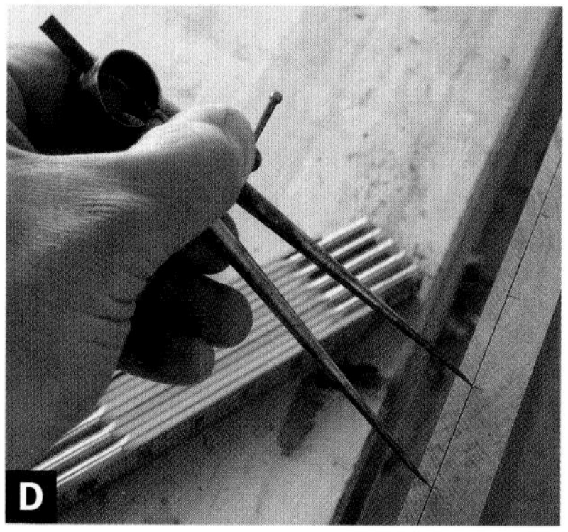
D

E

F

Cutting Half-blind Dovetails

Most dovetails on period furniture are half-blind to conceal them from view. (**A**) This follows the 18th-century practice of concealing joinery. Although half-blind dovetails can seem complex, they are really less fuss than through dovetails. I never cut dovetails with a jig, as the results are just not authentic. The pins of dovetails produced on a jig are too wide and the completed joint lacks the hand-worked look that is required of period work.

However, I do use a router freehand to remove the waste between the pins. Using a router dramatically reduces the time needed to cut the joint. Afterwards, I scribe the tails and saw them the traditional way. The result is a dovetail joint with a period look and feel without quite as much labor involved.

Begin by scribing the pin board for the thickness of the tail board (**B**). Next scribe the pin board for the length of the tails (**C**). Use dividers to space the distance to the center of each pin (**D**) and mark each pin with a knife (**E**). Next, clamp the pin boards together and transfer the layout lines (**F**).

Use a router and a fourteen degree dovetail bit to remove the wood between the pins (**G**). Afterwards, square the corners and work to the baseline with a chisel (**H**).

Now you are ready to begin the tails. Position the pin board over the tail board and align it with the baseline for marking (**I**). Now saw each tail carefully to the layout line (**J**). Chop the space between the tails with a chisel. The edge of the chisel will easily follow the knife line from your marking gauge (**K**).

The last step is to gently tap the joint together with a mallet (**L**). As you tap the joint, feel for any tight areas and pare a shaving away to prevent splitting.

G

H

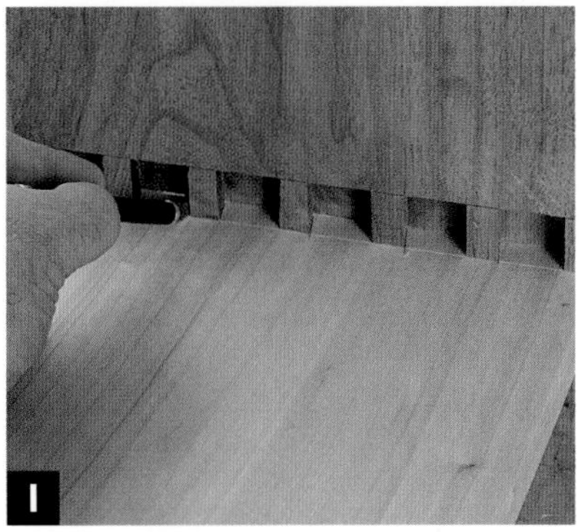
I

J

K

L

A

B

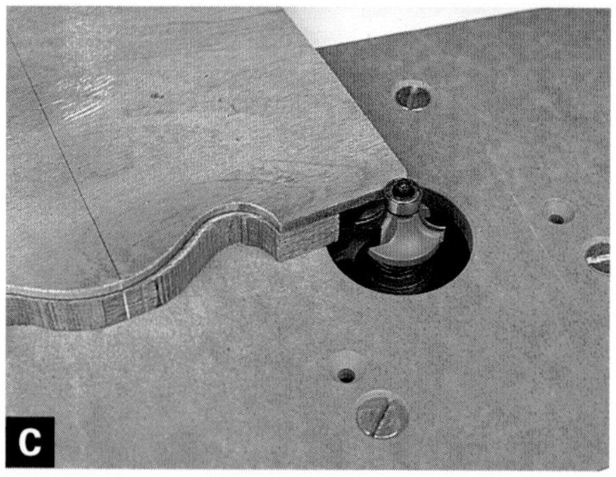

C

D

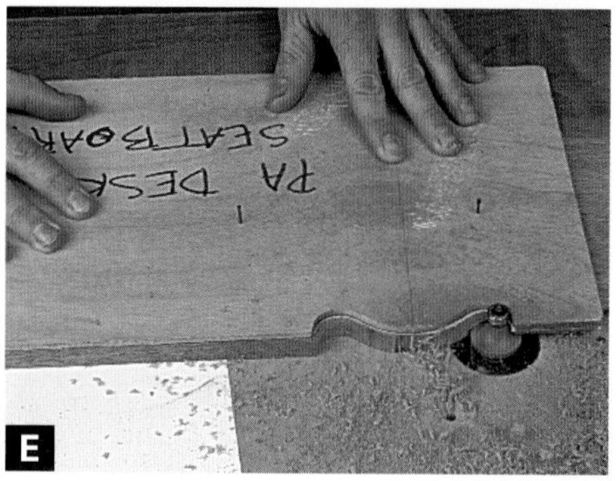

E

Seat Board on the Router Table

This example uses a seat board from a desk. The edge of the seat board has a thumbnail profile that must follow the curved contour at each drawer. The tight curves would be impossible to reach with a shaper and would be tedious to shape by hand.

➤ See *"Thumbnail Profile"* drawing on p. 6.

Begin by tracing the template onto the workpiece (**A**). Be careful to match the centerlines, because the eventual curves must align with two more sets of curves in the desk. After bandsawing heavy of the layout line (**B**), adjust the bit height so that the bearing contacts the template.

To make the cut, start by contacting the bearing with the extended portion of the template (**C**). This makes entry into the wood smooth (**D**). Now reposition the template and make the next cut (**E**). Shaping the seat board with this method takes just a few minutes.

Template Shaping Returns

These tiny blocks (**A**) measure approximately ½ in. by ⅞ in. by 3 in. and require a thumbnail profile along one edge and both ends. Because the entire edge is shaped, the setup requires either a fence or a template to limit the cutting depth. After shaping, the blocks will be mitered on the ends and carefully fit into a notch in the seat board.

Begin by milling the stock to the final thickness, but leave it oversize in width and length. Next, glue the stock to a piece of ¼-in.-thick plywood with heavy paper in the joint (**B**). The plywood will provide a template for the router bearing during the shaping process. After shaping, the paper will allow you to separate the plywood easily from the workpiece.

After the glue has dried, joint the edge of the assembly with a bench plane or jointer (**C**). Then rip the stock to final width and crosscut it to final length (**D**).

The next step is to shape the profile. There are a couple of keys to shaping such a small piece: add mass to reduce chatter and provide a method to grasp the part safely for shaping. One solution is to grip the part within the jaws of a wooden handscrew (**E**). The heavy wooden clamp effectively adds mass and positions hands a safe distance from the spinning router bit. Also, if the bit inadvertently contacts the jaws of the clamp, there's no dangerous metal-to-metal contact.

A

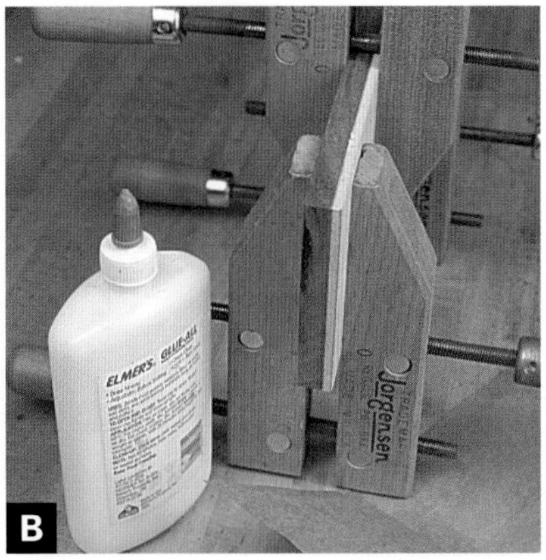

B

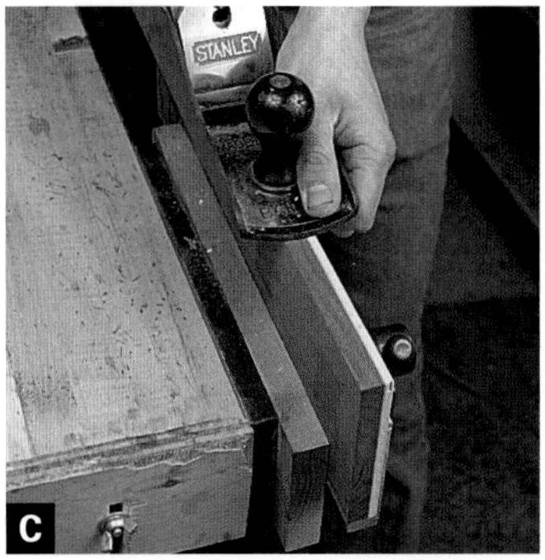

C

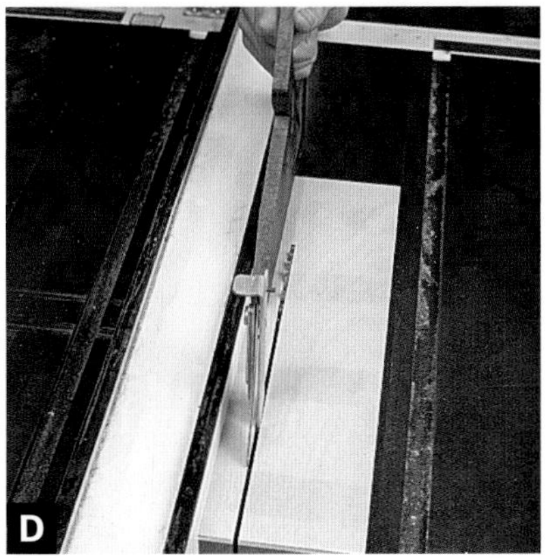
D

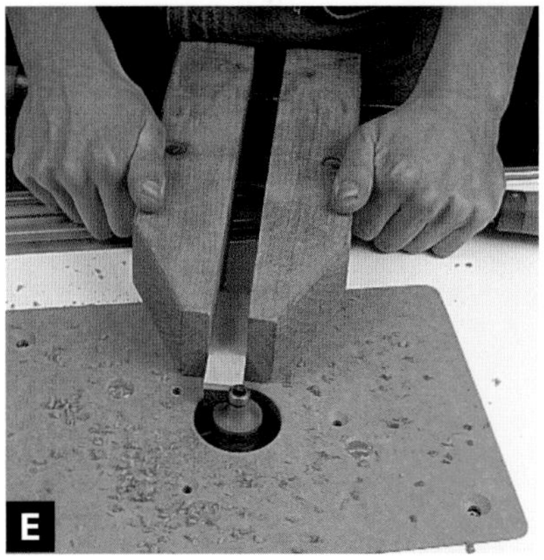
E

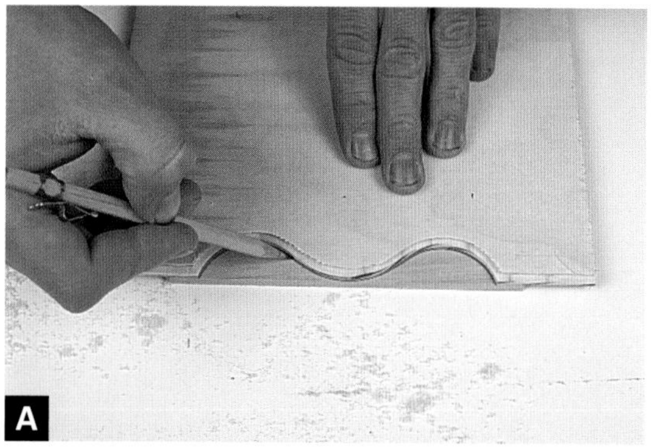

A

B

C

Divider

Here's a unique method for making the template: Make the template from the previous template.

For accuracy, trace the contour onto the stock directly from the template (**A**). After bandsawing, fasten the template to the stock with brads (**B**). Although the brads will leave small holes, they won't be seen in the finished desk and the process is fast to set up.

The bearing on the bit follows the template, cutting away the saw marks and creating the profile—all in one light pass (**C**).

[TIP] If you choose a bit that's slightly large, you'll avoid the ridges that occur with a smaller bit and the larger radius appears more refined.

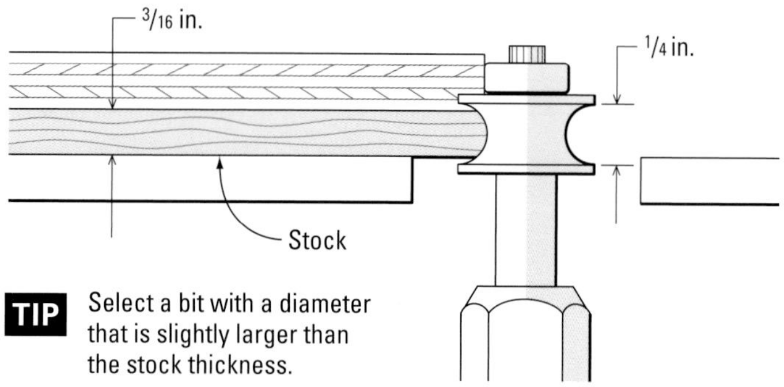
3/16 in.
1/4 in.
Stock
TIP
Select a bit with a diameter that is slightly larger than the stock thickness.

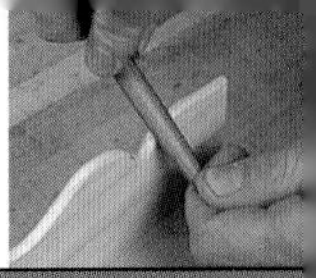

Shaping Inside Corners of a Divider

Begin by shaping the work with a template. Next, select a tool for the job; in this case, I'm shaping a 3⁄16-in.-thick divider from the gallery of a desk interior. The profile that I shaped was a 1⁄4-in.-diameter bead, so I want a small gouge that approximates the bead's curve (**A**).

Before you begin carving, sketch the outline onto the work (**B**). Next, carve from both directions into the corner (**C**). To remove any facets, smooth the area with a small file (**D**). The finished divider is a result of combining power-tool techniques with hand-tool skills to create detailed work efficiently (**E**).

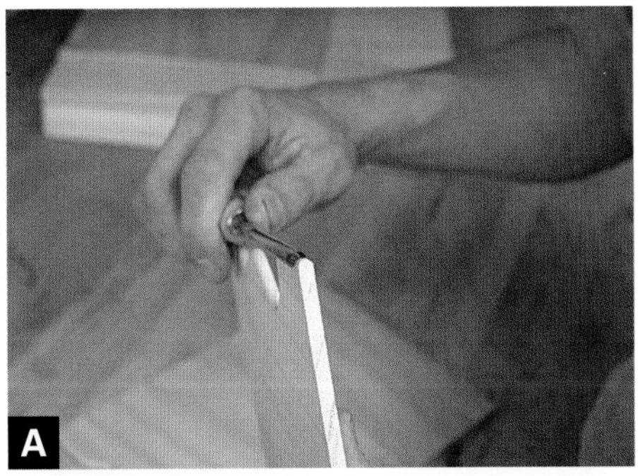
A

B

C

D

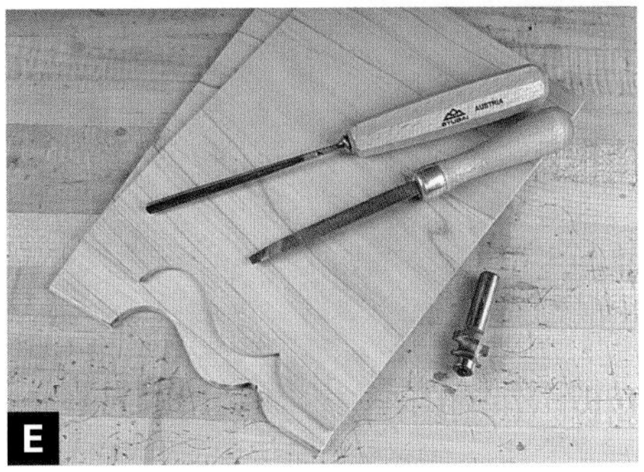
E

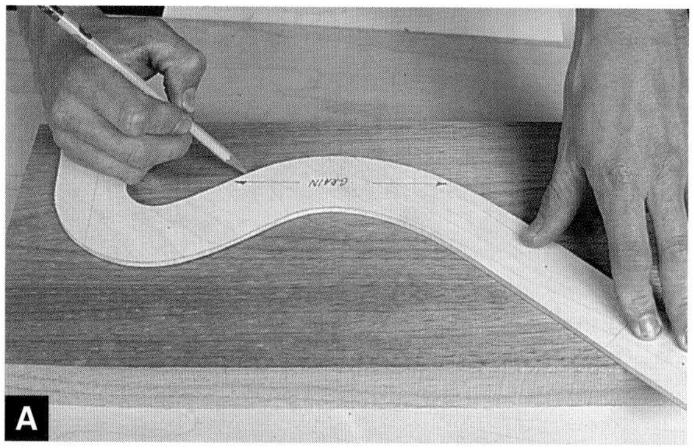

A

B

C

Gooseneck Molding on the Shaper

The shaper is the most efficient tool for shaping a gooseneck molding. By using a complex cutter and a template/jig to hold the stock, the profile can be shaped cleanly in just a few minutes.

Before shaping, you'll need to build a template/jig to hold the stock and guide the cutterhead in a curved path. Select a piece of ¾-in. plywood for the jig that's wide enough to position your hands a minimum of 8 in. from the cutterhead and long enough to extend several inches beyond the stock. After bandsawing the curve, attach a pair of toggle clamps to the jig to help hold the stock.

➤ See *"Making a Pattern for a Gooseneck Molding"* on p. 90.

Now select a wide piece of straight-grain stock for the molding and trace the inside curve directly from the pattern (**A**). Bandsaw the inside curve only (**B**) and fasten the stock to the jig with several screws. The screws, combined with the toggle clamps, keep the stock securely in the jig during shaping. Obviously, you'll need to locate the screws well out of the path of the cutterhead (**C**).

WARNING Safety is always an issue with any machine. But it's a special concern with the shaper, especially when shaping curved stock. I strongly urge you to gain plenty of experience with the shaper before using this technique.

The cutterhead shown here is one I designed; it was custom manufactured by Freeborn Tool Company. It's important to shape the profile in multiple passes to reduce the feed resistance and increase safety. This is accomplished by switching to a smaller rub bearing after each successive pass. I used three bearing sizes with this cutterhead; the smallest bearing allows the cutterhead to shape the full profile. Also, notice that I'm using a disk guard that mounts above the cutterhead. This guard is available from Delta. Although I removed the guard so the photos would be clear, I don't recommend using this technique without it.

Once the construction of the jig is complete, set up the cutterhead assembly on the shaper spindle. Slip the largest bearing on the spindle first, then the cutterhead, and finally the guard. Then lock the assembly in place with the lockwasher and spindle nut. Now position the jig and workpiece next to the spindle to make the height adjustment; then lock the spindle height (**D**).

Now you're ready for the cut. Remember always to feed the stock against the spindle rotation. In this case, I'm feeding from right to left.

Turn on the shaper and position the extended portion of the jig against the rub bearing (**E**). Now begin feeding at a steady pace (**F**). As you feed the work, keep the jig resting on the table and the edge against the bearing. As the chips fly, you'll soon be at the end of the cut (**G**).

Pull the work away from the spindle and turn off the shaper. Now switch to a smaller bearing and repeat the procedure (**H**). Remember to shape

(Text continues on p. 102)

D

E

F

G

H

I

J

K

L

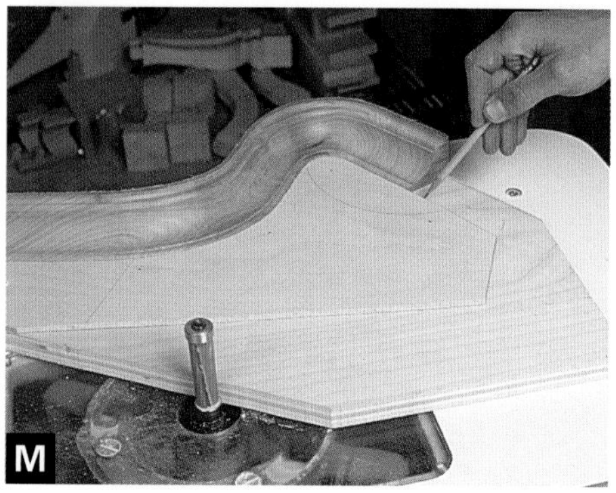

M

N

the matching gooseneck each time. Finally, install the smallest bearing (**I**) and shape the complete profile (**J**). Now remove the molding from the jig and bandsaw the outside curve. Invert the molding and bandsaw from the back for an accurate cut (**K**). Next, place the molding into a second jig for flush trimming (**L**). This jig has a negative pattern that acts as an alignment strip (**M**).

When you're finished (**N**), place the fence around the cutterhead and shape the returns that miter to the ends of the gooseneck.

Gooseneck Molding on the Router Table with Pin Jig

Another method for shaping gooseneck and arched moldings is to use a pin router. A pin or bearing is suspended over the router, which is mounted in a table. A template, which is positioned over the stock, follows the guide pin. Because the pin can be positioned offset to the router bit, interior cuts can be made.

Although pin routers are expensive, the jig shown here clamps to the edge of your router table to convert it to a pin router. A bearing is fastened to the end of the arm to guide the template (**A**). The arm is held in position on the base with a bolt. A tongue under the arm slides within a groove in the base to prevent the arm from moving sideways (**B**).

After constructing the jig, make a full-size pattern of the gooseneck curve. Next, use the pattern to lay out the curve on both the template and the stock. Extend the line on the template beyond the curve of the molding. This way the template will contact the bearing before the router bit contacts the stock, eliminating potential grabbing at the entry of the cut.

➤ See *"Making a Pattern for a Gooseneck Molding"* on p. 90.

Now fasten the workpiece to the template with several screws. Take care to keep them out of the path of the spinning bits. Allow the work to extend ¹⁄₁₆-in. beyond the template edge for flush

(Text continues on p. 104)

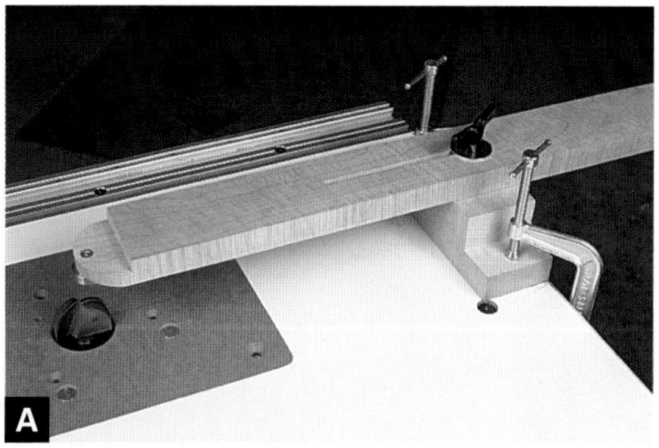

A

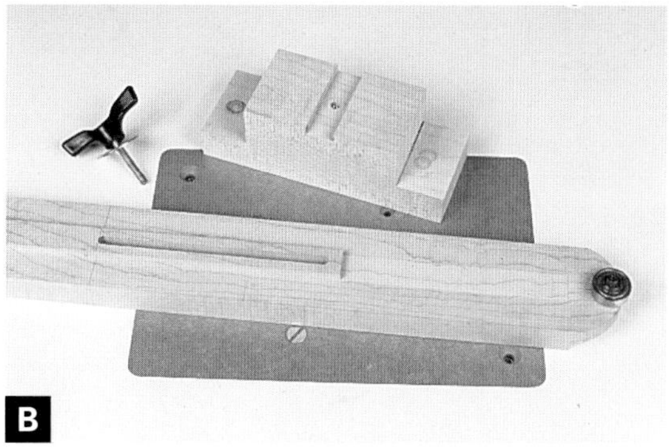

B

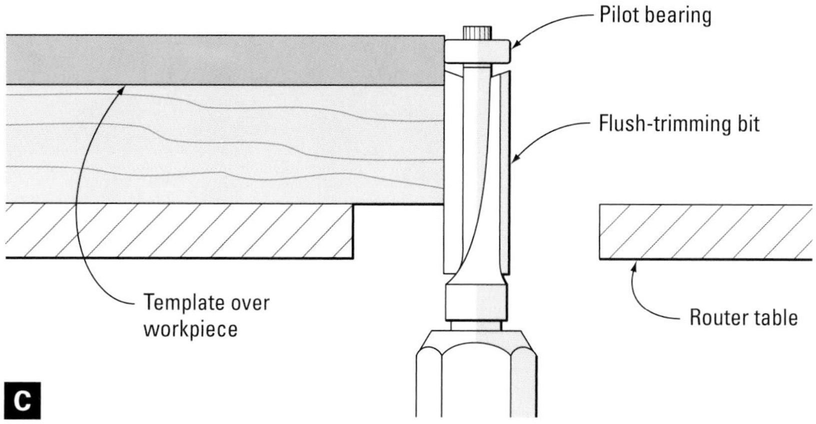

C

D

E

F

G

H

I

J

trimming. Next, fasten a large block of the same thickness toward the back of the template to stabilize it as you're shaping. Now you're ready to begin shaping.

Begin by flush trimming the work (**C**) with a flush-trimming router bit (**D**); you will not need the pin jig for this step. Next, begin shaping the cove. Because of the large size of the cove, it's necessary to make this cut in several passes. Mount the corebox bit in the router and clamp the jig to the table edge. Now slide the arm of the jig out and lock it in position for a light cut.

Before starting the cut, you must realize that it's necessary to keep the template edge in the same spot on the bearing throughout the cut; the location is a point tangent to the bearing at 90 degrees to the arm. This is necessary because the guide bearing and bit are not spinning on the same axis—they are offset. Performing this task is not difficult, but requires concentration. Also, realize that you'll gain experience as you go and keeping the template located properly is not extremely critical until the final pass.

Let's give it a try. Turn on the router, position the end of the template against the bearing, and begin feeding the stock (**E, F**). As the template curves, rotate it to maintain contact at the front of the bearing (**G, H, I**). Now turn off the router, retract the arm slightly, and repeat the process several times until the full profile of the cove has been shaped (**J**).

The next step is to shape the ogee at the top of the molding. If the router bit you're using has a bearing, you'll first need to remove it and grind off the stud (**K**). Now, mount the bit in the router and adjust the arm to position the bit correctly in relationship to the molding. Now make the cut (**L**).

The last step is to shape the thumbnail at the base of the molding (**M**). For this profile, you'll need a bit from CMT USA's crown-molding set. The inverted profile allows you to shape the thumbnail on the router table (**N**).

K

L

M

N

Mitering a Gooseneck Molding

Mitering a gooseneck molding is one of those processes that isn't nearly as difficult as it looks. The trick is to support the molding on the chopsaw for sawing the miter. To solve the problem, simply extend the molding horizontally when making the pattern. After shaping the molding, position it on the casework and mark the location of the miter. Next, align the layout mark with the kerf on the backboard of the chopsaw (**A**). Now clamp the molding in position and make the cut (**B**). After mitering the return, apply glue to each piece and attach them to the case (**C**). Photo (**D**) shows the molding in place ready for the rosettes and finials.

A

C

B

D

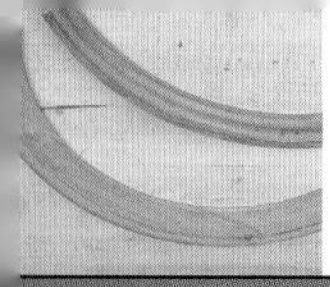

A

B

C

Arched Molding Edge on the Router Table

The process of shaping a curved strip molding is much like shaping a straight strip of molding. The difference is that you'll first have to bandsaw the curve into the stock (**A**). Then, when shaping, you'll guide the workpiece against a bearing instead of a fence (**B**).

After shaping, bandsaw the outside radius of the curved molding and smooth the edges (**C**).

> **WARNING** **Remember to use a starting pin as a fulcrum to enter the cut safely.**

Turning a Rosette

This rosette is a simple faceplate turning (**A**). To avoid scarring the work with a screw it's first glued to a scrap of plywood with heavy paper in the joint. Then the plywood is fastened to the faceplate with screws. After the turning and carving are completed, the glue joint is separated.

Begin by gluing the stock to a scrap of plywood; ¾-in.-thick plywood is sufficient to screw the faceplate. After the glue has dried, bandsaw an oversize circle out of the stock and mount it on the lathe.

Before turning, mark the dimensions of the rosette (**B**). Next, turn the rosette to diameter with a parting tool (**C**). Now you're ready to turn the beveled shape on the face of the rosette.

Position the scraper on the tool rest with the edge slightly lowered. This will cause the burr on the scraper to cut clean shavings from the face of the disk. Now simply pivot the tool side to side to create the desired shape (**D, E**). It's that easy!

Don't sand the turning; otherwise the fine abrasive grit will lodge in the pores of the wood and dull your carving tools. A sharp scraper will leave the surface relatively smooth; and besides, much of the surface is carved away.

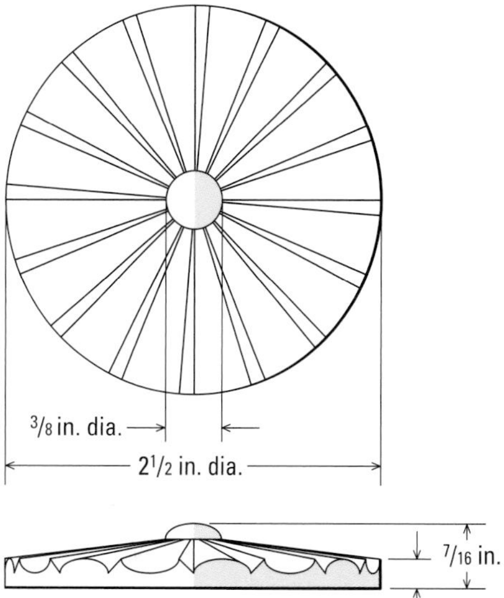

A

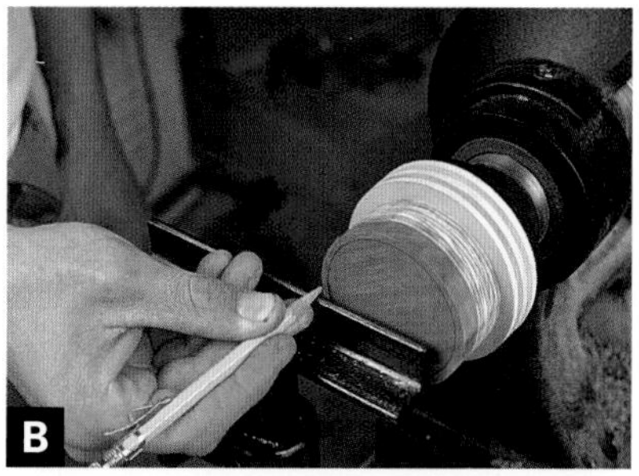

B

C

D

E

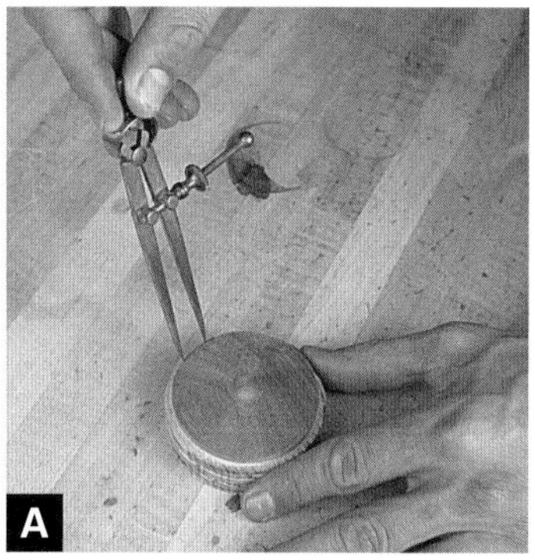
A

B

C

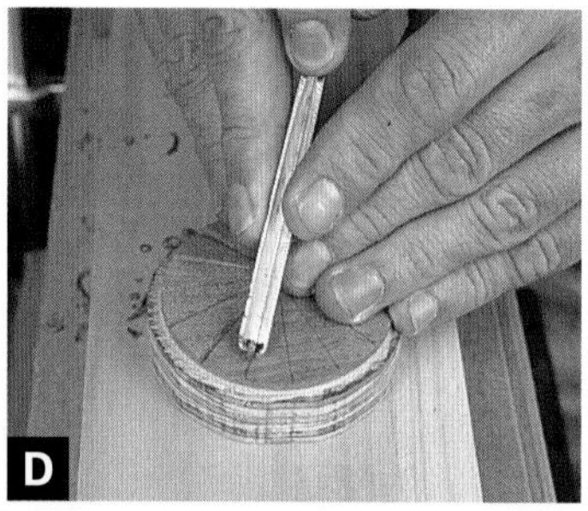
D

E

F

G

Carving a Rosette

A rosette is an ornamental terminus for a gooseneck molding on a pediment. The variations of this design are numerous. The example shown here is a small, simple design that is used on a clock.

Begin by turning the rosette on a lathe to the required shape. Next, step off an even number of spaces around the perimeter (**A**) with dividers and make a mark at each division (**B**). With the aid of a center head, draw a line from each division mark to the hub (**C**).

With the layout complete, you can turn your attention to carving. Begin by outlining each layout line with a V gouge (**D**). The depth of each V should be greatest at the perimeter and gradually diminish in size as it reaches the hub (**E**).

Next, use a ¼-in. no. 5 gouge to carve the rays and lobes (**F**). Begin carving at the perimeter and work back toward the hub. As you approach the hub, it will be necessary to carve from the opposite direction (**G**).

You can sand the carving lightly with 240-grit sandpaper to blend the facets from the gouge. Use care to avoid sanding away the crisp ridges on the V's.

Turning a Flame Finial

Finials are typically used as embellishment on casework such as clocks, desks, and chests. After turning the upper portion of the finial, the flame is carved.

See *"Carving a Flame Finial"* on p. 113.

This large finial (**A**) is easiest to turn as two pieces. Otherwise the narrow section at the base of the flame is quite fragile and causes considerable vibration and difficulty during turning. After turning and carving the urn and flame, the two are joined together with a round mortise-and-tenon joint.

Begin the urn by turning the blank round with a roughing gouge to the largest diameter (**B**). For accuracy, gauge the diameter with a spring caliper. Next, lay out the linear measurements with a story stick (**C**). With a parting tool, cut each of the diameters as indicated on the story stick (**D**). With the sizing complete, you're ready to turn the various shapes.

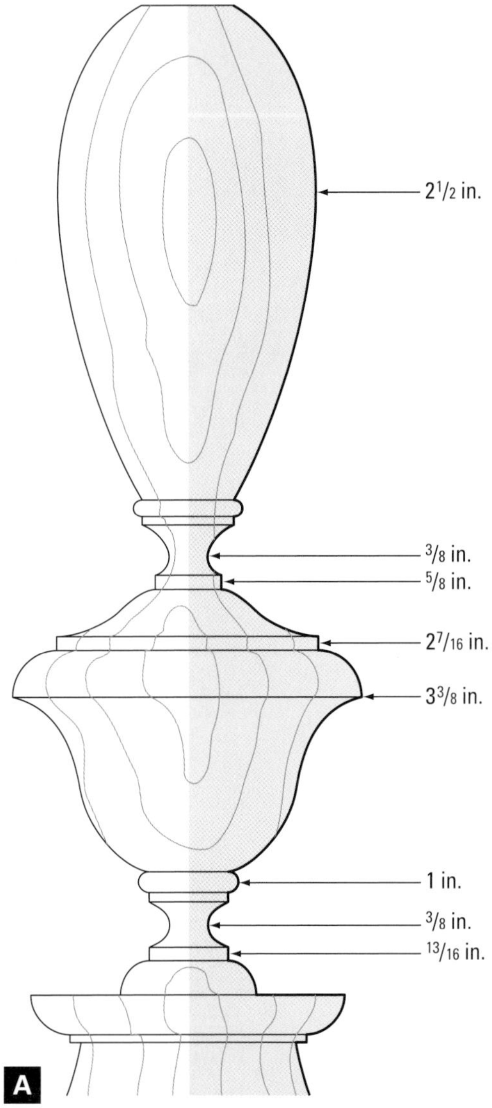

A

B

C

D

E

F

G

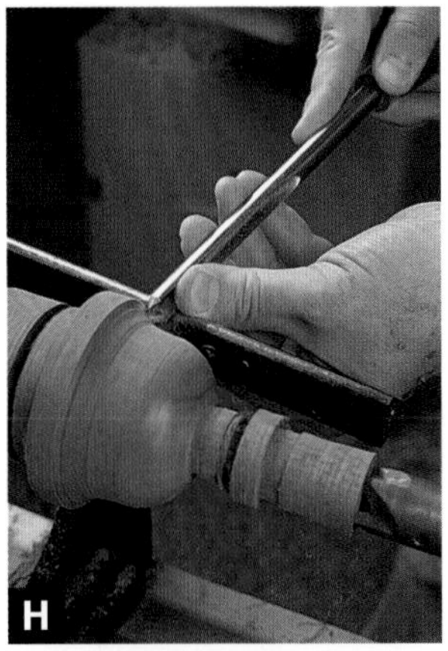

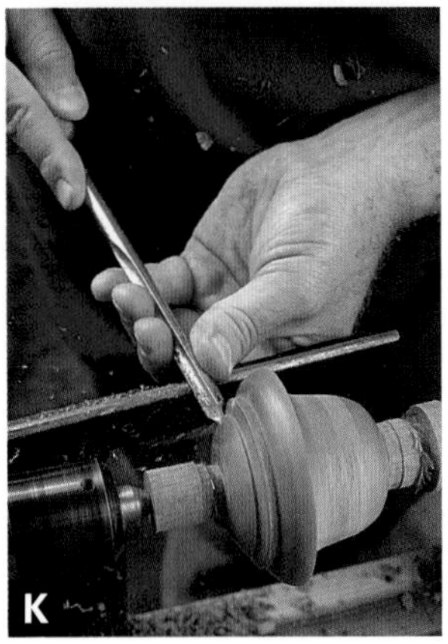

First turn the reverse ogee. Scribe a shallow line with the point of a skew at the start of the ogee (**E**). This incision will give you a positive start when shaping the profile. Begin turning by shaping the bottom of the ogee as a bead (**F**). Then turn the top portion as a cove (**G**) and blend the two to create a fluid cyma curve (**H**). Next, turn the bead at the top, which is adjacent to the fillet (**I**). Afterward, remove the extra stock to provide room to maneuver (**J**). Then cut the ogee at the top of the turning (**K**). If necessary, clean up the fillet to make the surface smooth and the corner crisp (**L, M**).

Now shape the bead at the base of the turning (**N**). Then direct your attention to the tiny bead at the base of the ogee. Shaping the bead requires a delicate touch with the heel of a small skew. You can gauge the width of this bead with a small set of dividers. The last profile is the small cove. Use a small spindle gouge and a light touch as you shape each side of the cove toward the bottom (**O**). If necessary, sharpen the fillets that flank the cove with a small skew.

Now lightly sand the turning (**P**) and burnish it with a handful of shavings (**Q**); then cut the top off with a parting tool. As you cut the top off you'll need to support the turning with one hand while controlling the tool with the other (**R**).

The next step is to bore the mortise that accepts the tenon on the flame. First mount a chuck equipped with a ⅜-in. bit into the tailstock. Next, center the bit on the turning and advance it into the spinning work with the handwheel on the tailstock (**S**).

To turn the flame, first remove the corners of the stock with a roughing gouge to the major diameter. Next, lay out the linear measurements with a story stick (**T**) and cut into the final diameters with a parting tool (**U**).

The next step is to turn the top of the flame. Simply approach this convex curve as a bead and roll it over with a spindle gouge (**V**). Next, shape

(Text continues on p. 112)

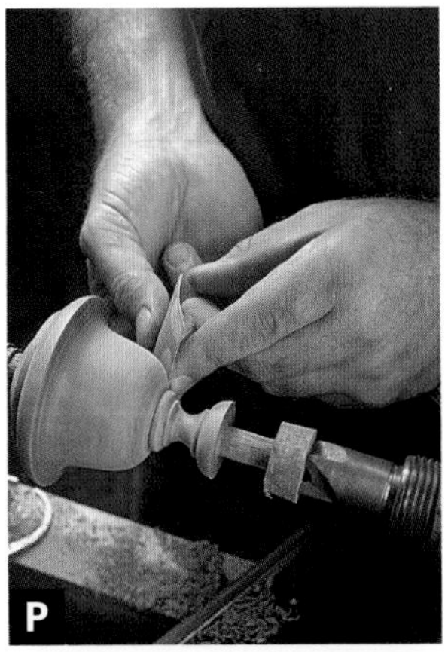

P

Q

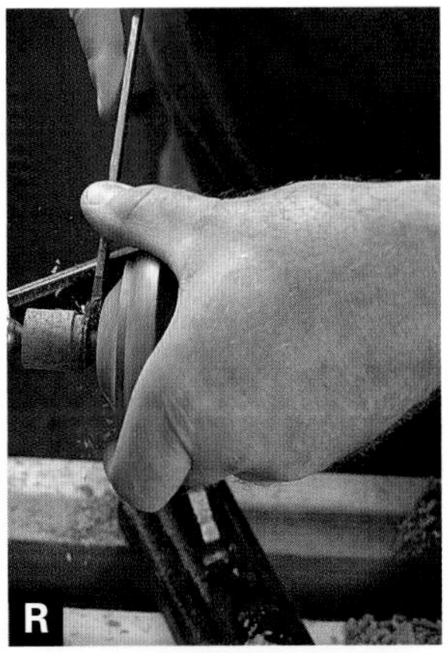

R

S

T

U

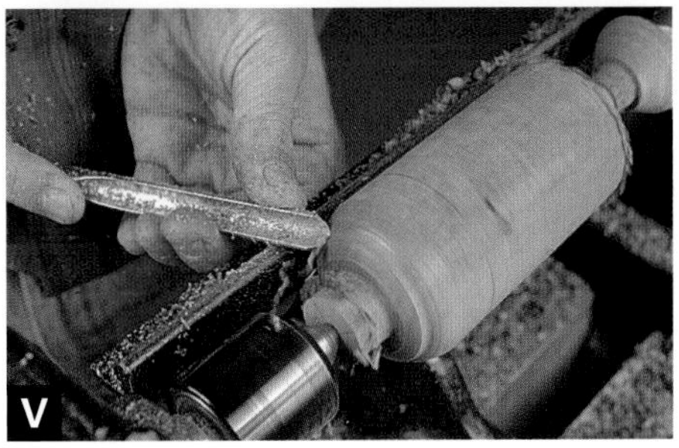

V

W

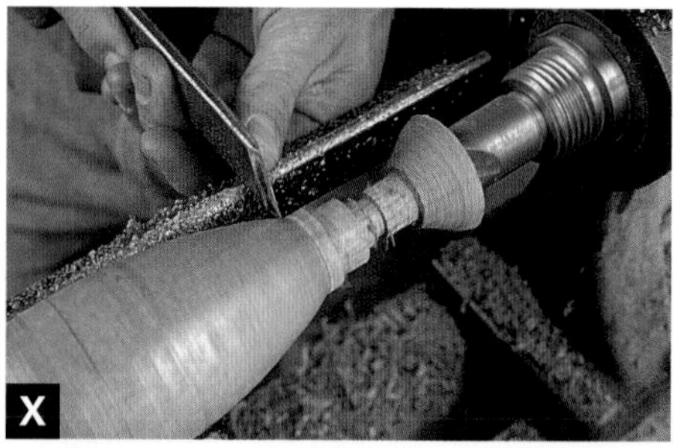
X

Y

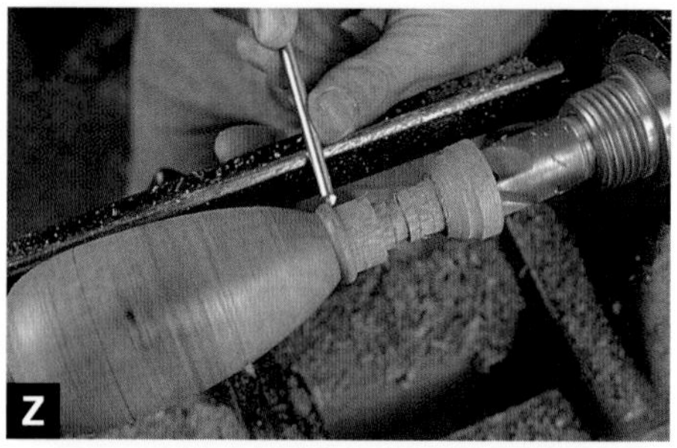
Z

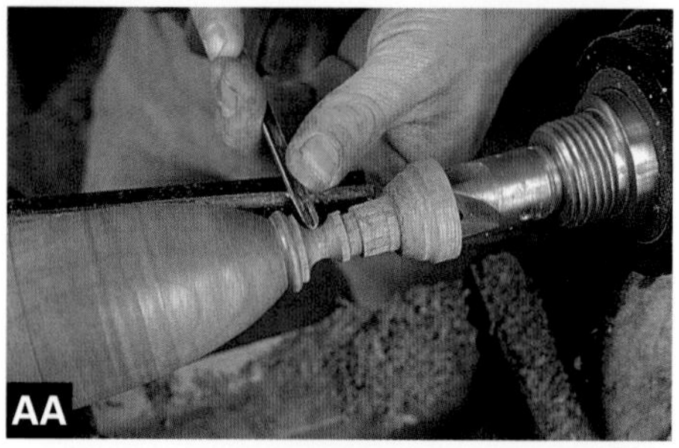
AA

BB

CC

DD

the tapered lower portion of the flame with a skew or large spindle gouge (**W**). Then incise the width of the bead with the point of a skew (**X**); then use the skew to turn the base of the flame further (**Y**). Next, roll the bead to the left and right until it is full and round (**Z**). The last shape is the small cove under the bead (**AA**).

After the turning is complete (**BB**), cut the round tenon for a snug fit within the mortise. To check the tenon for accuracy, make a gauge by boring a hole in a scrap of thin plywood (**CC**).

Don't sand the flame turning. If you do, abrasive grit will lodge in the pores and quickly dull your carving tools later on. Use a parting tool to cut the remaining stock from the end of the tenon and fit it into the mortise in the base (**DD**).

Carving a Flame Finial

Finials are a turned and carved decoration most commonly used on the pediments of casework. The stylized flame finial shown here was a popular ornament on Pennsylvania furniture during the 18th century. Although smaller finials are crafted from one piece of stock, large finials, such as this example, are easier to turn in two pieces.

After turning, the next step is to sketch the design. Good layout allows you to work through the design details and proportions before you begin to carve (**A**). It also provides an essential road map to give you direction as you're working. Although seemingly complex, the layout for this finial is relatively easy. It involves repeatedly sketching cyma curves around the perimeter of the turning. Spacing the curves is important, too, but it's easily accomplished with dividers.

➤ See *"Turning a Flame Finial"* on p. 109.

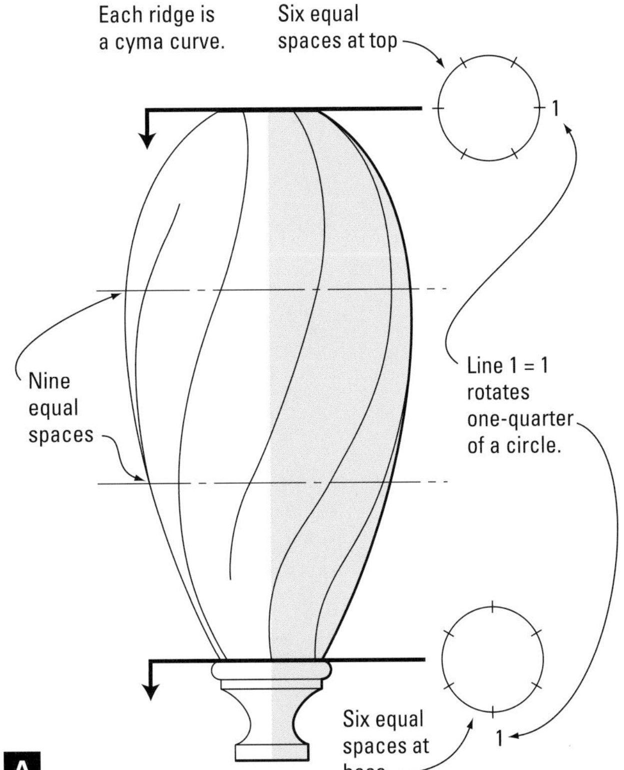

A

Begin layout by sketching the first curve. It becomes a ridge that rises from the base and spirals one-quarter of the circle as it reaches the top. Use the lathe dividing wheel to mark the beginning (**B**) and end (**C**) of the curve. It's most important that the curve is pleasing to the eye, especially because all the other ridges will be modeled according to the first one. You'll find it easier to sketch the curve if you pivot the pencil from your wrist or the knuckle of your little finger (**D**). Just below the midpoint of the turning is the transition point at which the curve changes direction. You'll probably find it easier to invert the turning to draw the upper portion of the curve.

(Text continues on p. 114)

B

C

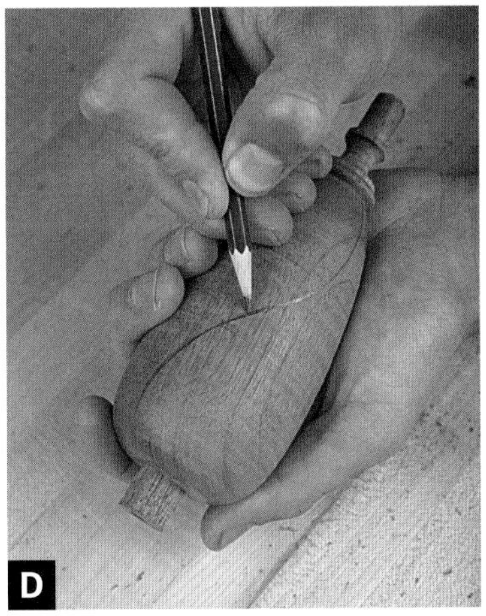

D

E

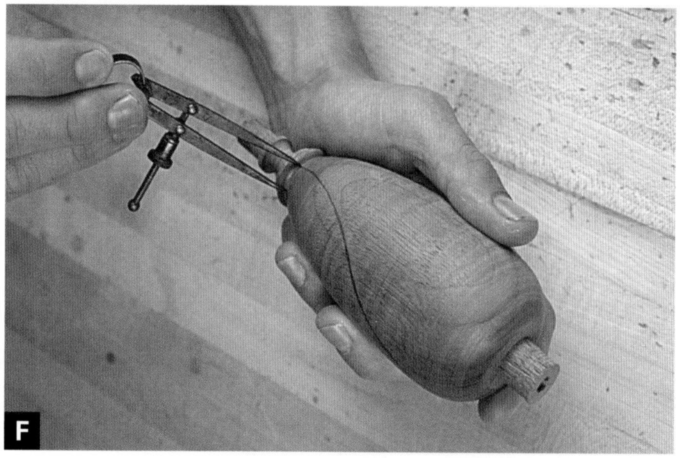
F

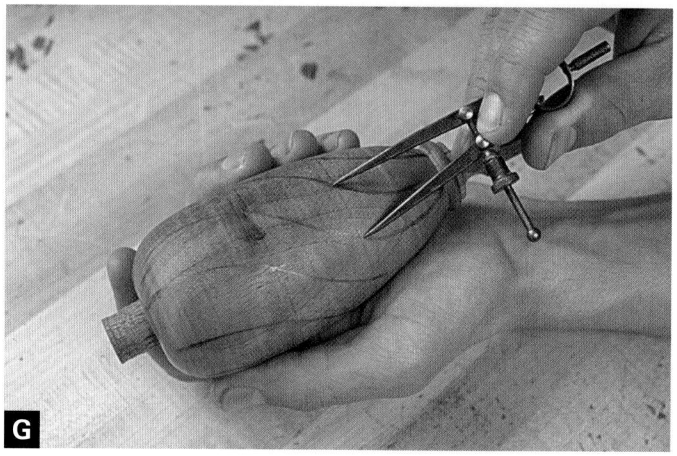
G

When you're satisfied with the first curve, the next step is to repeat the sketch around the perimeter of the turning. To make the spacing somewhat even, it's necessary to divide the turning into equal segments. But first, notice the pattern in the carving. The first ridge starts at the base and rises to the top. The second ridge begins at the base but it ends before reaching the top. The third ridge starts at the top and ends before reaching the base. Then the pattern repeats itself two more times for a total of nine ridges.

Before sketching the rest of the ridges, put the turning back in the lathe and divide the height of the flame into thirds. Next, draw a line around the circumference at the point of each division (**E**). Now you're ready to divide the turning into separate ridges—nine around the middle and six at the top and the base.

Beginning with the base, position one leg of the dividers on the first ridge and step off six spaces (**F**). Next, step off six spaces at the top starting with the ridge you've already drawn. Finally, divide the turning into nine equal spaces at each of the circumference lines, starting each time at the ridge (**G**). Now you're ready to sketch in the rest of the ridges.

Starting to the right of the first ridge, sketch in the adjacent ridge. It begins at the base and flows upward, ending before it reaches the top. Use the division points as guidelines, but remember that they are there as only a guide; it's not necessary to follow them precisely. It's most important to draw a smooth, flowing curve (**H**). The third ridge starts at the top and ends before reaching the base. Then the pattern is repeated twice more. When the layout is complete, you should have a total of nine ridges, yet only six points at the top and six at the base. Before carving, study your layout and check for spacing and irregularities in the curves. The layout doesn't require mechanical precision, but instead the lines should flow gracefully as they spiral toward the top. Spacing should look somewhat uniform; but it doesn't need to be, nor should it be, perfect. The idea is to create a carving that is well proportioned with pleasing curves.

Before you begin carving, take a few minutes to build the jig shown in photo I (at right) and photo M (on p. 116). It's essentially a V block with a build-in clamp for securing the work.

A sectional view of the carving reveals a series of ridges and V's. Each of the cyma curves that you sketched earlier becomes a ridge; the area between a pair of ridges forms a V. Carving is now simply a matter of removing the area between the ridges. And if you keep a couple of key points in mind as you carve, success is virtually ensured. First, keep the tools sharp; sharpness is critical to control of the tool. I keep a leather strop on my bench and hone the edges periodically. Second, always carve with or across the grain, not against it. If you attempt to work against the grain the wood will splinter and tear.

Begin by carving across the grain toward the bottom of each V (**I**). Alternate the cuts from either side of the V so that the wood between the cuts is removed cleanly (**J**). Work from the center of the V outward toward the ridges and from the base of the flame to the tip. Cutting across the grain will leave the surface slightly coarse; but the technique removes wood quickly, and you'll smooth and refine the surface later by carving with the grain.

As you carve, remember that each layout line becomes a ridge. Also, it's important that the line formed by the bottom of the V is smooth and flows in harmony with the ridges. As you deepen each V adjust the line, if necessary, to cause it to flow smoothly.

(Text continues on p. 116)

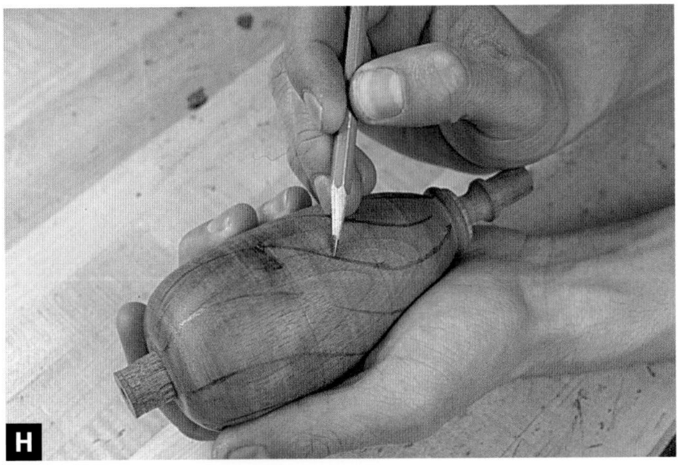
H

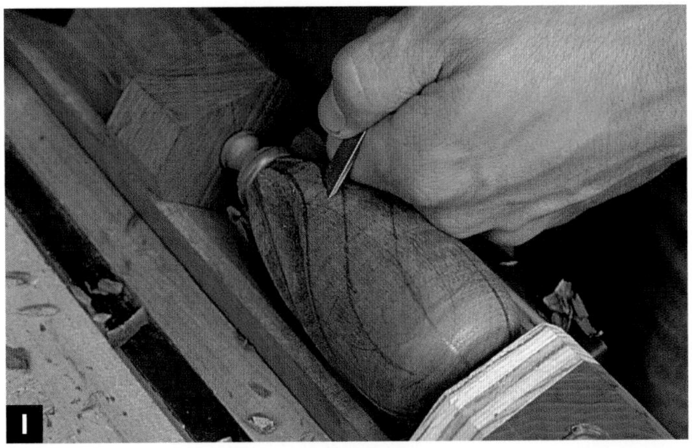
I

J

K

L

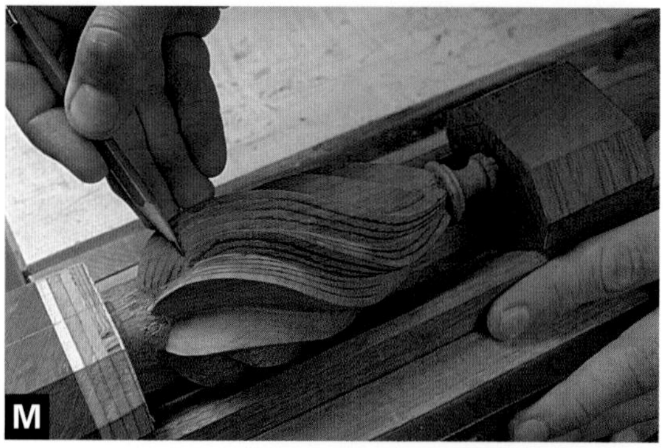
M

N

Avoid carving too deep at first. Once you've carved the entire circumference of the turning you'll have a better feel for the look you're trying to achieve, and you can deepen the cuts, if necessary. Unlike many other areas of woodworking, carving isn't a process of cutting to a set of precise dimensions. Instead, it's a matter of creating balanced, flowing lines. Often the lines can't be gauged or measured but are judged by a critical eye. In this case, each line should spiral along its length in a flowing, uninterrupted cyma curve.

As the carving progresses, the only remaining portion of the original turned surface will be each ridge. Be careful to leave the ridges intact—otherwise the flow of the curve that you created on the lathe will be spoiled. The only exception is the ridges that stop before reaching the base or the tip. Carve these ridges downward at the ends so that their lines flow smoothly toward the center of the work (**K**).

When you're satisfied with the initial carving, the next step is to refine the work. With a 12mm no. 2 gouge, smooth the surface of each curve by cutting with the grain (**L**). Sever the end grain at the base between the flames with the point of a skew.

The final touch is to carve the tiny veins on the surfaces of the flame. These shallow grooves break up the otherwise flat surface to give the carving greater detail and visual interest. But first, sketch them in with a pencil.

Depending on the width of the surface, each has three to five veins. Using your middle finger as a gauge, draw each vein beginning with the ones at the outer edges (**M**). The veins toward the inside may not flow entirely from top to bottom but may fade out as the surface narrows. Then with a steady hand, carve each vein with a 1.5mm no. 11 gouge (**N**).

Finial Pedestal

A router table will dramatically increase the versatility of your router. Here's a good example. This small fluted plinth is narrow, which makes it difficult to keep the router steady if it's handheld.

Begin with layout. You'll want to be accurate with the spacing, because it's used to set up the router. Also, mark the position of the end of the flute (**A**). Next, set the cutting depth of the bit and position the fence to cut the center flute. Finally, set stops at each fence to control the length of the flutes and keep them consistent. Now you're ready for shaping.

Position the workpiece against the infeed stop and lower it onto the spinning bit (**B**). Then push the stock to the next stop (**C**). Feed the stock slowly to avoid a fuzzy, torn surface; small-diameter bits have a relatively slow rim speed even at higher rotations per minute (rpms).

For each successive cut, move the fence closer to the bit (**D**). For each side of the center flute, each fence setting will make two flutes; simply turn the stock end for end.

A

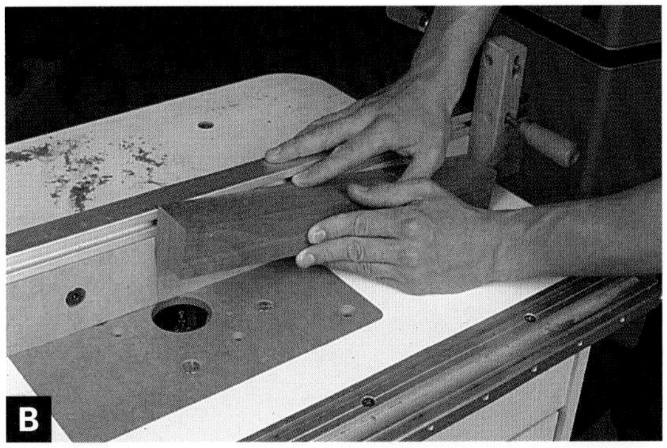
B

C

D

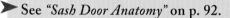

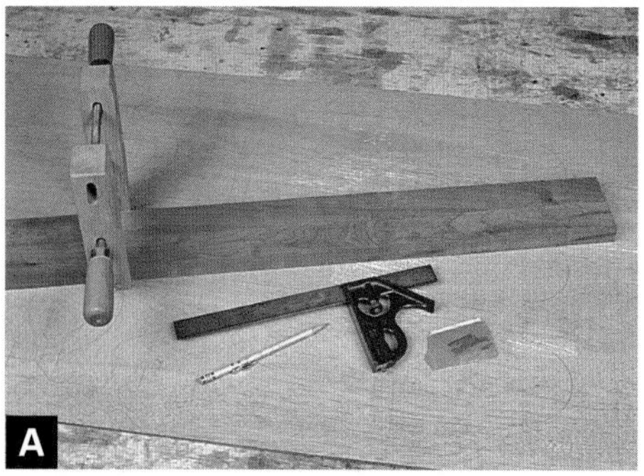
A

B

C

D

E

F

G

H

Arched Light Sash Door

Constructing a sash-type door with interlocking bars is a variation on the cope-and-stick construction. The key is accurate layout and machine setup.

➤ See *"Sash Door Anatomy"* on p. 92.

Check the fit frequently and make any necessary adjustments.

Begin by accurately milling the stock. Make the stock for the bars wide enough for two; this makes feeding the work through machines safer and more accurate. For greatest accuracy, clamp matching pieces together and transfer the lines (**A**).

The location of the mortise in relationship to the sticking is critical. For this reason, shape the sticking on the stiles first (**B**). Then cut the mortises with a hollow chisel according to the layout (**C**). When correctly positioned, the mortise falls just on the edge of the sticking (**D**).

Next cut the tenons. Since the tenon shoulders are offset, cut the face of each tenon (**E**), and then adjust the setup for the second shoulder (**F**).

Before bandsawing the curves, cut the cope on the tenon shoulder (**G**). Then bandsaw the arches in the top rail (**H**) and smooth them with a spindle sander.

[TIP] **Remember to check the cope for fit to the sticking; it may be necessary to adjust the cutter height, fence position, or both.**

The last two steps are to shape the sticking and the rabbet. But first you'll need to rip the narrow sash bars to final width. To shape the bars safely, take a few extra minutes to shape the jig shown here (**I**). This jig will add much-needed mass to the otherwise narrow stock (**J**). When cutting the second rabbet, fill the first rabbet with a stick tacked into the jig (**K**). To shape the sticking and to rabbet the arches, it's necessary to use a starting pin or block as a fulcrum when entering the cut (**L**).

Once all the cuts are made, fit each joint individually and check the fit. To assemble the framework, fit the sash bars into the rails first (**M**) and then the stiles. Gently tap the joints together with a mallet (**N**). Finally, clamp the door and set it on a flat surface while the glue dries (**O**).

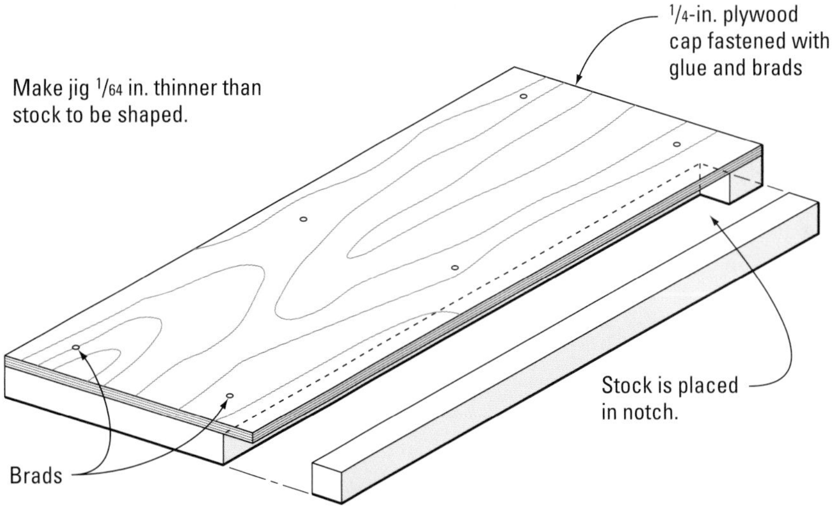

I

J

K

L

M

N

O

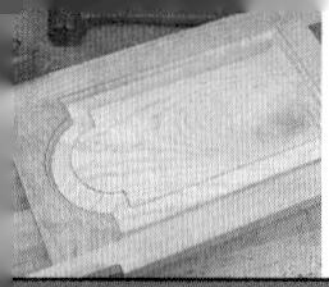

A

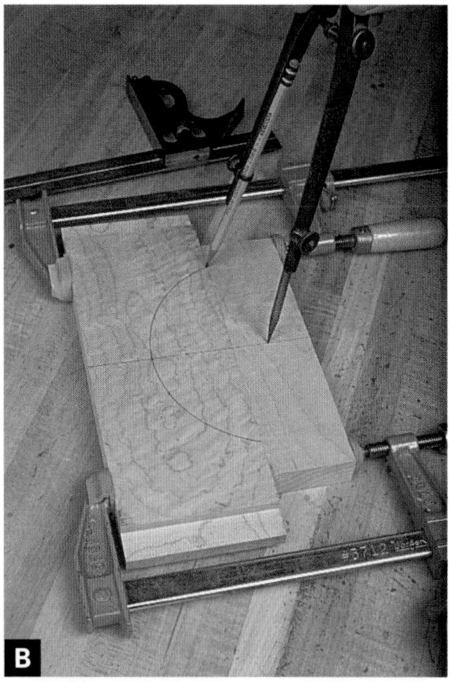
B

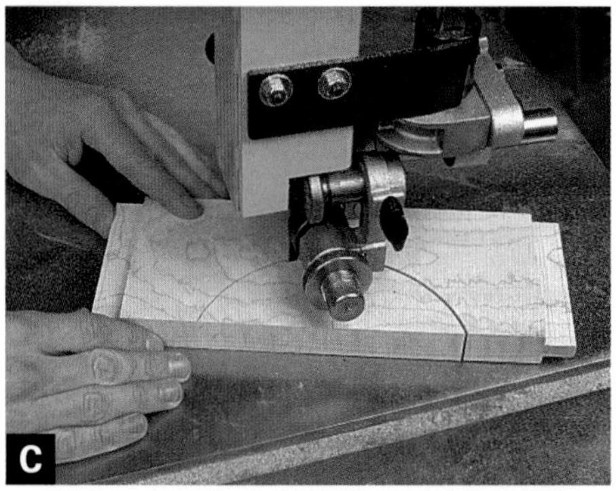
C

D

E

F

G

Tombstone Door

Mitered sticking adds structural strength to a door because it relies on longer tenons and deeper mortises than cope-and-stick joinery.

Begin by making an accurate, full-scale drawing of the door. This provides a layout reference to use throughout the process. Next, accurately mill the stock along with an extra piece or two for testing setups. Then lay out, cut, and fit the mortise-and-tenon joints (**A**). When laying out the tenons, add the sticking width to the shoulder at each end. This will compensate for the sticking around the mortise, which is removed before assembly.

The next step is to work the top rail. Begin by laying out the arch (**B**). After bandsawing (**C**), smooth the curve with a spindle sander (**D**).

Now you're ready to shape the frame. Begin by shaping the sticking profile; first on the top rail with a starting pin to begin the cut (**E**) and then on the stiles and bottom rail with a fence (**F**). Next, cut the panel groove using the same method as used for the sticking profile (**G**).

Once the sticking and panel grooves are shaped, you're ready to miter the sticking in the corners. First, tilt the table-saw blade to 45 degrees; then adjust the blade height to cut only the sticking.

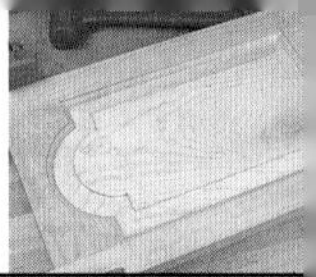

Next, mark a vertical line from the deepest point of the cut (**H**). Accuracy of the line is critical to the fit of the miters.

To use the setup, align the rail shoulders with the layout line and cut the miter (**I**). If you're mitering several pieces, clamp a thin piece of plywood to the miter gauge as a stop (**J**). To miter the stiles, align the mortise layout line with the layout line on the miter gauge (**K**). Before assembling the frame, you'll need to remove the excess sticking on the stiles with a chisel.

To make the panel, mill it to size and lay out the arch with a compass (**L**). The radius of the panel is typically ¼ in. greater than that of the top rail to allow for fitting into the panel groove.

(Text continues on p. 122)

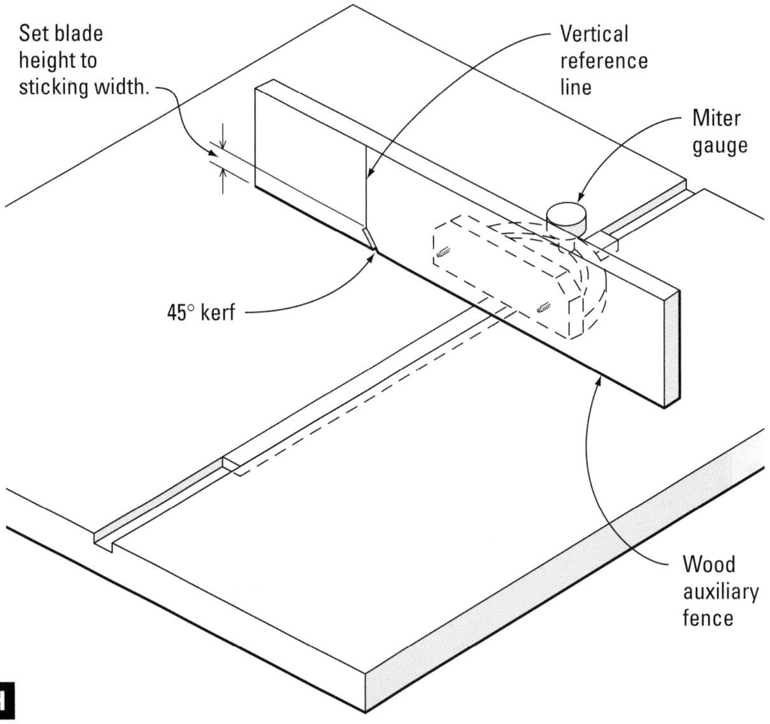

H

I

J

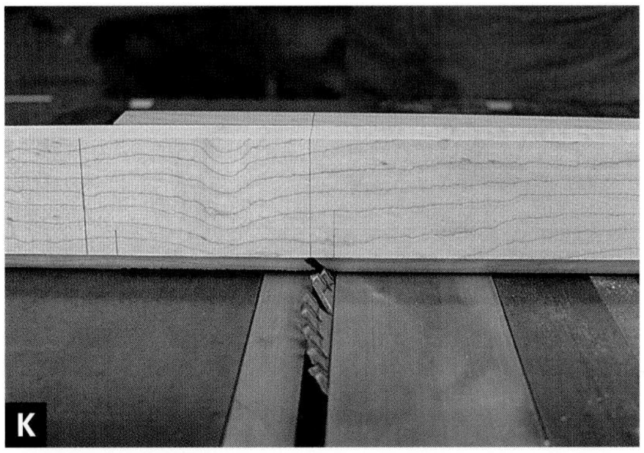

K

L

M

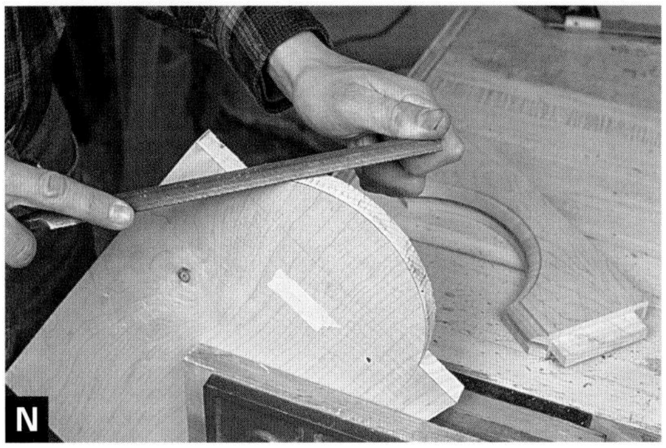

N

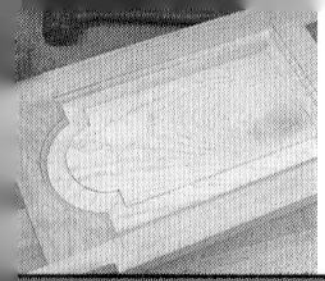

O

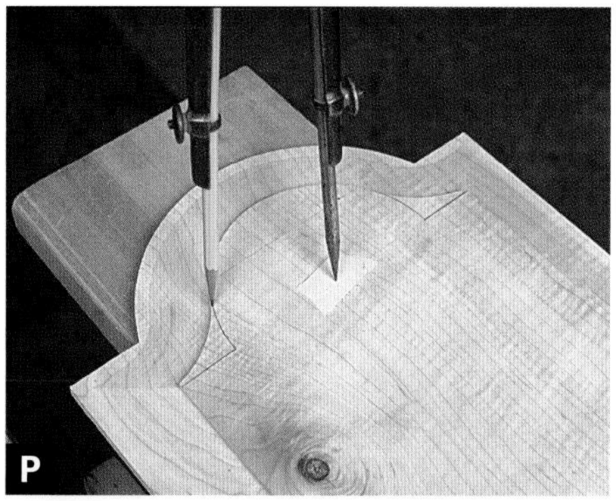
P

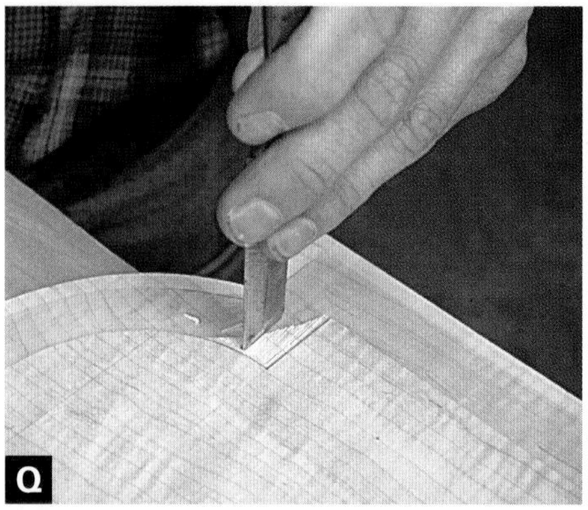
Q

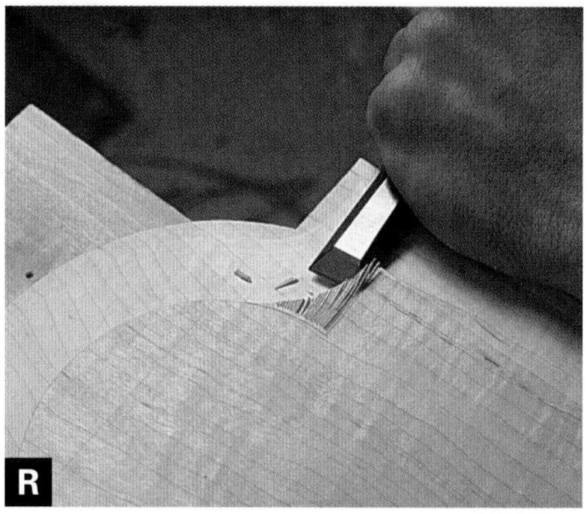
R

S

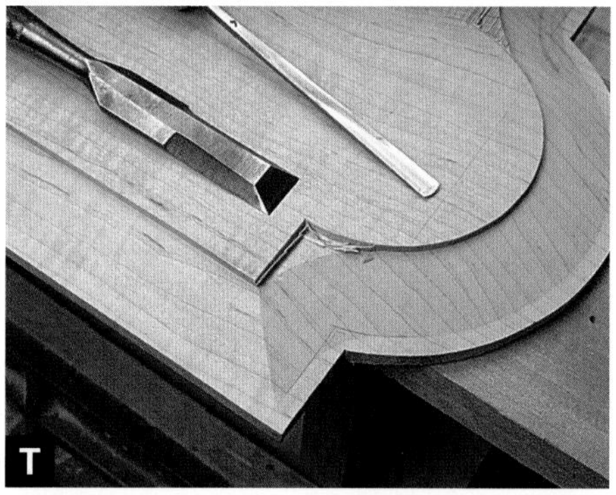
T

is ready for shaping. Shape the arch first, then the remainder of the panel (**O**).

To create an authentic panel, you'll need to carve the inside corners on each side of the arch. Although it's a bit time-consuming it's not at all difficult.

First, lay out the corner with a compass and square (**P**). Use the compass to complete the arch into the corner and the square to lay out the shoulder.

The next step is to cut away the excess stock in the corner (**Q**). Chisel across the grain to avoid splitting the panel (**R**). Next, incise the area indicated by the layout line. A chisel works well at the shoulder, but a carving gouge works best for the curve of the arch. Check the depth with a combination square to avoid cutting the area too deep (**S**).

With the initial carving done (**T**), you're ready to miter the intersection. First, incise the miter (**U**); then pare the beveled surfaces to the incision (**V**). You'll need left- and right-skewed chisels for this last stage of the carving.

Finally, sand the panel and assemble the door (**W**).

U

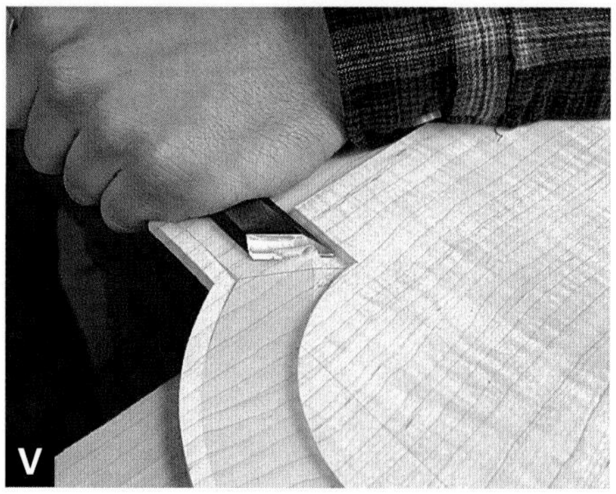
V

W

Small Tombstone Door

The process for making a small tombstone door is similar to the process for a large door. However, because the parts are very small, you'll need to use clamps and jigs to shape them safely.

Always begin with an accurate drawing, on which you've worked out details and proportions. After milling the parts of the door, lay out the arch in the rail (**A**). When bandsawing, follow the line carefully to avoid errors (**B**).

After smoothing the curve, shape the sticking (**C**) and then the panel groove. When shaping the curve of the top rail, use a large handscrew, which safely positions your hands and adds mass to the part being shaped.

When cutting the panel groove in the stile, remember to start the groove at one mortise and stop it at the other mortise (**D**). This will avoid having a gap in the top of the door frame after assembly. Use a stop block to prevent kickback. When milling the short bottom rail, always use a push block (**E**).

The next step is to miter the sticking.

With the frame complete. you're ready to shape the panel. The panel-raising bit has a bearing that follows the curve of the arch (**F**). To hold the panel safely while shaping, attach it to a push block with double-sided tape (**G**). This gives you plenty of leverage while distancing your hand from the router bit.

(Text continues on p. 124)

A

B

C

D

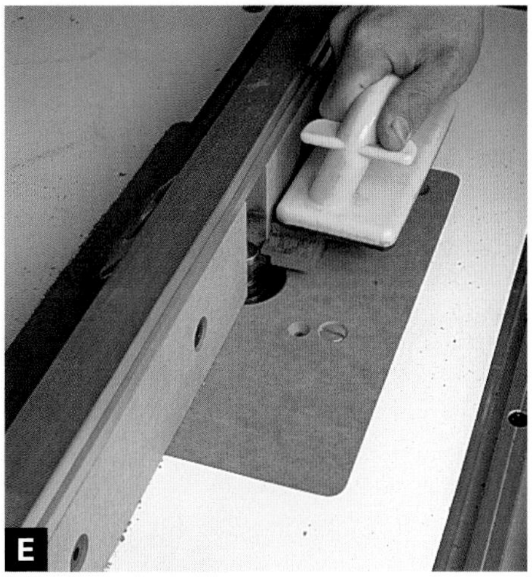
E

F

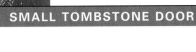

G

I

H

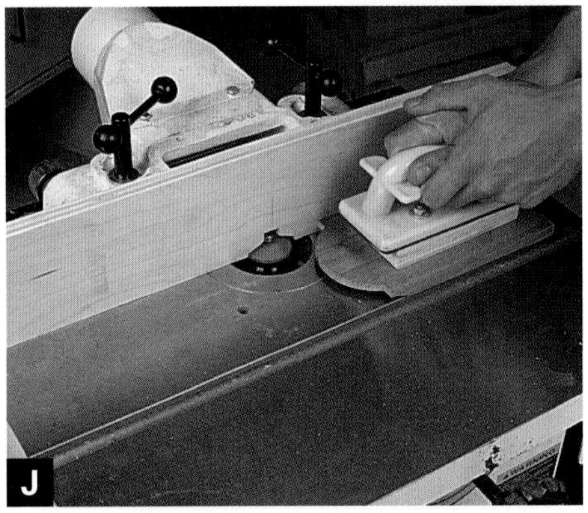
J

K

[TIP] When using double-sided tape, use woodturner's tape, which has tremendous holding power. Don't be fooled and use carpet tape. It doesn't work nearly as well.

Apply the tape to the push block and peel the paper. Then position it on the panel and clamp it momentarily to strengthen the bond (**H**).

Shape the arch first (**I**), which is primarily end grain; then shape the rest of the panel using a fence to guide the stock (**J**). When shaping the arch, it's crucial to use a pin or block for a fulcrum when starting the cut. Once the work makes contact with the bearing on the bit, it's safe to pivot away from the starting pin or block. Positioning the fence for straight cuts is easy; simply align the fence tangent to the bearing (**K**).

Finally, carve the corners and assemble the door.

Shaping a Lipped Door Edge

Unlike an overlay door that closes against the cabinet face, a lipped door looks refined. That's because most of the door's thickness fits inside the cabinet and the remaining lip is shaped with a delicate thumbnail profile.

The example I'm using here is the pendulum door from the waist of a tall clock. The top of the door has a decorative cutout. After bandsawing the top of the door, use a flush-trimming router bit and a template to remove the bandsaw marks (**A**). Then carve the inside corners where the router bit didn't reach (**B**). Next, use a roundover bit to shape the thumbnail profile around the perimeter of the door (**C**). Set the height of the bit to create a $\frac{1}{16}$-in. fillet next to the thumbnail profile. This fillet is important; it creates another fine detail to capture light and create a shadow line.

After the thumbnail, shape the rabbet that allows most of the door to fit within the opening. The bearing on the rabbeting bit can ride along the thumbnail without damaging it; just don't press too hard (**D**).

[TIP] A fence can be used to limit the rabbet's depth along the straight portions of the door.

Afterward, carve the inside corners on the top of the door to complete the thumbnail profile (**E**).

A

B

C

D

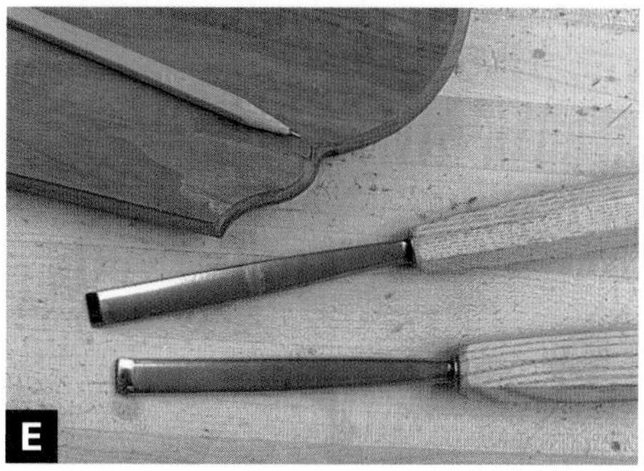
E

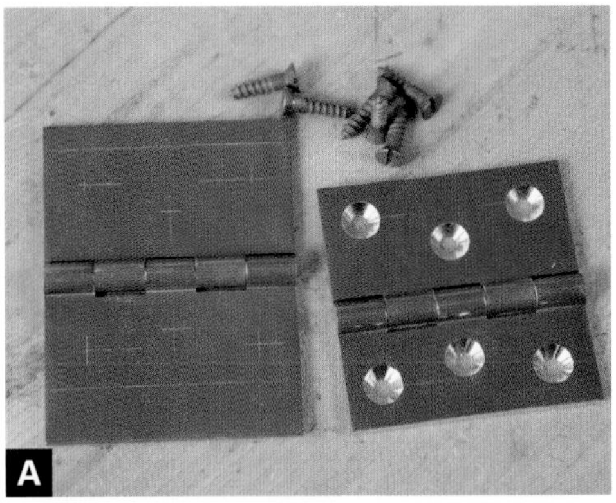
A

B

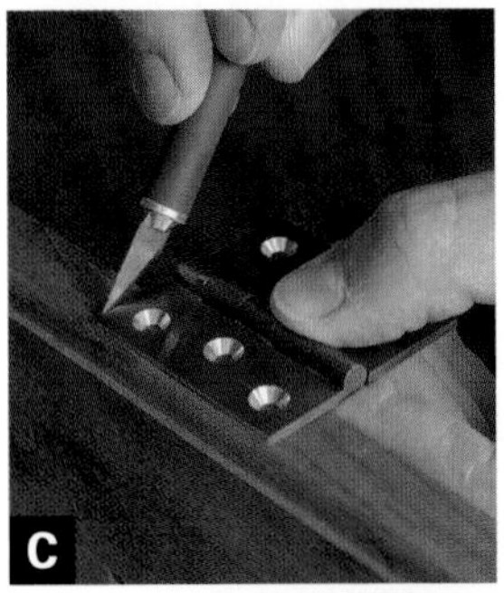
C

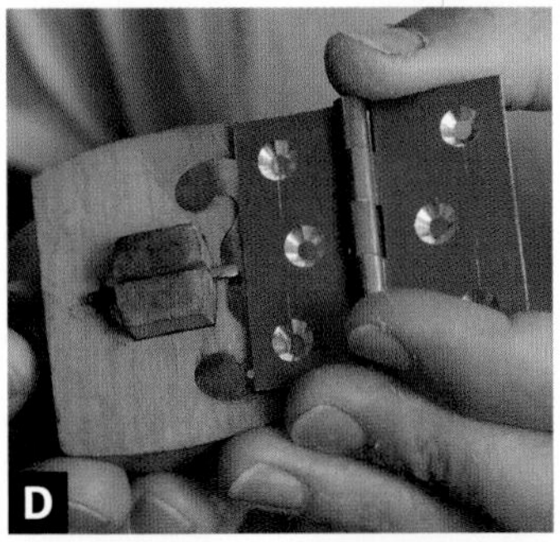
D

E

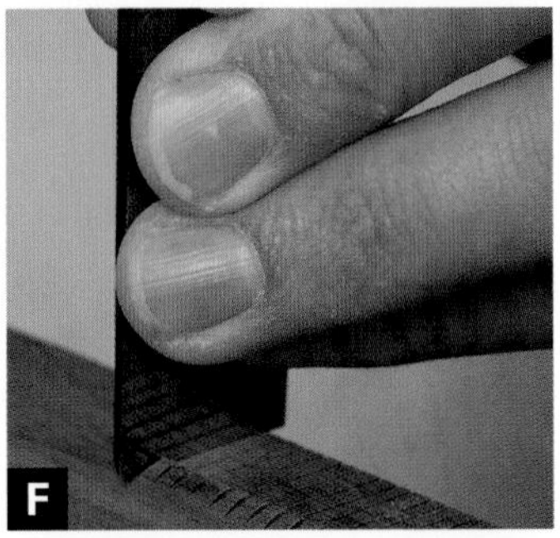
F

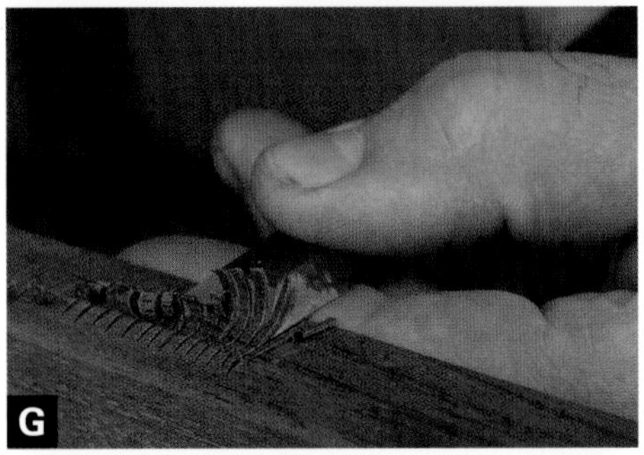
G

H

I

Hanging Lipped Doors

Lipped doors look refined because most of the door thickness rests inside the case and the lipped edge conceals the small gap around the door. Although they are a bit more work than a flush-fitting door, the results make it worth the extra effort.

It is important to note that the hinged edge of the door has just a small lip ($\frac{1}{16}$ in.) to prevent it from binding on the stile of the case. Also, you will need to purchase hinges with offset leaves. For the large doors of the upper case of a secretary, I modified blank hinges (**A**).

The first step is to layout the hinge mortise on the door stile. After marking the height (**B**), position the hinge and trace the opposite edge (**C**). Next, set a marking gauge to equal the hinge thickness (**D**) and scribe the mortise depth (**E**). Begin mortising by lightly chopping a series of cuts across the grain (**F**). Next, pare across the grain to the mortise depth (**G**). Install the screws (**H**) and fit the door in the case opening to mark the location on the cabinet stile (**I**). Cut the mortises on the case to complete the job.

Large Fluted Pilaster

Fluting lengthy stock, such as this pilaster for a corner cabinet, can be awkward when passed across the short top of a router table. In situations such as this, it's much easier to pass the router over the stock. Before you begin, you'll need a guide accessory, which attaches to the base of your router. Or you can make a guide as I did here (**A**).

After attaching the guide, adjust the cutting depth of the bit (**B**). Next, mill the stock for the pilasters. If you mill it oversize in length, you'll have an area to lay out the flutes and check each router setting (**C**).

After layout, clamp a stop block at each end to keep the flutes uniform in length. Begin by routing the center flutes and work outward (**D**). Afterward, cut two flutes with each new setting (**E**). Each time you start a new flute, position the router base against the stop block (**F**).

A

B

C

D

E

F

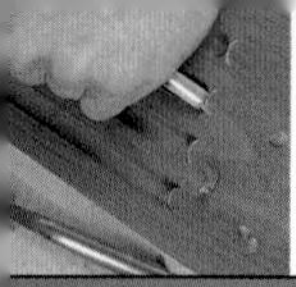

A

B

C

D

Carved Reverse-Stop Flutes

Before carving stop flutes, you'll need to modify the edge of the gouge. Carving gouges are somewhat square when you buy them. Although this profile is effective for most types of carving, the outside corners of the gouge will dig in when incising a stop flute. Instead, the end of the gouge must be semicircular to follow the contour of the flute.

The most efficient way to change the tool shape is to use a grinder. Roll the tool from side to side on the grinding wheel to grind away the corners. As you grind, keep the tool moving to avoid dead spots in the curve. After grinding, sharpen the tool to a mirror surface with benchstones.

A reverse-stop flute is a neat detail at the lower end of a flute. Rather than leave the flute end concave, as from the router, the end is carved to a convex profile. Like many details that add visual interest to a piece of furniture, reverse-stop flutes can't be created by machine. But for a special piece of furniture, the extra handwork is worth it.

Begin by routing stop flutes as shown on p. 127. Be certain to provide space for the carving. Next, lay out the stop flute. Use a combination square to extend the sides of the flute and a circle template to draw the arc (**A, B**).

Now select a carving gouge with a sweep that comes closest to the curve of the arc. Incise the curve by cutting vertically with the gouge (**C**). Then carve parallel to the flute to complete the profile (**D**).

Fluted Quarter Columns

Quarter columns, as the name implies, are one-quarter of a full circle. Typically fluted, the columns are inset within the front corners of casework such as desks, chest, and clocks. Like full-round columns and pilasters, quarter columns require a base and capital to complete them visually. Once complete, quarter columns provide a formal architectural look and additional detail.

To create quarter columns, you must glue four strips of wood together with heavy paper in the glue joints. After turning and fluting, the column is easily split into four segments, because the heavy paper in the joints allows the pieces to separate.

Begin by drawing a cross-section of the column full-scale (**A**). Columns typically have a 1¾ in. diameter, which yields a quarter column that's ⅞ in. across when viewed from the front of the case. Next, draw the flutes in place. The size and spacing of the flutes must look proportional to the column; spacing is determined by the index head on your lathe. More specifically, the number of flutes must divide equally into the number of divisions on the index head of your lathe.

The next step is to mill the stock for the columns. If you mill it slightly oversize, you'll easily be able to turn the column to the required diameter. After milling, you must glue the four sections together to create a full column. However, before you begin, remember that joint alignment is critical; the four seams must align perfectly. Otherwise the separate columns will not be exactly a quarter circle. Starting with the ends, align the joints with pressure from opposing clamps (**B**). You can check the alignment by examining the joint at the end of the assembly (**C**). After aligning

(Text continues on p. 130)

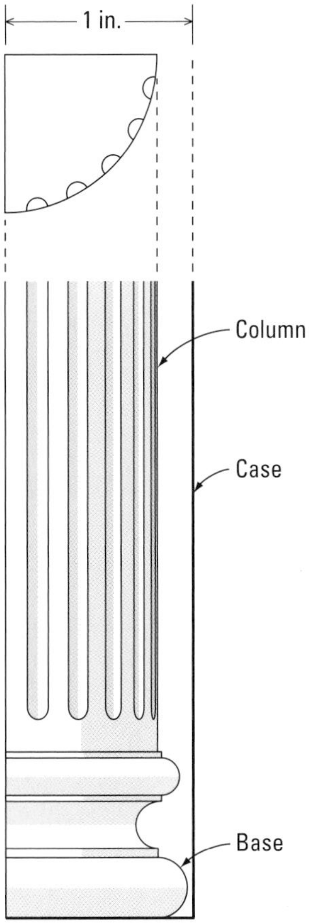

A

B

C

the ends, clamp the remainder of the work. For safety reasons, allow the glue to dry overnight before turning.

The next step is to turn the square to a uniform cylinder. Begin by squaring the ends of the turning blank. Then mark the centers for mounting in the lathe. Once again, alignment is critical. Mark the exact location with the point of an awl (**D**). Afterward, mount the blank securely in the lathe for turning.

Turning a straight, uniform cylinder isn't difficult if you follow a few easy steps. First, turn the blank round with a roughing gouge (**E**). Then carefully turn it to the required diameter. You can accomplish this by cutting to the diameter at several locations with a parting tool. As you lever the tool into the spinning stock with one hand, gauge the diameter with spring calipers in the other hand (**F**). Then turn the remaining portion of the cylinder to diameter with the roughing gouge. Afterward, smooth the cylinder with a block plane. Support the plane on the tool rest and push it slowly down the length of the slowly spinning stock (**G**). This is a great technique! The plane cleanly shears away the high spots to create a perfectly smooth, uniform surface (**H**).

The next step is to rout the flutes. But first you'll need to build a jig (**I**). The jig is actually a box that mounts to the bed of the lathe to support the router during the fluting process. Next, mount the box under the workpiece and, if necessary, attach a square base to your router to fit within the sides of the box (**J**). Finally, set the cutting depth of the bit and lock it in position.

Before you begin routing, remember that the flutes must be spaced equally around each quarter column; the first and last flute on each quarter column should be adjacent to a glue joint. For this spacing to occur, it may be necessary to reposition the cylinder between the centers. Lock the cylinder in place with the pin on the index head (**K**); then make a very short test cut on one end of the cylinder. If the flute falls next to the glue joint, fine. If not, release the pressure slightly at the tailstock and rotate the column to bring the router bit into alignment. Now tighten the handwheel at the tailstock and make a second test cut.

Once the column is aligned for the first flute, successive flutes will be correctly positioned in relation to the glue joints. Once the setup is complete, route the flutes (**L**). If you choose to stop the flutes, tack a wood block to the jig to act as a stop.

When fluting is complete, remove the column from the lathe and carefully split it into corners by placing a wide chisel at one end and tapping it gently (**M**).

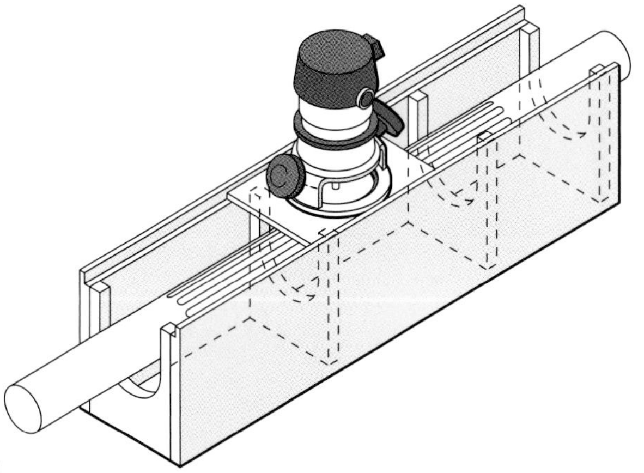

I

J

K

L

M

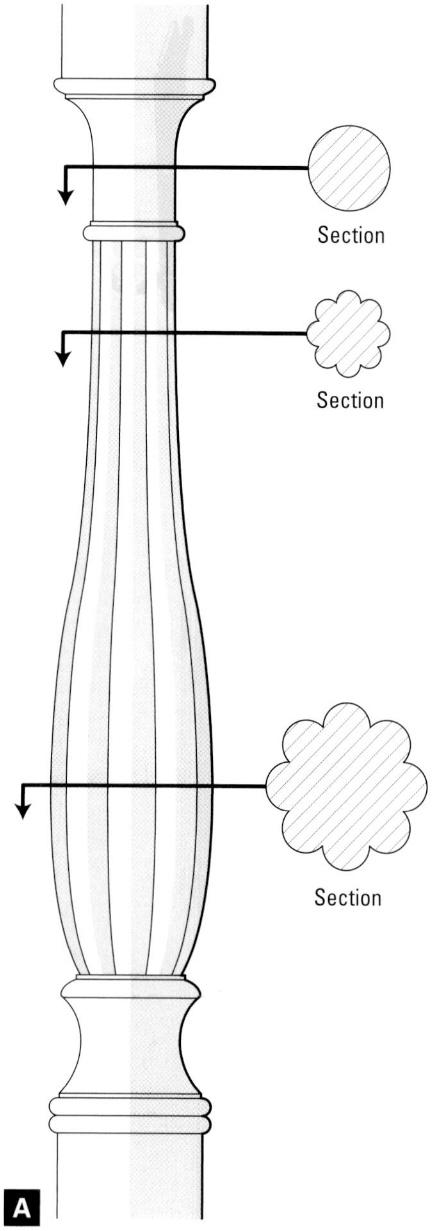

A

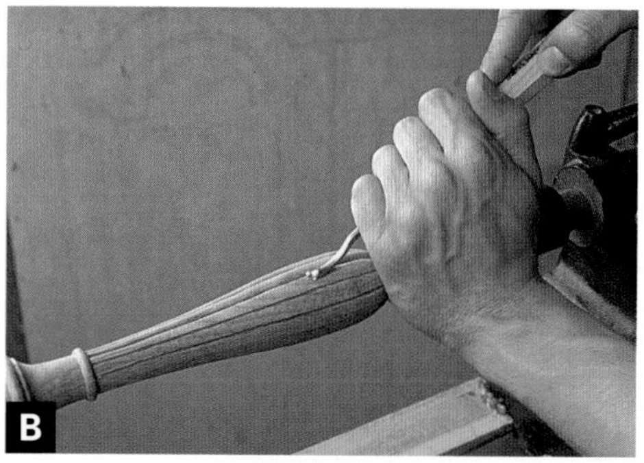

B

C

D

Reeded Turning

Reeding is a series of convex semicircular shapes, used as surface decoration (**A**). Although a router bit can be used for reeding, it's effective only when the surface to be reeded is straight. Surfaces that swell and taper, such as the example shown here, must be carved. Think about it this way: As the reeds flow down a tapered surface they must taper too (**B**). Furthermore, as they taper, the radius of each reed continually changes. Although a router guided by a tapered template will shape the reeds, it will not created a truly reeded surface—only a facsimile. This is because the radius of the router bit profile is constant.

Begin by turning the leg (**C**). Next, lay out the reeds equally around the circumference of the turning (**D**).

This is easy to accomplish with the simple jig shown here (**E**). Use the index head on your lathe to keep the spacing accurate. The next step is to outline each mark with a V gouge. First lock the turning in position with the pin on the index head. Then carefully follow each layout line with the gouge (**F**). Be sure to keep the lines running straight (**G**). Now round over the reeds with various sweeps of carving gouges (**H**). The wider portions of each reed will require gouges with a broader sweep; narrow areas require a gouge with a tighter sweep. Work carefully to keep each reed uniform as it tapers. Once you've carved each reed, inspect the surfaces for uniformity and make any necessary adjustments (**I**).

Complete the carving by sanding each reed lightly to smooth away any remaining facets from the gouges.

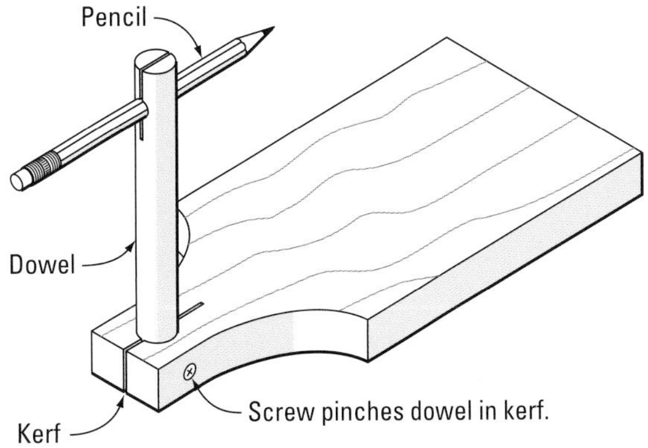

E

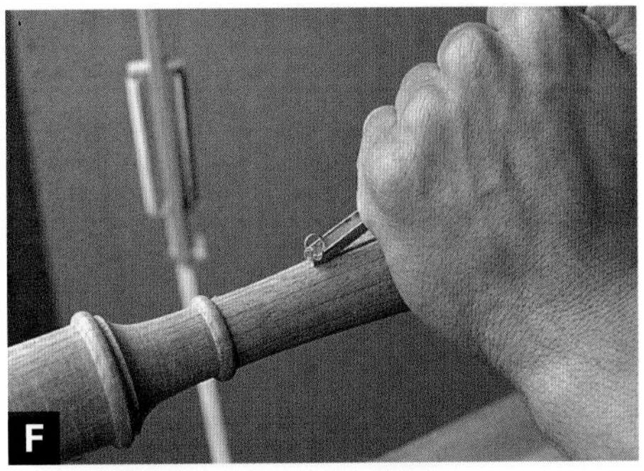

F

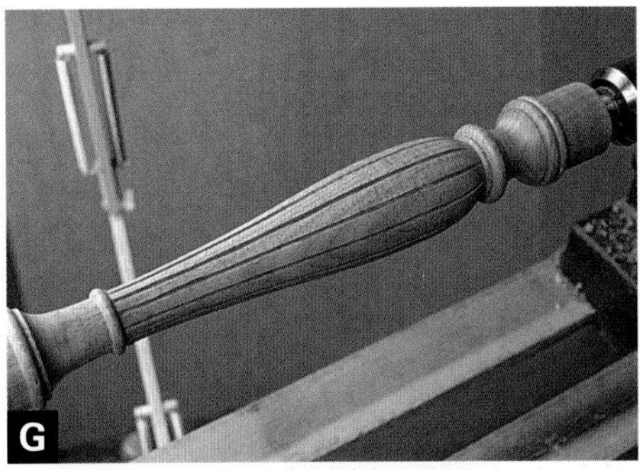

G

H

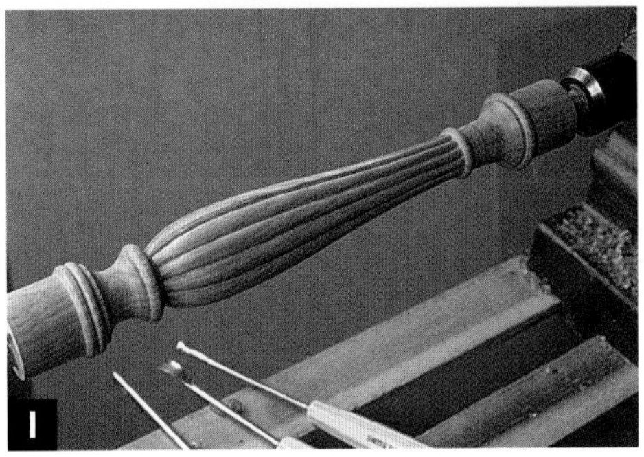

I

A

Base and Capital Molding

This small molding forms the base and capital on the fluted pilasters for a desk interior. After the strips are shaped, they are cut into small blocks and shaped on the ends to complete the detail.

[TIP] Whenever I design a new molding, I first make a drawing. It's a great aid for the setup; I can take measurements directly from the drawing to set the bit height. At each setup, I compare the test cut to the drawing to check accuracy.

B

C

The first step is to shape the bead. To set the bit height, I used a molding sample that I saved from a previous run (**A**). Shape the bead with the molding inverted (**B**). The next step is to lay the molding face down and shape the large cove at the top edge (**C**). Now turn the molding end for end, which will position the remaining flat surface against the fence, and shape the small cove (**D**). Finally, use a straight bit to cut the fillets next to the small cove (**E**).

D

E

TIP

Shaping the Edge of Base and Capital Molding

This small-part setup uses a miter gauge in conjunction with a backup board, which is fastened to the head of the gauge with a pair of screws. The router table fence is first secured parallel to the miter gauge slot; the small workpiece is then clamped to the backup board for safe shaping.

The parts being shaped in this example are the base and capital for a pilaster, or flat column. After shaping, the complete pilaster is added to the interior of a desk.

➤ See *"Fluted Quarter Columns"* on p. 129.

The first stage in this process involves shaping a strip of molding.

After shaping, short blocks of the molding are cut from the strip for use as the base and capital (**A**). But first, the ends of the blocks must be shaped, or "returned," with the same profiles used on the face of the block. This setup allows safe and accurate shaping of very small workpieces such as these.

For each profile, orient the stock on the edge (**B**) or end (**C**) and firmly clamp it to the backup board on the miter gauge.

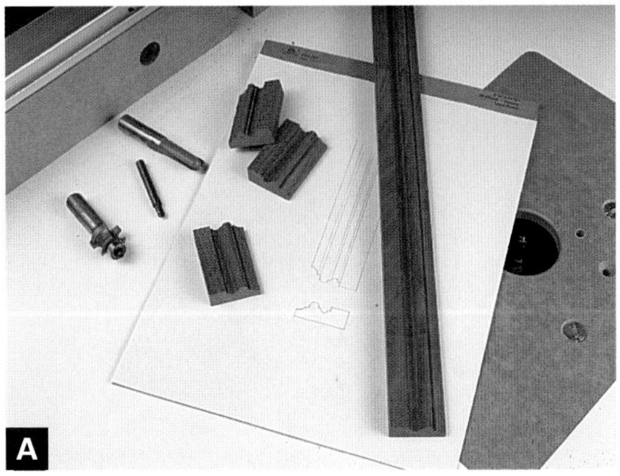

A

B

C

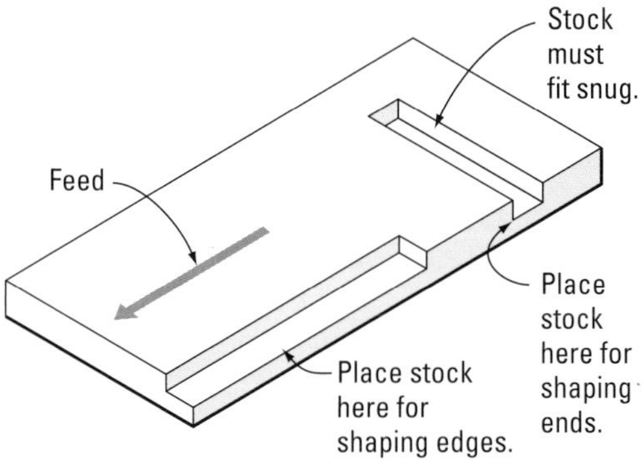
Stock must fit snug.
Feed
Place stock here for shaping ends.
Place stock here for shaping edges.

Note: Jig is pictured upside down.

A

B

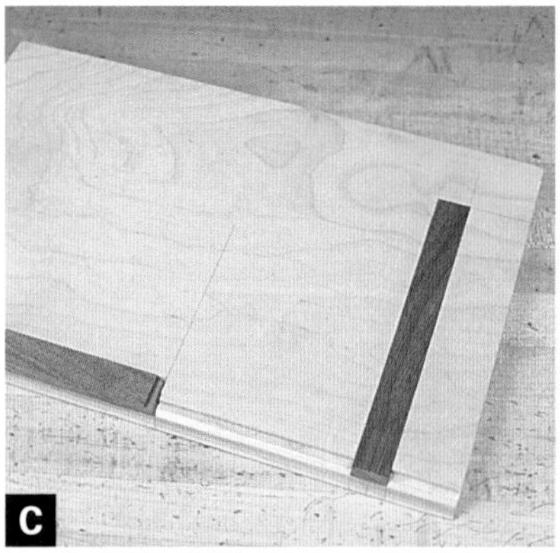

C

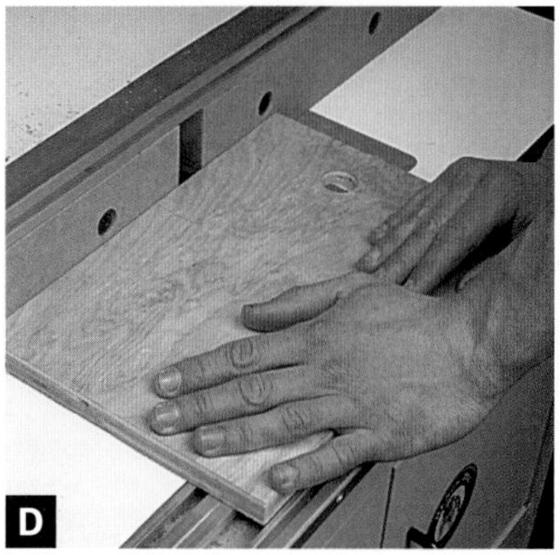

D

Candle-Slide Fronts

This method uses a simple jig that is designed for shaping multiple parts, such as the candle-slide front for a desk. The jig is a piece of ¾-in.-thick plywood with pockets for holding the work (**A**). A rabbet holds the first workpiece as it is shaped along the edge; the second workpiece is held within a groove as the end is shaped. The fit of the workpiece within the groove must be snug; a finger hole in the top of the jig provides a way to push the work free from the jig after shaping.

Furthermore, the rabbet that secures the work for shaping the edge must be slightly less in dimension than the stock being shaped. This way pressure is applied to the stock as it is shaped, preventing chatter.

After making the jig, mill the stock for a snug fit within the groove of the jig (**B**). Next, shape the ends of the stock. Then place it into the rabbet for shaping an edge. If you are shaping multiple pieces, you can also position a second piece into the jig for end shaping (**C**). As you use the jig, maintain firm pressure against the router table and fence (**D**).

Index